Topics in Applied Macroeconomics

Topics in Applied Macroeconomics

EDITED BY

DAVID F. HEATHFIELD

M

First published 1976 by
THE MACMILLAN PRESS LTD
London and Basingstoke
Associated companies in New York Dublin
Melbourne Johannesburg and Madras

SBN 333 11241 5 (hard cover)
333 11249 0 (paper cover)

Filmset at Universities Press, Belfast
and printed and bound in Great Britain at
The Pitman Press, Bath

Contents

List of Contributors

J. D. BYERS, Lecturer in Economics, University College, Aberystwyth.

E. GREENBERG, Professor of Economics, Washington University, St Louis.

DAVID F. HEATHFIELD, Lecturer in Economics, University of Southampton.

KENNETH HILTON, Professor of Financial and Managerial Controls, University of Southampton.

G. W. McKENZIE, Lecturer in Economics, University of Southampton.

ROBERT P. PARKS, Associate Professor of Economics, Washington University, St Louis.

P. G. SAUNDERS, Lecturer in Economics, University of Sterling.

D. J. TAYLOR, Lecturer in Economics, University of Sterling.

M. C. TIMBRELL, Lecturer in Economics, University of Southampton.

Editor's Preface

Students of economics, and observers of the discipline, may be excused for wondering at the profusion of theories directed at explaining economic phenomena. Indeed it has become something of a joke that any two economists will offer at least two different interpretations of the same problem. This springs in part from the normative nature of the social sciences which, being unfamiliar to those trained in the currently dominant physical sciences, is often interpreted, or rather misinterpreted, as woolly thinking. In some ways normative or prescriptive economic statements are of more interest than positive or descriptive statements. It remains true, however, that failure to make this distinction clear has caused, and continues to cause, confusion among economists and to suggest disagreement where none exists. Attempts to make economics more 'scientific', that is to say more positive, have given rise to injunctions for us to 'appeal to the facts'. This book is about appealing to the facts. It is designed to give critical surveys of the empirical work which has been undertaken on those economic relations which are discussed in most introductory or intermediate macroeconomic textbooks. As such it may be viewed as a companion volume to such texts.

Chapter 1 outlines the econometric problems involved in applied work. It is neither rigorous nor exhaustive but is intended to give the reader some understanding of the significance of various estimation procedures, alternative specifications of the structure of the error term and the summary statistics typically attached to empirical results. Chapter 2 deals with production functions and stresses the often implicit assumptions made about the form of the production function in most standard macroeconomic models. The discussion of production functions leads naturally to the discussion of the supply of labour and capital. The supply of labour is dealt with in Chapter 3 which discusses unemployment as a cost of searching for more appropriate employment and attempts to explain participation rates. Chapter 4 outlines various approaches to explaining fixed capital formation. Simple accelerator models are developed by the introduction of financial variables, time lags and uncertainty. Investment in inventories is taken up in Chapter 5. The relevance of so small a part of aggregate demand (or supply) is outlined and the various models used to explain both planned and unplanned inventories are critically examined. The difficulties which attend import and export functions are discussed in Chapter 6. A distinction is drawn between the determinants of the long-run pattern of trade and the short-term influences on imports and exports. Chapter 7 on the consumption function deals with the largest element of aggregate demand and compares the alternative theories, first explaining aggregate demand for non-durables, then taking up briefly the demand for consumer durables. Chapter 8 is concerned with the demand for money which is of continued and growing interest in both Keynesian and general-equilibrium models. Finally, Chapter 9 looks at ways in which macroeconomic models are used for policy-making, particularly for forecasting key economic variables. This may be a simple leading indicator or an auto-regressive model or a full economic model. The superiority of this last augers well for the application of economic theory to the problem of controlling economic events.

It will become clear that 'appealing to the facts' is no easy matter, nor is it as objective as the positivists imply. Selection of problems and of theoretical frameworks is normative and even the generation of data involves judgement as to what is the best representation of reality. Typically, in the social sciences, reality is not perceived by the researcher but is represented to him by a set of official statistics. Because of this it is tempting, for example, to assume that what the official statisticians labels as 'unemployment' is precisely what our particular theory calls 'unemployment'. It is also tempting to forget what actual 'raw' data were used in the generation of the published statistics and how much economic theory was implicitly used to derive the latter from the former.

With so many pitfalls it is of little wonder that the empirical work presented here is often inconclusive. It should also be clear that without some quantification of economic theory it is impossible to make any policy recommendations at all; we do not know whether it is better to use monetary or fiscal policy, whether to devalue and if so by how much. It does not seem unreasonable to expect economists to be able to answer such questions. It is hoped that this book will give students some idea of the problems faced by those doing empirical work and hence suggest why it is that 'appealing to the facts' has not yet realised its full potential.

ACKNOWLEDGEMENT

The original idea for this book and much of the early organisational work for it was due to David Pearce. He relinquished his editorial role on his appointment as Director of the Economic Research Unit at the University of Leicester.

D. F. H.

I

Econometric Introduction

Robert P. Parks

Washington University
St Louis

This chapter provides a brief overview of econometric methods, techniques and problems. There are many texts available for further reading both at the elementary level [11, 13, 15] and also at the more advanced level (see Johnston [10]).

In Section I, the method of least-squares estimation is explained, and the 'optimality' of these estimates and hypothesis tests are discussed. In Section II, the problems of specification error, multi-collinearity, heteroskedasticity and serial correlation are discussed. Section III deals with the problems of random independent variables with Friedman's permanent-income hypothesis as a model. Also lagged variables are discussed. Section IV contains a brief description of simultaneous-equation estimates.

I LEAST-SQUARES ESTIMATION

The two major topics of econometric analysis are to determine whether existing data are *consistent* with some hypothesis obtained from economic theory and to estimate values for the parameters in the theory. For example, suppose that we are interested in determining whether some data are consistent with the Keynesian consumption function, and determining the values of the parameters of the consumption function. The available data covering T periods (quarters for example) may be presented in an array such as

$$C_1 \quad C_2 \quad C_3 \cdots C_T$$

and
$$Y_1 \quad Y_2 \quad Y_3 \cdots Y_T,$$

where C_t and Y_t are the observations for consumption and income respectively during period t, and t may take any value from 1 to T.

This information may then be presented in the form of a scatter diagram as shown in Figure 1.1. The problem is to determine whether there is some regularity in these data that can be identified. The most common approach is to *assume* that the data are generated by a model of the following (linear) form, that is

$$C_t = a + bY_t + u_t, \qquad t = 1, \dots, T. \tag{1.1}$$

Unless all the points in the scatter diagram fall exactly on a straight line, they could not have been generated solely by a linear relationship of the form $C = a + bY$. In econometric analysis we assume that the true model is not exact, but rather that it includes a random error such as u_t in equation (1.1). The random error u_t is also known as a disturbance term, or a stochastic error, and is a random variable. One way to view or interpret a random error is that it is an unpredictable variable in the sense that weather is, although we may know something about the likelihood that it will take certain values. For example, the result of a flip of a 'fair' coin is unpredictable, but we believe there is a 50 per cent chance 'heads' will occur. Although we may be able to observe most random variables, random errors of econometric equations are, by definition, unobservable, that is we never know their value. This variable accounts for any deviations that consumption may take from the values that result from $a + bY_t$. These deviations or random errors may result from (*a*) some variables that influence consumption, possibly non-economic ones, being left out of the relationship for various reasons, (*b*) a theory of the

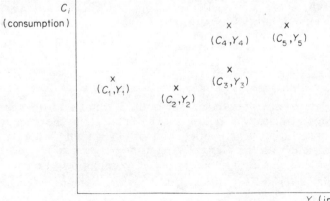

Fig. 1.1

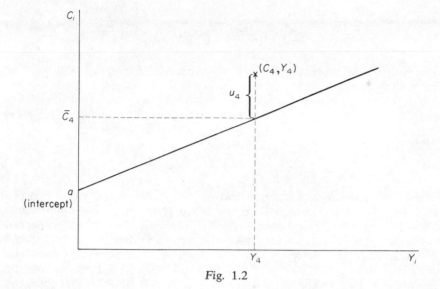

Fig. 1.2

consumption function that has a random element, and/or (c) the relation-ship is not exactly linear and so (1.1) is only an approximation. Usually any or all of these reasons for including u_t in the relationship are not explicitly mentioned in empirical work but are implicitly assumed.

Now we do not know the values of a and b. The problem for regression analysis is to estimate them, and the method most commonly used is the principle of 'least squares'. This principle requires that the estimates of a and b, $\bar{a}$ and $\bar{b}$, be chosen so that the sum of squared (estimated) errors is as small as possible. The estimated error in period t is

$$\bar{u}_t = C_t - \bar{a} - \bar{b}Y_t, \tag{1.2}$$

and the sum of squared errors is

$$\bar{u}_1^2 + \bar{u}_2^2 + \cdots + \bar{u}_T^2 = \sum_{t=1}^{T} \bar{u}_t^2 = \sum_{t=1}^{T} (C_t - \bar{a} - \bar{b}Y_t)^2. \tag{1.3}$$

By minimising equation (1.3) with respect to values of $\bar{a}$ and $\bar{b}$ we will obtain formulas for the values of $\bar{a}$ and $\bar{b}$ in terms of the data values C_t and Y_t. All that the principle of least squares does is to tell us one way of obtaining these values. In other words, it gives us a rule which determines a line, $\bar{C}_t = \bar{a} + \bar{b}Y_t$, approximating the data points. Such a line is drawn among the data points in Figure 1.2.

To minimise equation (1.3) we partially differentiate it with respect to $\bar{a}$ and $\bar{b}$, and set the two resulting equations equal to zero. We obtain

$$-2 \sum_{t=1}^{T} (C_t - \bar{a} - \bar{b}Y_t) = 0 \tag{1.4a}$$

and

$$-2\sum_{t=1}^{T}(C_t - \bar{a} - \bar{b}Y_t)Y_t = 0. \tag{1.4b}$$

By simplifying these expressions we obtain the *normal equations* of least-squares regression, that is

$$\sum_{t=1}^{T} C_t = T\bar{a} + \bar{b}\sum_{t=1}^{T} Y_t \tag{1.5a}$$

and

$$\sum_{t=1}^{T} C_i Y_i = \bar{a}\sum_{t=1}^{T} Y_i + \bar{b}\sum_{t=1}^{T} Y_i^2. \tag{1.5b}$$

Thus we have two simultaneous linear equations in the two unknown variables $\bar{a}$ and $\bar{b}$. The equations are linear in the unknown coefficients. This is what the term linear in linear regression refers to. It is not necessary that the variables enter the equation linearly but that the coefficients of the variables do. For example, equation (1.1) could be rewritten as $C_t = a + bT_t + dY_t^2$ without affecting the linearity of the parameters. But we could not write $C_t = (a + bY_t)^d$ since, in that case, the equation is not linear in the coefficients. Dividing equation (1.5a) by T, and solving for $\bar{a}$, we have

$$\bar{C} = \bar{a} + \bar{b}\bar{Y}, \tag{1.5a'}$$

where $\bar{C}$ and $\bar{Y}$ denote the sample means of C and Y, that is

$$\bar{C} = \sum_{t=1}^{T} C_t/T \quad \text{and} \quad \bar{Y} = \sum_{t=1}^{T} Y_t/T.$$

With some manipulation we can rewrite equation (1.5b) as

$$\sum_{t=1}^{T} c_t y_t = \bar{b}\sum_{t=1}^{T} y_t^2, \tag{1.5b'}$$

where $c_t = (C_t - \bar{C})$ and $y_t = (Y_t - \bar{Y})$. It is easily seen that the solutions for $\bar{a}$ and $\bar{b}$ are then

$$\bar{b} = \sum_{t=1}^{T} c_t y_t \Big/ \sum_{t=1}^{T} y_t^2 \tag{1.6a}$$

and

$$\bar{a} = \bar{C} - \bar{b}\bar{Y}. \tag{1.6b}$$

Notice that we have written the solution for $\bar{b}$ in terms of deviations from the mean data, that is in terms of $c_t = (C_t - \bar{C})$ and $y_t = (Y_t - \bar{Y})$. This is the direct solution for minimising the sum of squared errors, $\sum_{t=1}^{T}(c_t - \bar{b}y_t)^2$, which is analogous to the original problem if equation (1.1) were written as

$$c_t = by_t + U_t^* = by_t + u_t - \bar{u}. \tag{1.7}$$

In fact the relationship (1.1) implies the relationship (1.7) and we may work with raw data (*C*s and *Y*s) and an intercept (the parameter *a*), or deviations from the mean data without an intercept and obtain identical estimates of the parameter *b*. It is much easier to show properties of the estimates without the intercept and we will for the moment assume that equation (1.7) is our model.

The estimates in equations (1.6a) and (1.6b) result from the principle of least squares. The question is how good a principle is it. First of all, note that, by definition, it minimises the sum of squared (estimated) errors. As a principle of fitting a line among data points this is usually thought to be quite a good criterion. It places equal value on each error and treats positive and negative errors alike. Since there is no *a priori* reason to give unequal weights to the errors, and since negative errors are just as serious as positive errors, this would seem an appropriate criterion to use in fitting the line to the data.

That would be the end of the story if we did not want to make some assumptions about the random error in equation (1.7). But some assumptions have to be made about this random error, if we are to show that the principle of least squares results in estimates that have desirable statistical properties. After discussing some of these properties we will return to the question of whether the data are consistent with the hypothesis.

The two main properties that econometricians usually desire their estimates to have are 'unbiasedness' and 'minimum variance'. In order to explain these properties, note that $\bar{b}$ as defined in equation (1.6a) is a function of the random variable u_t (or U_t^* if we use the model (1.7)). This is most easily seen by substituting for the value of c_t in equation (1.6a) from equation (1.7). This results in

$$\bar{b} = b + \sum_{t=1}^{T} y_t U_t^* / \sum_{t=1}^{T} y_t^2, \tag{1.6a'}$$

and so $\bar{b}$ is a random variable itself.

Now two of the most important properties of a random variable are its expected value and its variance. The expected value of a random variable is defined to be the sum of the value of the random variable times the probability that that value occurs. For example, if heads of a coin was assigned plus 1 and tails minus 1, so that the random variable takes the value plus 1 with probability 1/2 and minus 1 with 1/2, then the expected value of that random variable is $-1 \times 1/2 + 1 \times 1/2 = 0$. For a continuous random variable integration is used rather than summation. The property of unbiasedness requires that the expected value of the estimate equals the parameter value, that is if $\bar{b}$ is unbiased, then $E(\bar{b}) = b$, where $E(\bar{b})$ is notation for the expected value of $\bar{b}$.

The variance of a random variable is defined to be the expected value of the difference between the random variable and its expected value, squared, that is $V(b) = E[(\bar{b} - E(\bar{b})]^2$. In the example above the variance is $(-1-0)^2 \times 1/2 + (1-0)^2 \times 1/2 = 1$. This number gives a measure of the spread that the random variable might take, that is how much the random variable can diverge from its expected value. If the variance were 0, then the random variable could take only one value.

Now to show that the least-squares estimate of b, $\bar{b}$ as defined in equation (1.6a), is unbiased, we need to make the following assumptions about the variables in equation (1.7):

(A.1) y_t is fixed, non-random, known number for each t;
(A.2) $E(U_t^*) = 0$ for all t;
(A.3a) $E(U_t^* . U_s^*) = \sigma_u^2$ if $s = t$; and
(A.3b) $E(U_t^* . U_s^*) = 0$ if $s \neq t$.

Under these assumptions it is possible to show that the least-squares estimates of a and b defined in equation (1.6) are best, in the sense that they are unbiased estimates, and have minimum variance in the class of all (linear) unbiased estimates of a and b. Linear here means that the estimate is linear in the dependent variable. The proof of this proposition, known as the Gauss–Markov Theorem, can be found in any advanced econometrics textbook. Application of the theorem, that is contending that one has best linear unbiased estimates, depends on the legitimacy of making these assumptions.

(A.1) is rather heroic and would not generally be true. Most economic variables are thought to be random variables, and hence for most applications this assumption would not be legitimate. But it may be weakened considerably without affecting the result and is stated here for ease of exposition. (A.2) states that we expect the random error to be zero on average for all periods. The reasonableness of this assumption depends on both the model and the data to which it is applied. Below, we will show at least three instances when it is untenable to make these two assumptions together (mis-specification error, errors in variables, and simultaneous-equation systems).

Now (A.1) and (A.2) can be used directly to show that $\bar{b}$ is unbiased for b. Under these assumptions $E(y_t . U_t^*) = 0$ for all t. Using this result in equation (1.6a′) directly obtains that $E(\bar{b}) = b$ since

$$E(\bar{b}) = E(b + \sum y_t . U_t^*/\sum y_t^2) = b + \sum E(U_t^* . y_t)/\sum y_t^2 = b + 0/\sum y_t^2 = b.$$

It should be noted that the key assumption used in order to show that $\bar{b}$ is unbiased for b is that $E(U_t^* . y_t) = 0$ and that (A.1) and (A.2) imply but are not implied by this, so that weaker assumptions may be made.

(A.3) is used to show that $\bar{b}$ has the least variance of all linear unbiased estimates of b. It requires two properties of the random error, U_t^*; that it have the same variance in each data period t, namely σ_u^2, and that the error in one data period is independent of the error in any other period. Independence here can loosely be taken to mean that the errors behave like the flips of a coin – the outcome of one flip in no way determines (gives information about) any prior or forthcoming flip – the errors have no inter-period correlation. For time-series data, this assumption is very strong, and below we will discuss how the estimates are affected if this assumption cannot be believed (the problem of auto-correlation).

The proof that $\bar{b}$ is the least variance estimate in the class of all linear unbiased estimates is rather long and we will not reproduce it here. Rather, we will derive the variance of $\bar{b}$ as it is used in hypothesis tests about b.

From equation (1.6a') we can see that $b - \bar{b} = (\sum U_i^* y_i / \sum y_i^2)$, and since we have shown that $E(\bar{b}) = b$, we have the variance of $\bar{b}$, $V(\bar{b})$, as

$$V(\bar{b}) = E((\bar{b} - b)^2) = E((\sum U_i^* y_i / \sum y_i^2)^2)$$

$$= E\left(\left(\sum U_i^{*2} y_i^2 + 2 \sum_{i<j} \sum U_i^* U_j^* y_i y_j\right) \Big/ \left(\sum y_i^2\right)^2\right).$$

The second equality may be easily derived by expanding the square and collecting some terms. Now (A.3) states that $E(U_i^* \cdot U_j^*)$ equals σ^2 when $i = j$ and equals 0 when $i \neq j$. Since the expected value of a sum of random variables is equal to the sum of the expected values, we have

$$V(\bar{b}) = \sigma_u^2 \cdot \sum y_i^2 / (\sum y_i^2)^2 = \sigma_u^2 / \sum y_i^2. \qquad (1.9)$$

Sometimes $V(\bar{b})$ is written as σ_b^2, which is the variance of the estimate $\bar{b}$.

The only remaining problem is to estimate σ_u^2, the variance of the random error in equation (1.1) (or (1.7)) since it is unknown. Normally,

$$\bar{\sigma}_u^2 = \sum U_i^2 / (T - 2) \qquad (1.10)$$

is used as an estimate of this variance. The reason for dividing by $T - 2$ is to make $\bar{\sigma}_u^2$ an unbiased estimate. The number 2 is due to the fact that in the original model (1.1) there were two 'explaining' or independent variables (the intercept and Y) on the right-hand side of the equation. If there had been k variables, then we need to divide the sum of squared errors by $T - k$ in order to have an unbiased estimate of the variance. Of course we cannot report the variance of $\bar{b}$ since it involves the unknown σ_u^2. What is normally done is to estimate this variance by using the estimate $\bar{\sigma}_u^2$ (defined in equation (1.10)) in the formula (1.9), and take its square root. This reported statistic is called the standard error of the estimate $\bar{b}$, and is defined by

$$\sigma_b = \sqrt{\bar{\sigma}_u^2 / \sum y_i^2}. \qquad (1.11)$$

Now the problem occurs that we might be interested in 'how well' we have done, that is how consistent are the data with the hypothesis. We know that we have minimised the sum of squared errors, and that $\bar{b}$ is an unbiased estimate which has minimum variance, often called 'best linear unbiased estimate' or *BLUE* for short. This means we have obtained good estimates (in some senses at least) but we do not know how good. The first measure of 'how good' is the 'multiple correlation coefficient'. It is defined as the percentage of variance of the dependent variable (C_t in our case) 'explained' by the regression variables, that is by the independent variables on the right-hand side of the equation (Y_t in our case). It may be shown to be the square of the correlation coefficient between the predicted dependent variable, $\bar{a} + \bar{b}Y$, and the dependent variable, C. Formally, it is calculated as one minus the percentage unexplained variance, or

$$R^2 = 1 - \frac{\sum U_t^2/T}{\sum (C_t - \bar{C})^2/T} = 1 - \frac{\sum U_t^2}{\sum c_t^2}. \tag{1.12}$$

This is a measure of the 'fit' of the estimated regression line $\bar{C} = \bar{a} + \bar{b}Y$ to the actual data points (C_t, Y_t). Higher values mean better fits, and $R^2 = 1$ means that the fit is perfect, that is $C_t = \bar{a} + \bar{b}Y_t$ which occurs only when $\bar{u}_t = 0$ for all t, and the theoretical relationships fit the data perfectly. Of course, $R^2 = 0$ implies that there is no relationship between C and Y, and that $\bar{b} = 0$.

Figure 1.3 graphs the observations of C and Y (represented by crosses). The lines drawn in represent $\bar{a} + \bar{b}Y = \bar{C}$, where $\bar{C}$ is the estimate of C. In Figure 1.3(a), R^2 is high as all the observations are close to the fitted line $\bar{C} = \bar{a} + \bar{b}Y$. In Figure 1.3($b$), R^2 is relatively low as many observations are far away from the fitted line. In this case, Y does not 'explain' C very well, that is a poor fit has been obtained.

Although R^2 is a useful number, and has a very convenient interpretation (percentage of the variance of the dependent variable explained), we do not know how large R^2 should be in order for us to conclude that the theory is either correct or consistent with the data. This is a problem of hypothesis testing. We want to test the theory, which in our example amounts to testing whether $b = 0$. If $b \neq 0$, then the theory is correct in stating that consumption is a function of income, no matter what the value of b is. If $b = 0$, then the theory is not correct, since consumption would not depend on income (for this particular set of data at least). Notice that assumptions (A.1) to (A.3) say nothing about the distribution of the random error, U. It could have any distribution and in fact could have different distributions in different periods so long as (A.2) and (A.3) hold true. But to test hypotheses we must assume that the underlying distribution of the random errors, U, is the normal distribution. This is a quite common distribution encountered in almost all statistical applications. The reader need not trouble himself with what a normal distribution is. He should note, however, that in some applications this assumption is untenable and hence the hypothesis tests discussed below are invalid. For example, if the dependent variable could only have the values 0 or 1 (0 if you didn't buy a car, 1 if you did) then the random error can only take one of two possible values, that is $-(a + bY_t)$ or $1 - (a + bY_t)$. But a normally distributed random error can be any real number and so the assumption of normality for a case in which the dependent variable has a limited range is untenable.

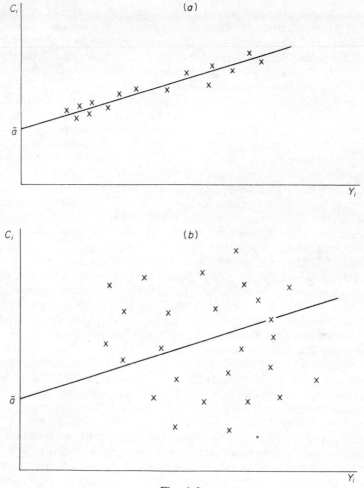

Fig. 1.3

If the errors are normally and independently distributed (equivalent to (A.3b)), then we can make some hypothesis tests about the estimated line $\bar{a} + \bar{b}Y = \bar{C}$. Notice that $\bar{b}$ is a linear function of the errors, (see (1.6a′) above) and hence is also normally distributed. It also turns out that $\bar{\sigma}^2$ is independently distributed as a chi-square variate, and under the hypothesis that $b = 0$, the ratio

$$\bar{F}_b = \frac{\bar{b}^2}{\bar{\sigma}_b^2/\sigma^2} \bigg/ \bar{\sigma}^2/\sigma^2 = \frac{\bar{b}^2/\bar{\sigma}_b^2}{\bar{\sigma}^2} = \bar{b}^2 \sum (Y_t - \bar{Y})^2 \qquad (1.13)$$

has an F-distribution. Again, the reader need not trouble himself over what a chi-square or an F-distribution is, since explicit knowledge of these distributions is not required in order to interpret econometric results. To test whether $b = 0$, we compare $\bar{F}$ with tabled values of the F-distribution which can be found in almost any statistics or econometrics book. If $\bar{F}_b$ is larger than the number in the table, we conclude that it is very unlikely that $\bar{F}_b$ was really distributed with an F-distribution, and hence reject the hypothesis that $b = 0$ in favour of $b \neq 0$. We actually reject the conjunction of the assumptions made in order to derive the fact that $\bar{F}$ was distributed with an F-distribution, for example the model (1.1), assumptions (A.1)–(A.3), the normality assumption and $b = 0$. Hence any one (or more) of them could be the fallacious one, and that is why one must believe that all the assumptions except $b = 0$ are tenable in order to reject $b = 0$.

In rejecting $b = 0$, we could have made an error, namely that b was in truth equal to 0. This is called a Type-I error. The other error, namely that we accept $b = 0$ when in truth $b \neq 0$ is called a Type-II error. Notice that the probability of rejecting $b = 0$ with the test above is exactly the probability that $\bar{F}_b$ is greater than the tabled value we picked for comparison. What is generally done is to specify this probability to be some number, usually $0 \cdot 05$ or $0 \cdot 01$, and find the tabled value corresponding to this probability of error. We then say that we have a hypothesis test with a five per cent (or one per cent) Type-I error, or significance level. The F-distribution also depends on two other numbers, namely the degrees of freedom of the denominator and the numerator of $\bar{F}$. In this specific case, the numerator has only one degree of freedom since it is based on only one estimate, $\bar{b}$. The denominator has $T - 2$ degrees of freedom. This is because there are T observations $\bar{u}_t$, the estimated errors, but two estimates, $\bar{a}$ and $\bar{b}$, had to be calculated before the $\bar{u}_t$s could be calculated. Actually there are only $T - 2$ independent observations $\bar{u}_t$. If we know $T - 2$ of them, we can use equations (1.6a) and (1.6b) to calculate the other two. The degree of freedom in the denominator is equal to the number of independent estimated errors, and this in turn is always equal to the number of observations, T, minus the number of estimates to be made in the equation. More formally, the denominator of $\bar{F}$ is a random variable which has a chi-square distribution of $T - 2$ degrees of freedom and the numerator is a random variable with a chi-square distribution of 1 degree of freedom. $\bar{F}$ is then the ratio of two (independent) chi-square random variables which is an F-distribution of the degrees of freedom of the two chi-square variables.

In general, there are k independent variables on the right-hand side of the equation to be estimated. In this case, the estimate of the variance of the equation's error, $\bar{\sigma}_u^2$, is $\sum \bar{u}_t^2/(T-k)$ and when this is used as the denominator in an F-statistic, it has $T - k$ degrees of freedom. We may then calculate $k \bar{F}_b$s, one for each coefficient estimate for each variable in the equation. Each has one degree of freedom in the numerator and $T - k$ in the denominator. Each $\bar{F}_b$ is compared to the tabled value of the F-distribution for the appropriate degrees of freedom (1 and $T - k$) in order to test whether each coefficient is significantly different from 0. Often the square root of $\bar{F}_b$ is reported since it has a tabled distribution called the t-distribution (that is the square root of a random variable which had an F-distribution with one degree of freedom in the numerator is a random variable which has a t-distribution). This is normally called the t-statistic of the coefficient, and it is reported more often since its distribution depends only on the degrees of freedom in the denominator, that is $T-k$.

In the general case where there are k independent variables, we may also wish to test whether all k coefficients are simultaneously zero. Although in our example we have only one independent variable, plus the constant term, in general there are k. We may desire to test not only whether *each* variable's coefficient is equal to zero separately, but also to test whether all of the coefficients are zero simultaneously. This may be done by calculating

$$\bar{F} = \frac{R^2/k-1}{(1-R^2)/T-k},$$
(1.14)

which again can be shown to have an F-distribution, this time of $k-1$ and $T-k$ degrees of freedom respectively. The reason for the number $k-1$ is that we are testing $k-1$ of the coefficients (not all k) with this test. The coefficient that is not being tested is that of the intercept which we exclude because it is not usually relevant in testing the theory. Recall that, in our example, the theory was that consumption was a function of income. If we test simultaneously that $a=0$ and $b=0$, we may incorrectly conclude that consumption is a function of income even though $b=0$, since $a\neq 0$ would lead us to reject the hypothesis that *both* coefficients are equal to zero. Even if $a\neq 0$ is accepted, it is not very interesting since the intercept is not really an economic variable and so we may not have explained anything economically. In fact if $\bar{b}=0$, then $\bar{a}=\bar{C}$ and the simultaneous test $a=0$ and $b=0$ would only determine whether the mean of the dependent was significantly different than zero.

However, the intercept *is* included in most regressions. Given (A.2) the null hypothesis that all the independent variables' coefficients are zero implied that the mean of the dependent variable is zero if an intercept is not included in the equation. Since most economic variables have a non-zero mean this is untenable and hence an intercept is included to avoid this implication.

In the discussion above, we stated that the null hypothesis was that $b=0$ in model (1.1). Now we might also wish to test whether $b=0\cdot75$ or any other number. Even more generally, we might wish to know what set of numbers is consistent with our estimate $\bar{b}$ where consistent here means that such a number, if used as the null hypothesis, would not result in its rejection. The set of numbers so constructed is called a confidence interval for the parameter b, that is we cannot reject the hypothesis (with our data) that b is actually equal to any number in the interval. In order to construct such an interval, first note that the more general null hypothesis, say $b = B$ (where B represents some number such as $0 \cdot 75$), can be tested with the statistic

$$\bar{F} = (\bar{b} - B)^2 / \bar{\sigma}_b^2 / \bar{\sigma}_u^2. \tag{1.15}$$

Notice that if $B = 0$, then we have our former statistic.

The actual test performed is to compare $\bar{F}$ with the tabled F-distribution of 1 and $T - 2$ degrees of freedom for some confidence level, for example $0 \cdot 05$ or 5 per cent. Let this number be represented as $F_{0 \cdot 05}(1, T - 2)$ which is found in the table. Now for any value of B such that

$$\frac{(\bar{b} - B)^2 / \bar{\sigma}_b^2}{\bar{\sigma}_u^2} \leqslant F_{0 \cdot 05}(k, T - k), \tag{1.16}$$

we cannot reject the null hypothesis that $b = B$. This defines a 95 per cent confidence interval for b. More commonly we take the square roots and obtain, with some manipulation,

$$\bar{b} - \bar{\sigma}_b \bar{\sigma}_u \sqrt{F_{0 \cdot 05}(1, T - k)} \leqslant B \leqslant \bar{b} + \bar{\sigma}_b \bar{\sigma}_u \sqrt{F_{0 \cdot 05}(1, T - k)}. \tag{1.17}$$

Often equation (1.17) is interpreted as defining an interval such that we can be 95 per cent certain (the probability is $0 \cdot 95$) that the true value of the parameter b is within this interval (of course assuming our model (1.1), (A.1)–(A.3) and normality of the u_ts).

Although we are interested in estimation of theoretical relationships, sometimes the main interest in the theory is how well it can predict future values. In our example, we predict values of the dependent variable C with $\bar{C}_t = \bar{a} + \bar{b} Y_t$. As a by-product of the least-squares estimation of a and b, we also obtain that $\bar{C}_t$ is an unbiased minimum variance estimate of C_t (given the model (1.1), and (A.1)–(A.3)). With the normality assumption on the errors we can also derive confidence intervals for (unknown) values of C. These intervals are derived much in the same way as the confidence intervals for b were, and given the interval we can state that the probability that the true value of C lies in the interval is, for example, $0 \cdot 90$. Choosing the level of confidence determines the size of the interval, and the higher the level of confidence that we want for C to lie in the interval the larger the interval will be. In Figure 1.4 the regression line is drawn in and two bands are drawn about it. Given the value Y_0, the 95 per cent confidence interval is the interval AB. The dashed band indicates 99 per cent confidence intervals. (One might think of weather forecasts in considering the idea of prediction in this context. The weatherman usually states that there is, for example, a 50 per cent chance of rain tomorrow. More precisely, he might mean that the probability of $\frac{1}{4}$ to $\frac{1}{2}$ inch of rain tomorrow is $0 \cdot 5$. If we asked him to be 90 per cent sure, he might state that he is 90 per cent sure that it will rain between 0 and 1 inch tomorrow.)

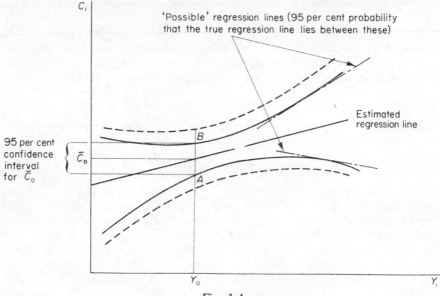

Fig. 1.4

One should also note that the bands bend away from the fitted line for observations of Y further from its mean. The reason for this shape may be most easily seen by considering data to be in deviation from the mean form (all this really does is to make the axes go through the means of the data, that is the means are then zero rather than their actual values. Now we have a confidence interval for the parameter b, for example expression (1.17), and with model (1.7), $\bar{c}_t = \bar{b}y_t = \bar{b}(Y_t - \bar{Y})$. The confidence interval for $\bar{c}_t$ will then be the confidence interval for $\bar{b}$ multiplied by $Y_t - \bar{Y}$, that is

$$y_t \, . \, (\bar{b} - \bar{\sigma}_b \bar{\sigma}_u \sqrt{F_{0 \cdot 05}(1, T-2)}) \leqslant c_t \leqslant y_t(\bar{b} + \bar{\sigma}_b \bar{\sigma}_u \sqrt{F_{0 \cdot 05}(1, T-2)}). \quad (1.18)$$

II SPECIFICATION ERROR

What we have done so far is to show that we can estimate theoretical relationships and test hypotheses about them given that (a) the correct theoretical relationship is the one estimated, and (b) that our econometric (statistical) assumptions are true. We now turn to an examination of departures from these two conditions.

A. *Specification Bias*

Suppose that we go ahead and estimate the relation between consumption and income as in model (1.1), but in fact consumption also depends on wealth or at least there is a theoretical reason for believing that it does, so that we might have

$$C = a + bY + dW + u', \qquad (1.19)$$

where W is wealth. Then if we estimate model (1.1) as before, we have left out a possibly relevant variable. This may cause the least-squares estimate of b to be biased. The least-squares estimate of b is

$$\bar{b} = \sum c_t y_t / \sum y_t^2. \qquad (1.20)$$

Substituting in for $c_t = by_t + dw_t + u_t^*$ (where the lower-case letters stand for deviations from the mean) we have

$$\bar{b} = b + d \sum y_t W_t / \sum y_t^2 + y_t u_t^* / \sum y_t^2. \qquad (1.21)$$

This can be expressed as $\bar{b} = b + d\bar{d}_{yw} + v$, where $v = \sum y_t u_t^* / \sum y_t^2$ is the error term at the end of the equation, and $\bar{d}_{yw}$ is the ordinary least-squares regression coefficient obtained from regressing y on w. If $\bar{d}_{yw} \neq 0$ then the estimate $\bar{b}$ will be biased, since $E(\bar{b}) = b + d\bar{d}_{yw}$ (under the assumption that the errors are independent of the right-hand variable, Y). In this simple case, we can tell the direction of the bias which is the sign of $d\bar{d}_{yw}$. If wealth is positively related to consumption, $d > 0$, and if wealth is empirically positively related to income, $\bar{d}_{yw} > 0$, then the least-squares estimate of b, $\bar{b}$, from estimating (1.1), is larger than it should be (on average or in expected value). This could lead to serious errors since we could have estimated the m.p.c. to be $\bar{b} = 0.9$ whereas an unbiased estimate would have been $0.7 = 0.9 - 0.2$ (supposing that $d\bar{d}_{yw} = 0.2$).

In order to avoid this specification bias on the coefficient(s), investigators generally include all the possible variables that are available and which might possibly influence the dependent variable. It may be shown that the estimated coefficient of y when equation (1.19) is estimated is an unbiased estimate of b, although equation (1.1) is true, and so, in terms of bias, it is better to include irrelevant variables. Estimating expression (1.20) we again obtain $E(\bar{b}) = b + d\bar{d}_{yw}$ but if wealth is irrelevant then $d = 0$ and $E(b) = b$. But there is a cost of doing so. The standard errors of the relevant variables (ones which have theoretical coefficients which are not zero) increase. One easy way to see this is that $V(\bar{b}) = \sigma_u^2 / \sum Y_t^2$ without an intercept in the equation, and is $\sigma_u^2 / \sum y_t^2$ with the intercept, regardless of whether the true coefficient of the intercept is zero or not. But $\sum Y_t^2 \geqslant \sum y_t^2 = \sum Y_t^2 - \bar{Y}^2$ and so the variance of b is larger when the intercept (or any other variable) is included in the regression than when it is not. With larger standard errors the confidence intervals of these coefficients will be larger than could have been obtained if we estimated the correct model. We might even be led to accept the hypothesis that $b = 0$ when in fact it is not, due solely to the inclusion of an irrelevant variable. This means that investigators must be quite careful in accepting the hypothesis that a coefficient is zero.

If the investigator accepts this hypothesis, then the equation should be re-estimated with that variable excluded from the equation. This is due to the fact that, if an error has not been made in accepting the hypothesis that the variable is irrelevant (coefficient equals 0), then more efficient (precise) estimates of the remaining variables will be obtained when the variable is dropped, since by excluding the variable the variances of the remaining estimates must decrease (or at least not increase). But if it is dropped erroneously, then biased estimates of the remaining coefficients will be obtained. The careful researcher is thus presented with a dilemma. If he excludes a variable which is relevant the estimated coefficients will be biased, while including an irrelevant variable will obtain inefficient (large variance) estimates which may lead to the rejection of truly relevant variables. In practice, one should take great care in either including or excluding a variable in a regression equation examining both empirical and theoretical reasons for doing so.

B.   *Multi-collinearity*

There is another reason that the F-statistic, testing whether or not a coefficient is zero, might be small although the coefficient is not zero. This is the problem of multi-collinearity. One simple way to see the problem is that in the simple regression of C on Y, if the variance of Y is quite small, b's estimated standard error will be quite large, as is seen in formula (1.11) (since $\sum_{t=1}^{T} y_t^2$ is the estimated variance of Y). A small variance of Y implies a small F, which will lead to acceptance of the hypothesis that the coefficient is zero more often than if Y has large variance.

In the more general problem in which there are many variables on the right-hand side of the equation, the problem of multi-collinearity is that some combination of the right-hand variables move together along a single line or plane. This line, formed by some combination of the right-hand variables, may explain the dependent variable quite well (high R^2) but the effects of each variable cannot be separated from each other since their observations all lie along a line. In such a case it is common to have all the coefficients separately test equal to zero, but the test of all simultaneously equal to zero fails. In our example consumption might be very well explained by income and wealth. But in time-series data, income and wealth tend to move together quite closely, and so we cannot determine the separate effect of income, since wealth moves with it. Now both of these problems, multi-collinearity and including irrevant variables, lead to large standard errors which in turn leads to a small $\bar{F}$ and hence it is more likely that we will accept the null hypothesis. In practice, to determine whether we should accept the null hypothesis and exclude the variable from the regression, the equation is generally estimated without the variable; if the remaining estimates are unchanged then the omitted variable is dropped (that is we accept the null hypothesis). If the estimates change dramatically, or if there is strong *a priori* (theoretical or previous empirical) reasons to believe that the coefficient is not zero, then the variable is left in the equation even though its coefficient is statistically tested to be equal to zero.

C. *Hetero-skedasticity*

We have discussed two problems with least-squares estimation above. The first concerned our specification of the equation to be estimated (generally known as specification error) and the second was a problem with the data. We now consider what happens to least-squares estimates when assumption (A.3) (concerning the errors of the equation) is untenable. It should be emphasised that in order to detect *any* specification error (whether it be about the model or the statistical assumptions made about the model) one must have some theoretical reason for believing that there might be one. Computer output does not generally tell us that we have mis-specified the regression equation or the errors except through careful examination of the estimated statistics *along with* the theory that generated the equation.

Returning to our consumption function, although consumption may be determined by income in the manner specified by our regression equation, for example model (1.1), it might be that for higher incomes the relation is less precise. The error on the equation in this case would have more variance with larger incomes than with smaller. We might then specify that the variance of the error depends on income. For example, $V(u_t) = \sigma_u^2 Y_t^2$ might be specified, which of course violates assumption (A.3a). Figure 1.5 illustrates this specification. The line drawn is the theoretical relation and the points represent data points. For larger incomes the points are further from the line than is the case with smaller incomes.

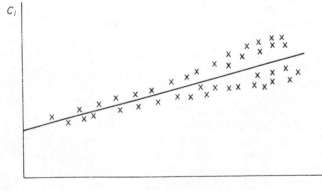

Fig. 1.5

Although with this specification we will still obtain unbiased estimates by regressing C on Y (if (A.1), (A.2) and (A.3b) are still true), it can be shown that these estimates are not efficient, that is they do not have minimum variance. In order to correct for the specification error (on the errors), we can divide equation (1.1) by Y obtaining

$$\frac{C_t}{Y_t} = \frac{a}{Y_t} + b + \frac{u_t}{Y_t}. \tag{1.22}$$

This equation now conforms to the original specification (A.3a) since $V(u_t/Y) = \sigma_u^2$, given our specification $V(u_t) = \sigma_u^2 Y_t^2$. More efficient estimates are obtained from equation (1.22) than from estimating (1.1) due to the fact that the latter does not have homoskedastic errors ($V(u_t) = \sigma^2$, for all t) while the former does. Intuitively, more efficient estimates are obtained since we use more information to obtain them. Estimation of (1.1) or (1.22) may result in estimates which are quite close, but with $V(u_t) = \sigma_u^2 Y_t^2$, the estimates from (1.22) will have smaller variance than those from (1.1).

This is quite a general practice, namely that of weighting the data by some other variable to obtain theoretically more efficient estimates. For example, in studies using cross-sectional data where the unit of observation is some geographical area (cities), one might divide the equation by the population of the area to alleviate the problem of hetero-skedasticity. Since all variables in the equation would be divided by the population to remove hetero-skedasticity, this is not equivalent to running an equation in *per capita* terms since in the latter some variables (average age of the city) do not have *per capita* interpretations.

There are some tests to determine whether the regression errors are homoskedastic *if* the investigator knows which variable might be related to the hetero-skedasticity. Basically, the data would be split into two groups, one having small values of the suspected variable and the other having large values. The regression is run on each subset of data and an F-statistic formed from the ratio of the estimated variances of each equation, that is $\bar{F} = \bar{\sigma}_1^2/\bar{\sigma}_2^2$ where $\bar{\sigma}_1^2$ and $\bar{\sigma}_2^2$ are the variance estimates from the two sub-samples. This statistic is then compared to tabled F-values as in the tests before. ($\bar{F} = \bar{\sigma}_1^2/\bar{\sigma}_2^2$ has $T_1 - k$ and $T_2 - k$ degrees of freedom where T_1 is the sample size of the first group, T_2 is the sample size of the second group, and k is the number of regressors.)

The null hypothesis here is that the errors are homoskedastic, so that if the estimated F-statistic is very large, the hypothesis of homoskedastic errors is rejected. (We are assuming that $\bar{F}$ is formed by the ratio of the larger variance to the smaller.) If it is rejected, then the equation should be estimated in another form such as (1.22). If it is not rejected, then least-squares estimates of the original equation would be used.

D. *Serial Correlation*

A second problem with the errors is that of serial correlation. Formally it means that $E(u_t u_{t-1}) \neq 0$. One general form of this problem is that

$$u_t = \rho u_{t-1} + v_t, \tag{1.23}$$

where v_t is normally and independently distributed with mean 0 and variance σ^2, that is v_t satisfies assumptions (A.3a) and (A.3b) and has a normal distribution. The normality assumption must be made in order to do hypothesis tests as before.

This error specification might occur if some variable(s) left out of the equation moved together over time, but do not in fact have any influence on the dependent variable (otherwise there would be a specification bias due to an excluded relevant variable). An illustration of serially correlated errors appears in Figure 1.6. The least-squares estimates are again

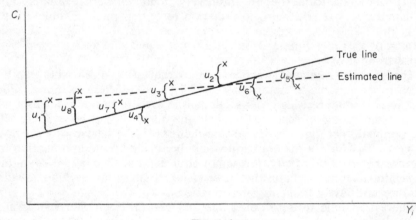

Fig. 1.6

unbiased but inefficient. Also, the statistics, such as the standard errors of the estimates, are incorrectly reported by the computer. This is due to the fact that computer programmes calculate these statistics assuming that (A.3a) and (A.3b) are true. Since equation (1.23) violates (A.3b), formulas derived with (A.3b) are incorrect if equation (1.23) is in fact true. In the case of positive auto-correlation (that is, $\rho > 0$) the reported statistics are generally biased in favour of rejecting the null hypothesis. The reported statistics are also miscalculated when the errors are heteroskedastic, but the direction of the miscalculation is generally unknown in that case. Even if we compute the correct statistics the estimates are inefficient, and so the general procedure is to estimate more efficient estimates rather than compute the correct statistics for the inefficient estimates.

The most common test for the presence of serial correlation is the Durbin–Watson test [7]. The Durbin–Watson statistic is calculated from

$$\bar{d} = \sum_{t=2}^{T} (\bar{u}_t - \bar{u}_{t-1} - 1)^2 \Big/ \sum_{t=1}^{T} \bar{u}_t^2. \qquad (1.24)$$

Unfortunately, the distribution of $\bar{d}$ depends on the values of the independent variables, and so its distribution cannot be conveniently tabulated. What has been done is to determine two random variables such that they bound the random variable d (of which $\bar{d}$ is an observation). In other words, there exist two random variables such that $d_l \leqslant d \leqslant d_u$. With tabled values of d_u and d_l we can then test for the presence of serial correlation. If $\bar{d} < d_l$, where d_l is taken from the table, one concludes there is serial correlation in the model. Actually, $\bar{d} < d_l$ implies that $E(u_t u_{t-1}) \neq 0$ is accepted. The form of the correlation of the errors is *not* determined though, and so equation (1.23) may or may not be true even though $d < d_l$. If $\bar{d} < d_u$, one concludes there is no serial correlation (accepts $E(u_t u_{t-1}) = 0$) and uses ordinary least-squares estimates. The values of d_u and d_l are tabled for 0·05 and 0.01 probability of Type-I error. The distribution is also tabled for the number of observations and the number of independent variables. The tables only include up to five (six including the intercept) independent variables.

When $\bar{d}$ is between the tabled values of d_u and d_l the test is inconclusive, and no decision is indicated. Many researchers reject the null hypothesis of no serial correlation when $d < d_u$. Although this increases the probability of Type-I error over the amount chosen (to determine d_u), it decreases the probability of Type-II error. The more serious error is to accept the null hypothesis when it is false (since the presence of serial correlation makes ordinary least squares inefficient and reported statistics are biased). Since this error, Type-II (rejecting serial correlation when it is true), is more serious, we would rather make a Type-I error than this one. Hence we trade some increase in the probability of Type-I error (rejecting the null hypothesis when it is true) for less of Type-II error. Although we do not know what this trade-off is, the procedure implies that the cost of Type-II error is much greater than that of Type-I.

Again taking (1.1) and (1.23) as our model, it is seen that if we know ρ we could write the equation as

$$(C_t - \rho C_{t-1}) = (1 - \rho)a + b(Y_t - \rho Y_{t-1}) + v_t, \qquad t = 2, \ldots, Y, \qquad (1.25)$$

and estimate the values of a and b efficiently (or almost so since we lose an observation by estimating the equation above). But we also have to estimate the value of ρ. Two methods are generally used in practice to do this. We may rewrite equation (1.25) as

$$C_t = \rho C_{t-1} + (1 - \rho)a + b Y_t - b\rho Y_{t-1} + v_t, \qquad t = 2, \ldots, T, \qquad (1.26)$$

and then use it to obtain an estimate of ρ with the coefficient estimated on the lagged dependent variable (C_{t-1}). This estimate would then be used to calculate the variables in (1.25), from which a and b would be estimated. This procedure was proposed by Durbin [4]. The other procedure is an iterative one, called the Cochrane–Orcutt method [3].

Initially, ρ is set equal to 0 in (1.25) and the equation estimated. The estimated errors from this regression are then used to determine an estimate of ρ by regressing $\bar{u}_t$ on $\bar{u}_{t-1}$, that is ρ is estimated from the regression equation, $\bar{u}_t = \rho \bar{u}_{t+1} + v'_t$. This estimate of ρ is then used in (1.25) to determine a new estimate of a and b. These estimates are in turn used to create new estimates of the errors, $\bar{u}_t = C_t - \bar{a} - \bar{b} Y_t$, which are then used to determine a new estimate of ρ. Various stopping rules can be used, the most common of which is to stop the iterations when the old estimate of ρ is close (say within 0·001) of the new estimate.

The problem with both these estimates is that the $\bar{a}$ and $\bar{b}$ so determined are no longer unbiased, since they are determined in part by an estimate of ρ which in turn theoretically involves the random errors u_t. This means that we cannot (easily) evaluate $E(\bar{b})$ as before and can no longer determine whether the estimates are biased. Note that since $\bar{\rho}$ is a function of u_t, $\bar{b}$ will now be a ratio of functions of u_t where before u_t was only in the numerator. But the estimates do have another property if some additional statistical assumptions are made. This property is called consistency, which means (loosely) that if the sample size grows infinitely large, then the estimate (from the infinite sample) will equal the true value of the parameter. For example, the sample mean is a consistent estimate of the mean of the distribution from which the observations were drawn. It turns out that both the Durbin and the iterative Cochrane–Orcutt estimates are consistent estimates.

Recall that the reason for worrying about serial correlation is that inefficient estimates are obtained from ordinary least squares, and that in general the reported statistics are miscalculated. Among the three estimates discussed so far, some studies have shown that the estimate proposed by Durbin is better (in a certain sense) than ordinary least-square estimates in small samples [9]. Seemingly, this means that sacrificing unbiasedness of the O.L.S. estimate yields a much more precise estimate. But, of course, whether these results can be generalised for all data (since these studies create their own data to determine which estimate is better) is an open question. Most researchers tend to use the iterative Cochrane–Orcutt method to obtain their estimates.

E.   *Pooling of Data: The 'Chow' Test*

In many cases, such as with investment behaviour, we not only have data for different periods but also for different firms. In this case we would like to be able to combine the data into one sample rather than a sample on each firm, since increasing the sample size improves the estimates. This 'pooling' of data would imply that the effects of the independent variables on the dependent are the same for all firms. We might want to test this assumption alone ignoring the fact that, if it is true, we could combine the samples. Rather than assume this, we may wish to test this specification. Formally, we might have the following specification:

$$C_{it} = a_i + b_i Y_{it} + u_{it}, \qquad t = 1, \ldots, T, \qquad i = 1, \ldots, m, \qquad (1.27)$$

so that there are m units of observation (firms, consumers, and so forth) – i indexes these units – and T observations for each unit. The hypothesis that we would like to test is that $a_i = a_j = a$ and $b_i = b_j = b$ for all units i and j. The procedure for doing this is really quite simple, and again is based on a statistic which has an F-distribution. We run the m regressions each having T observations and obtain the m estimates of the variance of the m regressions, $\bar{\sigma}_i^2$, $i = 1, \ldots, m$. We also estimate the equation using the pooled (combined) sample of mT observations and its estimated variance, $\bar{\sigma}^2$. Then the statistic $\bar{F}$, defined as

$$\bar{F} = \frac{(\sum \bar{\sigma}_i^2 - \bar{\sigma}^2)/2m}{\bar{\sigma}^2/(mT - 2)}$$

has an F-distribution of $2m$ and $mT - 2$ degrees of freedom and we compare the value of $\bar{F}$ with an appropriate tabled value and reject the hypothesis that we can pool the data (all the a_is and all the b_is are equal) if $\bar{F}$ is too large. This test is frequently called a Chow test, after Gregory Chow who first presented it [2].

III STOCHASTIC VARIABLES: MEASUREMENT ERRORS

In all of the preceding analysis the independent variables were assumed to be non-random and the dependent variable was then 'created' from a linear function of the independent variables plus some error term. But in many (if not all) problems it is a rather strong assumption at best that the right-hand variables are not random themselves. Even if the right-hand variables in the equation are random variables (or functions of random variables) all is not lost. For many applications, the estimates obtained from least squares are unbiased and efficient conditional upon the ob-served values of the independent variables (given the correct model and error specification).

But there is a case in which the observed independent variables are in part random variables where all the properties including consistency are lost. It is really a form of specification error, but is more commonly known as a measurement-error problem. One of the best illustrations of the problem comes from consumer theory. We suppose that consumption is a linear function of 'permanent' income but permanent income cannot be observed. What is observed is 'measured' income, Y_t, which is perma-nent income, Y_t^*, plus transitory income, V_t. Formally,

$$C_t = a + b Y_t^* + u_t \qquad (1.28a)$$

and

$$Y_t = Y_t^* + V_t. \qquad (1.28b)$$

If we could obtain data on Y^* then ordinary least-squares estimates will have all of the properties we desire. But if observations on Y^* are unavailable (non-measurable) and only data on Y_t is observed, then ordinary least squares applied to

$$C_t = a + bY_t + u_t^*$$

(1.29)

will be biased and inconsistent. The problem is that the regression line cannot determine the effect of Y^* on C since Y^* is not observed. This is illustrated in Figure 1.7. The dots on the graph represent the observed

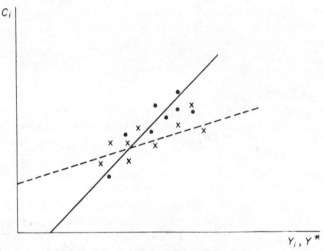

Fig. 1.7

data points (C_t, Y_t), while the crosses represent the unobserved points (C_t, Y_t^*). The dashed line represents the line which would be estimated if we could observe Y^* while the dark line represents the actual estimation from the data (C_t, Y_t). It should be noted that the larger the error between Y and Y^* (that is V) the more chance we have of estimating an incorrect line. One should also note that the problem is that we do not observe the variables in the true theoretical equation, not that the independent variable is random. If consumption were based upon measured income this problem would not arise, since Y would be the variable that belongs in (1.28a) and not Y^*.

Unlike the cases of hetero-skedasticity and serial correlation, there is no statistical test for the presence of measurement error. It is a theoretical specification that cannot be detected empirically and so the theory must tell us whether or not we should suspect this problem. The solutions offered for the problem have been many and we will discuss only two of them. The problem can be seen easily if we write out the formula $\bar{b}$ as in

(1.6a′) above, that is

$$\bar{b} = b + (\sum Y_t(U_t - V_t b)/\sum Y_t^2$$
$$= b + \frac{(\sum Y_t^* U_t - \sum Y_t^* V_t b + \sum V_t U_t - b \sum V_t)}{\sum (Y_t^* + V_t)^2}. \qquad (1.30)$$

This is obtained by substituting $Y_t^* + V_t (= Y_t)$ for y_t in (1.6a). Before, when there was no measurement error, the expected value of the last term equalled zero. Here, even though we cannot evaluate the expected value of the term (due to the fact that Y_t is a random variable), we cannot assume that it is zero, unless the variance of V_t is 0 (no measurement error) or b is 0 (no relationship) due to the term $b \sum V_t^2/\sum Y_t^2$.

The solutions to the problem are not all that happy, and in many cases it is not clear that the cure is better than the disease. One method which is consistent (ordinary least squares applied to the observed data is not) is the technique of instrumental variables. The estimate of b is computed according to

$$\bar{b}_{iv} = \sum z_t C_t/\sum z_t y_t = b + \sum z_t(u_t - v_t b)/\sum z_t y_t. \qquad (1.31)$$

If the instrumental variable z_t is uncorrelated (theoretically) with the error $(u_t - bv_t)$, then $\bar{b}_{iv}$ will be conditionally unbiased and consistent. Durbin [4] has shown that if z_t is chosen to be the ordinal rank of the variable with measurement error, then there is no serious loss of efficiency in using $\bar{b}_{iv}$ compared to estimates by ordinary least squares applied to the theoretically correct data.

Durbin's method generalises easily to the case with more than one right-hand variable. In this general case all the estimates would lose consistency, etc., even if only one variable is measured with error, and so the solution becomes quite important. Sometimes, especially when there are many variables in the analysis, the variable with measurement error is regressed on variables not in the analysis. The predicted value for this variable is then used as a proxy variable for it. This procedure is somewhat better than just choosing a proxy variable since the predicted values of the secondary regression will have a higher correlation with the actual variable than if just one variable is used as a proxy. This predicted variable may also be used as an instrumental variable rather than the ranks that Durbin used. But, in using the secondary regression (regressing the variable with measurement error on other variables not in the equation), one must be careful to choose variables for this regression which can be safely assumed to be uncorrelated with the error in the original equation ($u_t - bv_t$ in the simple equation). Determining which variables to use in these secondary regressions is somewhat of an art and in general one is limited to variables for which the researcher has data available.

Lagged Variables

In many theories, the dependent variable is not only affected by current values of other variables, but also by lagged values of the variables. Current consumption might be affected by one's current income and also lagged values of income so that we have

$$C_t = a + \sum_{i=0}^{\infty} b_i Y_{t-i} + u_t. \tag{1.32}$$

Direct estimation of the equation cannot be made since there are an infinite number of the coefficients (b_is) to estimate. Even if we are willing to ignore the effects of income far in the past, there may still be too many coefficients to estimate. Compounding this problem is the fact that Y_t, Y_{t-1}, Y_{t-2}, etc. may be highly correlated with one another, and hence the equation will have multi-collinearity problems. The solution to estimation is to assume that the b_is are related in some way. One common relation is that the b_is are declining over time, and we might postulate that

$$b_i = \lambda^i (1 - \lambda). \tag{1.33}$$

This is generally called a geometrically declining lag and is due to Koyck [12]. If we lag equation (1.32) by one period and multiply by λ and then subtract this from the original equation, we obtain

$$C_t - \lambda C_{t-1} = (1-\lambda)a + (1-\lambda)\sum_{i=0}^{\infty} \lambda^i Y_{t-i} - (1-\lambda)\sum_{i=0}^{\infty} \lambda^{i+1} Y_{t-(i+1)} + u_t - \lambda u_{t-1}$$

$$= (1-\lambda)a + (1-\lambda)Y_t + u_t - \lambda u_{t-1}, \tag{1.34}$$

which leads to the regression equation

$$C_t = \lambda C_{t-1} + (1-\lambda)Y_t + u_t - \lambda u_{t-1}. \tag{1.35}$$

This equation can also be derived from other theoretical considerations such as a partial-adjustment model or an adaptive-expectations model. Of course, different statistical properties will be derived for the errors in equation (1.34) depending from which model the equation is derived. Hence there is great interest in estimating such an equation. Various assumptions about the original errors will lead to different 'optimal' properties. If the errors of the regression equation, $v_t = u_t - \lambda u_{t-1}$, are serially independent and independent of Y_t, then ordinary least-squares estimates of the equation provide consistent and efficient estimates (in large samples). This would imply that the original errors are serially dependent ($E(u_t u_{t-1}) = \lambda$). This is not a very happy assumption. If the v_ts are serially correlated serious problems develop. Recall that serial correlation alone does not affect the unbiasedness or consistency of ordinary least squares, and that a lagged dependent variable as a right-hand variable still allows consistency. The two problems together, though, cause ordinary least squares to be completely off as in the case of measurement error. Of course, the test statistics are also invalid in this case, and this is especially true for the Durbin–Watson statistic which we might use to test whether v_t is serially correlated. Recently, Durbin [5] has proposed a test of serial correlation in the case where there is a lagged dependent variable among the right-hand variables.

The test is based on the statistic

$$\bar{h} = (1 - 1/2\bar{d}) \cdot \sqrt{T}/\sqrt{1 - T \cdot V(\lambda)}, \ \bar{d} \text{ as defined in (1.24)} \quad (1.36)$$

where $V(\lambda)$ is the variance of the estimate of the coefficient of the lagged dependent variable. The test only works when $T \cdot V(\lambda)$ is less than one although a much more complicated test can be formed if this is not true. The statistic $\bar{h}$ has a standard normal distribution in the absence of serial correlation, and hence, by comparing its value to the tabled values of the standard normal variate, the test may be made.

If the null hypothesis is rejected with such a test, so that we accept serial correlation, then ordinary least-squares estimation will yield rather poor estimates. The problem is much like that of measurement error, depending on the particular set of assumptions made about the errors v_t. For example, with a particular specification of the errors, Y_{t-2} might be used as a proxy for Y_{t-1} to obtain consistent estimates. In other cases, sequential estimation techniques might be used to determine the serial-correlation coefficient and then estimate the parameters of the equation using weighted first-differenced data, the weight being the value of the estimated serial-correlation coefficient.

Not all lag specifications run into the problem of having a lagged dependent variable and serial correlation. One procedure, due to Almon [1] is to assume a finite lag distribution. In order to estimate the lag parameters and to avoid the serious loss of degrees of freedom and multi-collinearity of the lagged variables, Almon proposed the following technique. New variables are formed by weighted sums of the lagged variables, that is

$$z_{lt} = \sum_{i=1}^{r} w_{il} x_{t-i}, \qquad l = 1, \ldots, s, \quad (1.37)$$

where r is the number of lagged periods assumed to affect the dependent variable and s is the number of new variables. If $s = r$, then nothing will be gained, but if $s < r$, we will have gained degrees of freedom and possibly reduced the multi-collinearity problem. The regression

$$Y_t = \sum_{i+1}^{s} c_i z_{it} + V_t \quad (1.38)$$

is run to obtain estimates of c_i, $\bar{c}_i$. These are then used to calculate the estimates of the lagged coefficients by

$$\bar{b}_j = \sum_{i=1}^{s} \bar{c}_i w_{ij}, \qquad j = 1, \ldots, r. \quad (1.39)$$

If the weights are created from a polynomial approximation of the coefficients b_i, the technique seems to have some meaning, that is the coefficients b_i are considered as arising from a polynomial function such that $f(i) = b_i$. The weights are determined by approximating the general polynomial of degree s, $f(i)$. If the weights first rose and then fell, a polynomial of degree 2 would suffice (Figure 1.8 illustrates this).

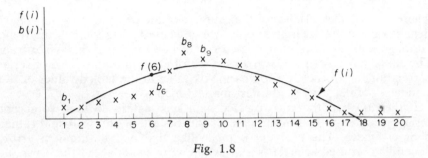

Fig. 1.8

Of course, the method may yield biased estimates due to specification error (the estimated equation does not have the true independent variables in it) and the properties of such estimates will be dependent on the approximation formula used, and how 'good' the function 'fits' the values, b_i. Hence these estimates are tenuous at best, but possibly better than assuming some other form of the lag distribution, such as the Koyck method.

IV SIMULTANEOUS SYSTEMS

We now turn to estimating relationships where some of the variables are determined simultaneously. In the most simple Keynesian model income is determined from two relations, the consumption function which is behavioural and the identity that aggregate demand (consumption plus investment) equals aggregate supply (income). Firms' supply and consumers' demand may be influenced by variables such as the rate of inflation, wealth, capital stock, and so on. Our intention is to present a model in which consumption and income are simultaneously determined and the other variables are either determined by past relationships or by independent authorities (the government for example). We then classify the variables whose values are determined within the system as endogenous variables and variables which are determined outside the model as exogenous. Of course, in some systems a variable may be endogenous and in other systems exogenous, depending on what the model is explaining. Let our model be

$$C_t = b_{11} + b_{12}Y_t + b_{13}X_{1t} + b_{14}X_{2t} + b_{15}X_{3t} + u_{1t} \qquad (1.40a)$$

and

$$Y_t = b_{21} + b_{22}C_t + b_{23}X_{1t} + b_{24}X_{2t} + b_{25}X_{3t} + u_{2t}. \qquad (1.40b)$$

In the simple Keynesian cross diagram, the intersection of the consumption function and the line $C = Y$ determines income and consumption. In our two-equation model, the solution of the two equations determines them. The variables X_1, X_2 and X_3 are the exogenous variables of our system. These variables might be (exogenous) investment, the interest rate, price level, and so forth. Notice that our model does not have an identity; however, most macroeconomic equation systems do. Our purpose is not to present a theoretically based model, but to present one in which we can explain estimation procedures for simultaneous equations. Given the values of these variables, consumption and income adjust to obtain equilibrium (both equations satisfied simultaneously). Observations are then values of C and Y determined jointly from this system, noting of course that there is some error in the equations.

There are two problems in trying to estimate each of these equations.

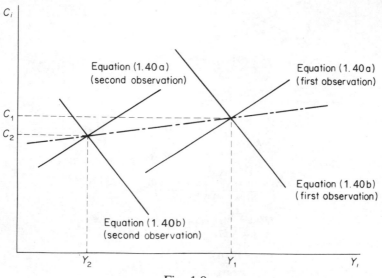

Fig. 1.9

First, without some knowledge of the value of the parameters, they are observationally identical. Between two points of data, we cannot tell whether the two points lie on one consumption function, one supply function, or both functions shifted (due to changes in the X variables) to create the second data point. This is illustrated in Figure 1.9 and is known in general as the problem of identification. If we know that $b_{13} = b_{14} = b_{15} = 0$, then all the points would have to lie along the consumption function since only the supply functions shifts, as is illustrated in Figure 1.10. We will return to this problem later.

The second problem is that, even if we can distinguish (identify) the two behavioural relations, it can be easily seen that in both equations one of the right-hand variables is not only a random variable but is determined by the random errors of both equations. This is most easily seen by solving the system for the endogenous variables (those determined within the system) in terms of the exogenous variables and the errors. For our

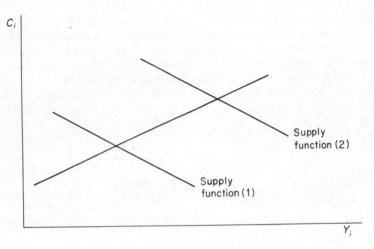

Fig. 1.10

system we have,

$$C_t = \frac{b_{11} + b_{12}b_{21}}{1 - b_{12}b_{22}} + \left(\frac{b_{13} + b_{12}b_{23}}{1 - b_{12}b_{22}}\right)X_{1t}$$
$$+ \left(\frac{b_{14} + b_{12}b_{24}}{1 - b_{12}b_{22}}\right)X_{2t} + \left(\frac{b_{15} + b_{12}b_{25}}{1 - b_{12}b_{22}}\right)X_{3t}$$
$$+ \frac{u_{1t} + b_{12}u_{2t}}{1 - b_{12}b_{22}} \ldots \tag{1.41a}$$

or

$$C_t = P_{11} + P_{12}X_{1t} + P_{13}X_{2t} + P_{14}X_{3t} + v_{1t} \tag{1.41a'}$$

$$Y_t = \frac{b_{21} + b_{22}b_{11}}{1 - b_{12}b_{22}} + \left(\frac{b_{22} + b_{22}b_{13}}{1 - b_{12}b_{22}}\right)X_{1t} + \left(\frac{b_{24} + b_{22}b_{14}}{1 - b_{12}b_{22}}\right)X_{2t}$$
$$+ \left(\frac{b_{25} + b_{22}b_{15}}{1 - b_{12}b_{22}}\right)X_{3t} + \frac{u_{2t} + b_{22}u_{1t}}{1 - b_{12}b_{22}} \tag{1.41b}$$

or

$$C_t = P_{21} + P_{22}X_{1t} + P_{23}X_{2t} + P_{24}X_{3t} + v_{2t} \tag{1.41b'}$$

where

$$P_{11} = \frac{b_{11} + b_{21}b_{12}}{1 - b_{12}b_{22}}, \qquad P_{12} = \frac{b_{13} + b_{12}b_{23}}{1 - b_{12}b_{22}}$$

$$P_{13} = \frac{b_{14} + b_{12}b_{24}}{1 - b_{12}b_{22}}, \qquad P_{14} = \frac{b_{15} + b_{12}b_{25}}{1 - b_{12}b_{22}} \qquad (1.42a)$$

$$P_{21} = \frac{b_{21} + b_{22}b_{11}}{1 - b_{12}b_{22}}, \qquad P_{22} = \frac{b_{23} + b_{22}b_{13}}{1 - b_{12}b_{22}} \qquad (1.42b)$$

$$P_{23} = \frac{b_{24} + b_{22}b_{14}}{1 - b_{12}b_{22}}, \qquad P_{24} = \frac{b_{25} + b_{22}b_{15}}{1 - b_{12}b_{22}}$$

This system is generally called the reduced form of the simultaneous system. These equations show that Y and C are functions of the random errors in both equations and so ordinary least-squares estimates of the behavioural equations (1.40a) and (1.40b) will be biased and inconsistent, just as in the measurement-error case.

Now so long as there is no serial correlation of the errors, within each equation and between equations, and the equation errors are independent, (that is $E(u_{it}, u_{jt-s}) = 0$ for all i, j, t, s except when $i = j$ and $s = 0$. The reduced-form equations can be estimated by ordinary least squares to obtain unbiased and efficient estimates of the parameters in the reduced-form equations. We will obtain eight of these estimates, $\bar{P}_{ij}$, $i = 1$ and 2: $j = 1, 2, 3$ and 4. Since we know that these estimates are related to the structural coefficients (structural coefficients are those that occur in the original system, that is the b_{ij}s in (1.40a) and (1.40b)) by equations (1.42a) and (1.42b), we might try to solve these equations for b_{ij} in terms of the $\bar{P}_{ij}$. What should be obvious is that we have eight estimates and ten structural parameters, so that no exact solution is possible. Another way of looking at this is that there are eight equations and ten unknowns, so that the best that we can do is to solve for eight of the unknowns in terms of the two others and the eight estimates $\bar{P}_{ij}$. This again is the problem of identification, namely can we identify the structural coefficients from the reduced-form coefficients.

If we were to assume known values for two of the structural parameters, say zero, then we may be able to identify the structural parameters from the reduced-form parameters. But if one looks at equations (1.42a) and (1.42b) carefully, it is seen that we must assume values for one parameter in each equation, rather than just assuming two arbitrary structural parameters are zero.

For example, assume that $b_{14} = b_{15} = 0$. Then we can estimate b_{11}, b_{12} and b_{13} by solving the equations

$$b_{11} = \bar{P}_{11} - b_{12}\bar{P}_{21}$$
$$b_{13} = \bar{P}_{12} - b_{12}\bar{P}_{22}$$
$$0 = b_{14} = \bar{P}_{13} - b_{12}\bar{P}_{23} \qquad (1.43a)$$
$$0 = b_{15} = \bar{P}_{14} - b_{12}\bar{P}_{24}$$

and

$$b_{21} = \bar{P}_{21} - b_{2i}\bar{P}_{11}$$
$$b_{23} = \bar{P}_{22} - b_{2i}\bar{P}_{12}$$
$$b_{24} = \bar{P}_{23} - b_{2i}\bar{P}_{13} \tag{1.43b}$$
$$b_{25} = \bar{P}_{24} - b_{2i}\bar{P}_{14}$$

which are obtained from equations (1.42a) and (1.42b). Specifically, we have

$$\bar{b}_{12} = \bar{P}_{13}/\bar{P}_{23}$$
$$\bar{b}_{11} = (\bar{P}_{11} - \bar{P}_{13}\bar{P}_{21})/\bar{P}_{23}$$
$$\bar{b}_{13} = (\bar{P}_{13} - \bar{P}_{13}\bar{P}_{23})/\bar{P}_{22} \tag{1.44}$$
$$\bar{b}_{14} = \bar{b}_{15} = 0 \text{ (assumed).}$$

These estimates are called the indirect least-squares estimates. They can be obtained only in case the system is identifiable. In this particular case we can solve for the first equation's structural parameters but not the second. The parameters of the second equation cannot be solved for since they are determined by model (1.43b) which is four equations in five unknowns. The general rule, to determine whether a structural equation is identifiable, called the order condition, is that *the number of variables in a structural equation* (including the intercept and the dependent variable) *must be less than or equal to the number of exogenous variables* (including the intercept as an exogenous variable) in the entire system. If the number of variables is exactly equal to (strictly less than, strictly greater than) the equation is exactly identifiable (over-identifiable, under-identifiable). This will translate directly to the more commonly used rule, but one harder to remember and verify, that the number of excluded exogenous variables must be at least as great as the number of included endogenous variables less one (the left-hand variable is not counted as an included endogenous). Excluded of course means that the coefficient is *a priori* assumed equal to zero. There are more complicated rules when the parameters are restricted by equations rather than just set equal to zero and when one can make assumptions about the variances and covariances of the random errors in both equations, but these are rarely used in practice.

Now indirect least squares (solving for estimates of the structural coefficients in terms of the reduced-form estimates) will provide consistent estimates of the structural coefficients but may provide more than one estimate (usually the estimates are biased except when the specification is such that one of the reduced-form parameters is identically equal to the structural parameter). With our assumption that $b_{14} = b_{15} = 0$, it is seen that we can estimate b_{12} by $\bar{P}_{13}/\bar{P}_{23}$ or by $\bar{P}_{14}/\bar{P}_{15}$. If the sample size grew infinitely, then these two estimates would have the same value since both are consistent. But for finite sample sizes they will generally give quite different estimates of b_{12}. The problem is that indirect least squares provides more than one estimate when the equation is over-identifiable, which in terms of our rule means that the number of variables in the equation is strictly less than the number of exogenous variables.

A second method of estimation is called two-stage least squares. It is very much like one of the solutions offered to the problem of a variable with measurement error. The trouble with directly estimating the structural equations of a simultaneous model is that the right-hand variables which are endogenous to the system are correlated with the error term of the equation. This is much like the case of measurement error, and one solution is to obtain proxy variables for the endogenous variables which are not correlated with the errors. In the simultaneous-system case, a natural choice would be the predicted values of the endogenous variables obtained from the reduced-form estimation, that is we would obtain predicted values of Y_t, $\bar{Y}_t$, from estimating equation (1.40b), and then estimate the structural parameters from the regression equation

$$C_t = b_{11} + b_{12}\bar{Y}_t + b_{13}X_{1t} + b_{14}X_{2t} + b_{15}X_{3t} + u_t^*. \tag{1.45}$$

Now it appears that we have avoided the problem of identification with this method. This is not the case. If all of the parameters of the exogenous variables are assumed to be non-zero in this equation, then $\bar{Y}_t$ is an exact linear combination of these variables, $\bar{Y}_t = \bar{P}_{11} + \bar{P}_{12}X_{1t} + \bar{P}_{13}X_{2t} + \bar{P}_{14}X_{4t}$, and hence is exactly collinear with the variables X_1, X_2 and X_3 (considered as a set). Although we would have to present the general form of the estimates in matrix notation to provide a direct proof, the intuition is clear. When one of the variables on the right-hand side of the equation is an exact linear combination of some or all of the other variables on the right-hand side, estimates cannot be made. It is a case of extreme collinearity, and is equivalent to having the same variable appear twice on the right-hand side. Estimates in this case cannot be made.

Hence the two-stage least-square estimates can be obtained only when the system is identifiable. Now it turns out that more efficient estimates are obtained with two-stage least squares (at least for large samples) than with indirect least squares, when the structural equation is over identifiable. This fact has led most investigators to use two-stage estimates rather than indirect least-squares estimates in practice. There are also some other methods, such as least variance ratio-limited information maximum likelihood estimates which involve maximising the likelihood function of all the endogenous variables. These estimation techniques are quite costly computationally compared to two-stage estimators, and since they generally involve iterative solutions to non-linear equations, they are numerically less accurate. Monte Carlo studies of different estimators have been made to determine whether one estimator is better, in terms of various criteria, than another for small sample sizes. In the Monte Carlo study, data are created where the true parameter value is known, and the different estimators applied to the created data. There seems to be no general agreement among the various studies (or even within the same study) as to which estimator is best for small samples. One of the studies (Summers [14]) concludes that two-stage least squares 'may well be the best estimator to choose since it is the cheapest and easiest method to compute'.

BIBLIOGRAPHY

[1]   S. Almon, 'The Distributed Lag Between Capital Appropriations and Expenditures', *Econometrica*, vol. 30, no. 1 (1965).
[2]   G. Chow, 'Tests of Equality between Subsets of Coefficients in Two Linear Regressions', *Econometrica*, vol. 28, no. 3 (1960).
[3]   D. Cochrane and G. H. Orcutt, 'Application of Least-squares Regression to Relationships Containing Auto-correlated Error Terms', *Journal of the American Statistical Association*, vol. 44, no. 245 (Mar 1949).
[4]   J. Durbin, 'Estimation of Parameters in Time-Series Regression Models', *Journal of the Royal Statistical Society*, series B, vol. 22, no. 1 (1960).
[5]   —, 'Errors in Variables', *Review of the International Statistics Institute*, vol. 22 (1954).
[6]   —, 'Testing Serial Correlation in Least-Squares Regression when some of the Regressors are Lagged Dependent Variables', *Econometrica*, vol. 38 (1970).
[7]   — and G. S. Watson, 'Testing for Serial Correlation in Least Squares Regression', *Biometrika*, vol. 37 (1950) and vol. 38 (1951).
[8]   F. Fisher, 'Tests of Equality Between Sets of Coefficients in Two Linear Regressions: An Expository Note', *Econometrica*, vol. 38 (1970).
[9]   Z. Griliches and P. Rao, 'Small Sample Properties of Several Two-Stage Regression Methods in the Context of Autocorrelated Errors', *Journal of the American Statistical Association*, vol. 64 (1969).
[10] J. Johnston, *Econometric Method* (New York: McGraw-Hill, 1972).
[11] H. H. Kelejian and W. E. Oates, *Introduction to Econometrics* (New York: Harper & Row, 1974).
[12] L. M. Koyck, *Distributed Lags and Investment Analysis* (Amsterdam: North-Holland, 1954).
[13] J. L. Murphy, *Introductory Econometrics* (Homewood, Ill.: Irwin, 1973).
[14] R. M. Summers, 'A Capital Intensive Approach to the Small Sample Properties of Various Simultaneous Equation Estimators', *Econometrica*, vol. 33, no. 1 (1965).
[15] A. A. Walters, *Introduction to Econometrics* (New York: Norton, 1970).

2

Production Functions

David F. Heathfield

University of Southampton

INTRODUCTION

A production function describes the relationship between what is put into a productive process and what emerges in the form of output. There may be a number of ways of combining inputs to achieve a given output or it may be that a unique combination is required. In so far as we are interested only in scarce inputs we can limit our definition to the set of efficient combinations of such inputs. By efficient is simply meant that no more than is necessary is used up to produce the required output; it does not limit us to the least-cost combination.

Inputs may be treated at various levels of aggregation as may outputs. In macroeconomic models it is usual to deal with only two inputs (labour and capital) and only one output. In such models production functions sometimes turn up in an implicit form explaining the demand for labour when output, capital stock and technology are known. In the Brookings Model ([26] p. 234), for example, 'production functions will be developed in the guise of man hour demand equations'.

In some expositions of the classical macroeconomic model the relationship between output and labour input is used to generate a demand curve for labour. This requires assumptions about the constancy of technology and capital stock and the substitutability of labour for capital. This demand curve together with a supply curve of labour then determines equilibrium output, employment and wage rate.

The classical derivation of the labour-demand function is questioned by Keynes ([46] n. 1, p. 272). He argues that it is unrealistic to assume that labour inputs will be changed without changes in the supply of other factors. The diminishing-returns argument used to impose some shape on the classical demand for labour curve and on the Keynesian aggregate supply function is therefore mistaken. Also Keynes suggests that aggregate supply curve slopes upwards because of the 'diminishing efficiency of labour employed ... not due to internal diseconomies' ([46] n. 1, p. 42). It is not clear why the least-efficient workers should be employed last nor is it clear why increasing returns to scale (since all inputs can now be changed) cannot overcome any decreased labour efficiency.

These confusions may have arisen because the classical model was concerned with the relationship between the *flow* of output, the *flow* of labour input and the *stock* of capital. The stock of capital clearly can be regarded as fixed in the short run (and indeed Keynes assumes this too) but it is evident that not all capital stock is currently being worked for 24 hours every day and so output can be increased either by mixing more labour with fixed capital for a fixed working day, or by employing more labour to work the same stock when it would otherwise be idle. The first approach implies substitutability of factors and is susceptible to the diminishing-returns argument but the second approach, which seems to be that adopted by Keynes, gives no clue as to the likely cost curves.

Why it is that some factors are idle is discussed in Winston [79] and Winston and McCoy [80]. They discuss optimum idleness of resources and some work has been done on measuring capacity usage (see Hilton [39]).

It is clear that macroeconomic models, of both the classical and the Keynesian type, rely for their solutions upon some, often implicit, assumptions about the nature of the productive process. It is the purpose of this chapter to consider some well-known specifications of production functions and to see what empirical support there may be for these different forms. Before doing so it is first necessary to describe the data typically used for these studies and to indicate some of the difficulties attending them.

MEASURING THE VARIABLES

Typically, aggregate production functions relate labour and capital inputs to a single output. Measurement of each of these presents some formidable problems. They are partly theoretical (deciding what it is we are trying to measure) and partly practical (how to go about measuring it).

The theoretical problems are not our prime interest here and are beyond the scope of a chapter such as this but it is clear that aggregating dissimilar quantities will present the usual kind of index-number problems and the time-honoured device of using prices (constant or current) as weights gives rise to a number of problems. Joan Robinson has been particularly active in showing how measures of capital suffer in this regard. (See Harcourt [35] but cf. Pearce [60].)

As far as production functions are concerned we are interested in measuring the amount of human effort and intelligence (labour) applied directly to production, the amount of previously produced, stored up 'output' currently within the production process (capital) and the amount of output per time period.

The amount of human effort and intelligence is usually measured by time spent at place of work (in man-hours). Clearly not everyone at his place of work is working (see Taylor [69] on hoarding) and not everyone who works supplies the same quantity of labour services per hour. The latter problem has been overcome partly by disaggregating labour into different types and aggregating it by using wage rates which it is hoped will reflect relative 'efforts'. Hopefully this will reflect the 'capital' tied up in the labour force, that is human capital. (This was suggested by Keynes.) Sometimes labour hours are not available and, simply, employment figures are used.

Output is the quantity of goods and services supplied per period and the weights used to aggregate the different products are chosen to reflect the relative values placed by society on these goods. Rita Maurice ([54] p. 14) writes that 'broadly speaking the justification of market prices is that they represent the relative value to the individual of different goods and services on the usual assumption that the price paid for each commodity is proportional to its marginal significance'.

There are attempts to adjust for quality changes which tend to be unmeasured when base-period prices are used as weights. The output of services which constitute some 50 per cent of U.K. output can only be measured by valuing the inputs. This is in fact not so different from the output measures used elsewhere. The output of any particular sector is made up partly of the contribution of labour and capital supplied by that sector and partly by the value of raw materials, fuel and other single-use intermediate goods which are bought by that sector from others. This adds up to gross output which can be changed simply by buying more single-use intermediates and hence is not properly the measure of the output of this one sector. There are two ways of deriving net output. It may be possible to value intermediates and output and deflate them both by their appropriate price indices and subtract one from the other; this is called double deflation. The other method is to simply measure the income generated by the sector (the value added by capital and labour) and deflate that. The problem is that there is no appropriate price index for 'value added'. In fact, output is usually represented by the index of industrial production [17]. This is based on censuses of production [10] which are taken every five years or so. Interpolation is done by various proxies for value added, for example labour input, raw material inputs and gross output. These proxies are crucial for production-function analysis since they are justified precisely by an assumed production function. Estimating functions as if the index were an independent measure of output may be misleading in simply revealing the kind of production function assumed by the compiler of the statistics. Perhaps the most that can be said for generated output measures is that they may well reflect *changes* in output at any rate over fairly short time periods.

Capital measures, in so far as it is stored up output, should present no separate problems but its durability gives rise to some difficulties. National Income accounts distinguish between fixed and circulating capital, and further subdivides the fixed item into 'buildings and works' and 'plant and equipment'. These latter two are measured by the perpetual inventory method. Each type of investment is given a 'life' and investment expenditure on each item is deflated by an appropriate price index to give replacement cost new at 1963 prices. Capital stock is computed since new investment flows are added and capital retirements are simply investments L years previous, where L is the life of the item. It turns out that errors in estimated life do not greatly influence stock estimates. This is a gross-capital concept and it may be argued that wear and tear affect the stock so that its productive power as well as its value is better represented by gross stock less depreciation. One can either assume a straight-line depreciation (instead of the sudden death used for gross estimates) or one can use some valuation of the assets of the productive sector. This might be insurance valuations or stock-market valuations or discounted expected earnings. These latter include valuation of all income-earning assets (including patents for example) and one might question the inclusion of this in a capital stock. (For an early discussion of this see Barna [7].)

A second and equally well-recognised problem is that of generating capital-service data from capital-stock data. Clearly one could work a machine for eight hours a day or two machines for four hours and obtain the same output and the same labour requirements. Some argue that the usage of capital can be estimated from the usage of labour but if this is done then it is difficult to see how they can be independently entered into the production function. One would require to know the stock of capital and the number of men simultaneously working with it. In other words, the employment statistics have to be modified to allow for shift-working. (For another attempt to measure capital usage using electricity-consumption data see Heathfield [37].) Bearing those data limitations in mind we now consider some specific production functions.

THE COBB-DOUGLAS PRODUCTION FUNCTION

Perhaps the first attempt to specify and empirically quantify an aggregate production function was that of Douglas [25]. Professor Douglas came to specify his production function by observing that the share of national output going to labour had remained constant for some time. Thus

$$WL = \alpha Y, \tag{2.1}$$

where W is the wage rate, L is man-hours worked, Y is national income and α is a constant.

The problem was to work back from this relationship to the production function implied by it. Douglas took the problem to his mathematical colleague, Cobb, who suggested the form

$$Y = AL^{\alpha}K^{1-\alpha}, \tag{2.2}$$

where K is capital input. Thus the Cobb–Douglas production function was born. Reborn perhaps since it had previously been used by Wicksteed [77].

The derivation of (2.1) from (2.2) requires further assumptions. Consider a profit-maximising entrepreneur deciding on the level of output, the employment of labour and the use of capital. His profit is

$$\pi \equiv YP - LW - Kr, \tag{2.3}$$

where π is profit (to be maximised), P is the price of the product and r is the return going to capital (interest rate). To maximise π, partially differentiate (2.3) with respect to L and K and equate the partials to zero. Thus

$$\frac{\partial \pi}{\partial L} = \frac{\partial Y}{\partial L}P + Y\frac{\partial Y}{\partial L}\frac{\partial P}{\partial Y} - W - \frac{\partial W}{\partial L}L = 0.$$

Therefore

$$\frac{\partial Y}{\partial L}P\left[1 + \frac{Y}{P}\frac{\partial P}{\partial Y}\right] = W\left[1 + \frac{\partial W}{\partial L}\frac{L}{W}\right], \tag{2.4}$$

while for capital we have

$$\frac{\partial Y}{\partial K}P\left[1 + \frac{Y}{P}\frac{\partial P}{\partial Y}\right] = r\left[1 + \frac{\partial r}{\partial K}\frac{K}{r}\right], \tag{2.5}$$

where $\frac{Y}{P}\frac{\partial P}{\partial Y}$ is the inverse of the elasticity of demand for the product ($\sum PY$), $(L/W)(\partial W/\partial L)$ is the inverse of the elasticity of the supply of labour ($\sum LW$) and $(K/r)(\partial r/\partial K)$ is the inverse of the elasticity of the supply of capital ($\sum Kr$). In a perfectly competitive world all these elasticities are zero. Thus

$$\frac{\partial Y}{\partial L} = \frac{W}{P} \tag{2.6}$$

and

$$\frac{\partial Y}{\partial K} = \frac{r}{P}. \tag{2.7}$$

If P is a suitable price deflator for the wage good, equation (2.6) can be taken to mean that real wage equals marginal physical product. Otherwise money wage equals marginal-revenue product.

If we differentiate the Cobb–Douglas function with respect to labour, we have

$$\frac{\partial Y}{\partial L} = A\alpha L^{\alpha-1}K^{1-\alpha} = \frac{\alpha Y}{L}. \tag{2.8}$$

Combining (2.6) and (2.8) yields $LW = \alpha YP$ which is (2.1), that is Douglas's original observation.

Thus, Douglas's observation that the share of National Income going to labour was constant could arise from the existence of an aggregate production function of the Cobb–Douglas variety if the system profit maximises in perfectly competitive markets. Cobb's original form imposed on to the function the parameter $\alpha - 1$ as the exponent of K. There is no need for such a constraint on the evidence so far since

$$Y = AL^{\alpha}K^{\beta} \tag{2.9}$$

also yields (2.1) if the same assumptions are made. The significance of this constraint is twofold; first, $a + \beta$ determines the returns to scale of the function and secondly, they determine the level of profits. Returns to scale are defined as the percentage change in output consequent upon equiproportionate changes in each factor. If we take the differential of (2.9) we have

$$dY = AK^{\beta}L^{\alpha}\alpha\frac{dL}{L} + AL^{\alpha}K^{\beta}\beta\frac{dK}{K}.$$

$$\therefore \qquad dY = \alpha Y\frac{dL}{L} + \beta Y\frac{dK}{K}.$$

$$\therefore \qquad \frac{dY}{Y} = \alpha\frac{dL}{L} + \beta\frac{dK}{K}.$$

But, by definition of returns to scale, $(dL/L) = (dK/K) = (dF/F)$.

$$\therefore \qquad \frac{dY}{Y} = \frac{dF}{F}(\alpha + \beta). \tag{2.10}$$

Thus, if $\alpha + \beta > 1$ the percentage change in output is greater than the percentage change in factors and we have increasing returns to scale; if $\alpha + \beta = 1$ we have constant returns to scale; and if $\alpha + \beta < 1$ we have decreasing returns to scale.

Profits, from (2.3), are $\pi = YP - LW - Kr$. In real terms, dividing throughout by P, we obtain

$$\pi_R = Y - LW_R - Kr_R. \tag{2.11}$$

Substituting from (2.6) and (2.7) we have

$$\pi_R = Y - L\frac{\partial Y}{\partial L} - K\frac{\partial Y}{\partial K}, \tag{2.12}$$

but $\dfrac{\partial Y}{\partial L}=\dfrac{\alpha Y}{L}$ from equation (2.8), and, similarly, $(\partial Y/\partial K)=(\beta Y/K)$. Thus $\pi_R = Y - \alpha Y - \beta Y$, and hence

$$\pi_R = Y(1-(\alpha+\beta)). \tag{2.13}$$

Hence, if returns to scale are constant, $\alpha+\beta=1$, and $\pi_R=0$ for all levels of output. If increasing returns to scale prevail, $\alpha+\beta>1$, and π_R is everywhere non-positive then Y goes to zero. If there are decreasing returns, $\alpha+\beta<1$, profits are positive and Y goes to infinity. (The requirement that the sum of factor rewards equals the total product is the so-called 'adding-up problem'.) The scale of output cannot be determined for a Cobb–Douglas function operating in perfectly competitive markets.

Returns to scale typically do not appear in the discussion of single-commodity macroeconomic models which concentrate on diminishing returns to a factor. We have already shown in equation (2.8) that for the Cobb–Douglas function

$$\frac{\partial Y}{\partial L}=\alpha\frac{Y}{L}=AK^{\beta}\alpha L^{\alpha-1}.$$

A, K, β and α are (by assumption) constant, and so $\partial Y/\partial L$ diminishes as L increases if $\alpha<1$. Thus, the requirements of diminishing returns are satisfied by Cobb–Douglas production functions.

ESTIMATING THE PARAMETERS

It will be recalled that we are dealing with stochastic relationships and must add an error term to the equation. The simplest possible form of error term would be multiplicative and exponential. Thus we have

$$Y = AL^{\alpha}K^{\beta}e^{u}. \tag{2.14}$$

Taking logs, this gives

$$\log Y = \log A + \alpha \log L + \beta \log K + u, \tag{2.15}$$

which is linear and susceptible to simple ordinary least-squares estimation procedures.

Quite a lot of empirical work has been done using this error specification, much of it by Douglas. The constraint that the exponents of L and K sum to unity was imposed on the early estimates [25] by estimating

$$\log Y - \log K = \log A + \alpha(\log L - \log K). \tag{2.16}$$

This yielded (for U.S. manufacturing industry, 1899–1922) $Y = 1 \cdot 01 L^{0 \cdot 75} K^{0 \cdot 25}$ with a coefficient of correlation of $0 \cdot 97$. Clearly, the three variables Y, L and K each grew over time and Menderhausen [56] suspected this multi-collinearity would give rise to specious estimates of α. If each series is detrended, Douglas found $\bar{Y}=\bar{L}^{0 \cdot 84}\bar{K}^{0 \cdot 16}$, where the bar represents the detrended variable.

Durand's estimate [27] of the function without the constraint on the exponents gave $Y = 1 \cdot 01 L^{0 \cdot 765} K^{0 \cdot 246}$. Thus constant returns to scale seem to exist and the constraints satisfied. Subsequently Douglas with Gunn published for the Australian economy the estimates of α and β [33] as shown in the table. In the main, constant returns prevailed and the function was, at minimum, not being rejected on the basis of all this testing. The foregoing estimates each assume a multiplicative-error term which, though convenient for logarithmic linearising, does not seem to be any more justifiable than additive-error terms. Furthermore, it is assumed that the production model can be adequately described by a single equation.

		α	β	$\alpha + \beta$
Victoria	1910–11	0·74	0·25	0·99
Victoria	1923–4	0·62	0·30	0·92
Victoria	1927–8	0·59	0·27	0·86
New South Wales	1933–4	0·65	0·34	0·99
Australia	1934–9	0·64	0·36	1·00

Relaxing the first assumption requires some form of non-linear estimation: relaxing the second requires simultaneous-equation estimation.

SIMULTANEOUS-EQUATION ESTIMATION

It will be remembered that the profit-maximising entrepreneur equates the marginal physical product of labour to the real-wage rate and the marginal physical product of capital to the real rate of interest (see equations (2.6) and (2.7)). Combining these gives

$$\frac{r}{w} = \frac{\beta L}{\alpha K},$$

which together with the production function constitutes a two-equation model which, given an expected level of output, a wage rate and an interest rate, determines L and K. The two equations may be given additive or multiplicative errors such that

$$Y = A 10^{\lambda t} L^{\alpha} K^{\beta} U$$

$$\frac{r}{w} = \frac{\beta L}{\alpha K} v$$

or

$$Y = A 10^{\lambda t} L^{\alpha} K^{\beta} + U$$

$$\frac{r}{w} = \frac{\beta L}{\alpha K} + v$$

The notation is that of Bodkin and Klein [9] and λ is the rate of technical progress (see p. 41).

We could estimate the production functions as single equations ('straight' estimates as previously) or by a stepwise procedure of estimating $\frac{\beta}{\alpha}$ from the marginal-productivity equation and then imposing this constraint on to the production function to yield estimates of α and β. A third approach would be to estimate the equations by some non-linear simultaneous estimation procedure. This has been done by Bodkin and Klein [9] whose results are reported in Table 2.1 (p. 42).

Constant returns to scale are imposed by using Y/L as the dependent variable and K/L as the independent variable. Constant returns are not suggested by the unconstrained estimates but, if imposed, decreases the productivity of capital, β, and labour, α, and increases the rate of technical progress, λ.

The most satisfactory result, as far as the foregoing analysis is concerned, is that of the constrained simultaneous estimation, which yields estimates of α and β of 0·660 and 0·340 respectively. It is nevertheless disturbing that for the other three specifications the original estimates are not confirmed, and apart from the somewhat worrying suggestion of economies of scale there is also the negative productivity of capital in the straight constrained case.

The increasing returns are 'worrying' since it implies negative profit (see equation (2.13)) but this is only true in the perfectly competitive case. If we use the marginal-productivity equations (2.4) and (2.5) we obtain

$$\pi = Y\left[1 - \frac{\alpha}{1+\Sigma_L} - \frac{\beta}{1+\Sigma_K}\right],$$

where π is profit, Σ_L is the elasticity of labour supply with respect to the wage rate and Σ_K is the elasticity of capital supply with respect to the interest rate. Given suitable values for Σ_L and Σ_K we can have increasing returns to scale $(\alpha + \beta > 1)$ and non-negative profits. But the marginal-productivity equation used in our simultaneous model will only be valid if $\Sigma_L = \Sigma_K$.

Notice that the technical-progress term is introduced by Bodkin and Klein by means of an exponential time trend, $e^{\lambda t}$. It is to this aspect of the production function that we now turn.

TECHNICAL PROGRESS

We have defined the production function as being the known set of most-efficient production techniques. It is therefore susceptible to change as our knowledge of production technique changes. This is called *technical progress* which may be variously categorised [36], and which bears a close relationship to what is called total factor productivity. This extension of our knowledge may be regarded as endogenous to our economic model, either in the passive sense of learning by doing [2] or in the active

TABLE 2.1*

Estimates of the parameters of the Cobb–Douglas production function, with unconstrained returns to scale

	A or log A (1)	α (2)	β (3)	α + β (4)	λ (5)	10λ (6)	R̄² S_u (7)	$\frac{\delta^2}{\delta^2}$ (8)
Straight regression, multiplicative error (1)	1·9564 (0·0202)	1·167 (0·0505)	0·035 (0·054)	1·202 (0·048)	0·00696 (0·00033)	1·0162	0·9925 0·01353	1·38
Straight regression, additive error (2)	88·31 (5·66)	1·145 (0·0696)	0·062 (0·073)	1·207 (0·064)	0·00690 (0·00043)	1·0160	0·9899 2·807	1·07
Simultaneous estimation, multiplicative errors[a] (3)	1·7947 (0·0044)	0·960 (0·061)	0·496 (0·032)	1·456 (0·093)	0·00484 (0·00054)	1·0112	0·9795 0·02234	0·66
Simultaneous estimation, additive errors[b] (4)	61·87 (0·78)	0·964 (0·065)	0·501 (0·034)	1·465 (0·098)	0·00526 (0·00063)	1·0122	0·9811 3·839	0·64

[a] $r_{uv} = -0 \cdot 0101$.
[b] $r_{uv} = -0 \cdot 0063$.

Estimates of the parameters of the Cobb–Douglas production function, with constant returns to scale

	A or log A (1)	α (2)	β (3)	α + β (4)	λ (5)	10λ (6)	R̄² S_u (7)	$\frac{\delta^2}{\delta^2}$ (8)
Straight regression, multiplicative error (1)	1·9803 (0·0232)	1·081 (0·055)	−0·081 (0·055)	1·00 (· ·)	0·00806 (0·00025)	1·0187	0·9712 0·01623	0·841
Straight regression, additive error (2)	97·6 (5·90)	1·102 (0·062)	−0·102 (0·062)	1·00 (· ·)	0·00311 (0·00025)	1·0189	0·9658 3·725	0·762
Simultaneous estimation, multiplicative errors[a] (3)	1·8037 (0·00445)	0·658 (0·0028)	0·342 (0·0028)	1·00 (· ·)	0·00705 (0·00030)	1·0164	0·9322 0·02489	0·335
Simultaneous estimation, additive errors[b] (4)	63·8 (0·73)	0·660 (0·0028)	0·340 (0·0028)	1·00 (· ·)	0·00745 (0·00035)	1·0173	0·9244 5·539	0·302

* See notes 1–5 on pp. 63–4.
[a] $r_{uv} = -0 \cdot 377$.
[b] $r_{uv} = -0 \cdot 394$.
Source: Bodkin and Klein [9].

sense of research and development expenditure [13]. Alternatively, as is more usual, technical progress is assumed to be exogenous and is expressed as a function of time. Thus, for a Cobb–Douglas function,

$$Y = A e^{mt} L^\alpha K^\beta. \qquad (2.17)$$

Thus, if both labour and capital remained fixed then

$$\frac{\partial Y}{\partial t} = AL^\alpha K^\beta e^{mt} m = mY. \qquad (2.18)$$

Therefore
$$\frac{\partial Y/\partial t}{Y} = m. \qquad (2.19)$$

Output changes at a constant proportionate rate of m. This gives rise to the so-called 'residual' which is that amount of output not explained by labour and capital inputs (see [21, 45, 58]).

In short-run macroeconomic models, such as the classical and the Keynesian, technical change is assumed away on the grounds that it is a long-run phenomenon, and these are short-run models.

Researchers differ as to its importance. These differences seem to arise from alternative ways of specifying inputs rather than from alternative specifications of the production function. Denison [21] attempted to correct the input of labour for quantity and quality changes and having done so concluded that some 33 per cent of the growth of output in the United States in the period 1929–57 was due to this 'residual factor' or technical progress. On a *per capita* employed basis, 50 per cent is residual (see Table 2.2 on p. 44). Jorgenson and Griliches [45] conclude that had Denison corrected for measurement errors in output and capital services, the amount of the residual would be very small indeed (see the table below).

Total output, input and factor productivity, U.S. private domestic economy, 1945–65, average annual growth rates

	Output	Input	Productivity
Initial estimates	3·49	1·83	1·60
corrected for			
Errors of aggregation	3·39	1·84	1·49
Errors in investment goods prices	3·59	2·19	1·41
Errors in relative utilisation	3·59	2·57	0·59
Errors in aggregation of			
capital services	3·59	2·97	0·58
Errors in aggregation of labour			
services	3·59	3·47	0·10

Source: Jorgenson and Griliches [45].

Apart from this distinction between endogenous and exogenous changes, it is also customary to distinguish between 'embodied' and 'disembodied' technical change. The former requires a change in the

TABLE 2.2

Growth rates for real National Income and underlying series, total and per person employed
(per cent per annum)

	Total			Per person employed		
	1909–29	1929–57	1909–57	1909–29	1929–57	1909–57
Real National Income	2·82	2·93	2·89	1·22	1·60	1·44
Increase in total inputs	2·33	2·10	2·20	0·74	0·78	0·77
Labour, adjusted for quality change	2·30	2·16	2·22	0·71	0·84	0·78
Employment and hours	1·62	1·08	1·30	—	—	—
Employment	1·58	1·31	1·43	—	—	—
Quality of a man-year's work due to shorter hours	0·03	-0·23	-0·12	0·03	-0·23	-0·12
Annual hours	-0·34	-0·73	-0·57	-0·34	-0·73	-0·57
Quality of a man-hour's work due to shorter hours	0·38	0·50	0·45	0·38	0·50	0·45
Education	0·56	0·93	0·78	0·56	0·93	0·78
Increased experience and better utilisation of women workers	0·10	0·15	0·13	0·10	0·15	0·13
Changes in age-sex composition of labour force	0·01	-0·01	0·00	0·01	-0·01	-0·00
Land	0·00	0·00	0·00	-1·58	-1·32	-1·43
Capital	3·16	1·88	2·41	1·55	0·56	0·97
Non-farm residential structures	3·49	1·46	2·30	1·87	0·13	0·86
Other structures and equipment	2·93	1·85	2·22	1·33	0·52	0·78
Inventories	3·31	1·90	2·49	1·70	0·58	1·15
U.S.-owned assets abroad	4·20	1·97	2·89	2·58	0·64	1·45
Foreign assets in the United States (an offset)	-1·85	1·37	0·03	-3·46	0·06	-1·39
Increase in output per unit of input	0·47	0·81	0·67	0·47	0·81	0·67

Source: Denison [21].

capital stock before it can be realised, but the latter occurs independently of the factors of production.

The introduction of embodied technical change is a critical one for macroeconomic models. Essentially, it destroys the assumption that capital is a single homogeneous input. Each piece of capital equipment has characteristics determined by its date of manufacture and which are unalterable throughout its lifetime. Capital is therefore disaggregated into vintages. The range of vintages is, according to Salter [63], very wide, and substantial gains in productivity could be realised by bringing all capital in line with 'best-practice' techniques (see Table 2.3 on p. 46). If capital were homogeneous, then no meaning can be attached to the notion of embodied technical change.

The immediate question is if there exists an alterable number of unalterable production processes, is it possible to retain the notion of an aggregate production function. The short answer is no, at least not without imposing very strong assumptions about the form of the individual production functions (see [40, 47]). What is immediately apparent is that if one has individual processes which obey the Cobb–Douglas function, then the aggregate function cannot be Cobb–Douglas. Nevertheless, Cobb–Douglas functions are successfully fitted to both aggregate and sub-aggregate production processes.

For short-run macro models, it seems legitimate to assume a fixed structure of vintages, but even so neither a demand curve for labour nor a supply curve of aggregate output can be deduced without some additional assumptions on the relative usage rates of the various vintages as output changes. This in turn raises the question of how far factors are substitutes for each other and hence whether factor proportions change as relative prices change, that is, what is the elasticity of substitution between factors?

THE ELASTICITY OF SUBSTITUTION

One of the implications of the Cobb–Douglas function is that factor rewards remain in fixed proportions. This distributional aspect of the function is summed up by a single parameter which is due to Hicks and is the elasticity of substitution. This determines (or is determined by) the shape of the isoquants and is defined as

$$\sigma = \frac{d(K/L)}{(K/L)} \frac{(dK/dL)}{d\left(\frac{dK}{dL}\right)} = \frac{d(K/L)}{(K/L)} \frac{(w/r)}{d(w/r)}. \tag{2.20}$$

For a Cobb–Douglas function, $\sigma = 1$ (see [36] p. 36) so that a 10 per cent change in relative factor prices brings about a 10 per cent change in relative factor proportions. Income distribution therefore remains unchanged.

TABLE 2.3

Variation in labour content per unit of output in selected industries

Industry, time and place	No. of plants	Unit of output	Man-hours per unit of output			Ratio of range to mean	
			Mean	Range of all plants	Range of middle 50 per cent of plants	All plants	Middle 50 per cent
Bricks, U.K. 1947	17	1000 bricks	1·36	2·12–0·54	1·75–0·93	1·16	0·61
Houses, U.K. 1948	160	Standard house	3080	4300–2150	3530–2630	0·66	0·29
Men's shoes, U.K. 1949	12	Dozen pairs	9·70	12·34–7·30	11·02–8·53	0·53	0·26
Cement, U.S. 1935	60	100 barrels	46·7	86·0–25·3	57·9–39·3	1·30	0·40
Beet sugar, U.S. 1935	59	Ton of beet sliced	1·46	2·81–0·88	1·98–1·20	1·32	0·53
Sole leather, U.S. 1949	8	1000 lb.	48	—	61–39	—	0·47

Source: Salter [63].

Since Douglas's work, his function has been subjected to wider and wider generalisations. These are summarised in Vazquez [75] and we shall consider only the first stage of generalisation, which is to consider elasticities other than unity.

THE CONSTANT ELASTICITY OF SUBSTITUTION FUNCTION

The history of the constant elasticity of substitution function (C.E.S.) bears remarkable similarity to that of the Cobb–Douglas function. Empirical investigation of it was prompted by the observation that the share of national income going to labour was not fixed but varied as the wage rate varied. Thus

$$\frac{Y}{L} = \frac{W^{\chi}}{\alpha}. \tag{2.21}$$

Arrow, Chenery, Minhas and Solow [3] tested the Douglas assumption that χ was unity (see Table 2.4). They found it to be significantly different from unity and deduced a production function of the form:

$$Y^{-\theta} = \gamma^{-\theta}(\delta K^{-\theta} + (1-\delta)L^{-\theta}), \tag{2.22}$$

where $\theta = 1/\chi - 1$ (see [36]) which under perfectly competitive profit-maximising conditions gives rise to equation (2.21).

The elasticity of substitution of (2.22) is

$$\sigma = \frac{1}{1+\theta} = \chi \tag{2.23}$$

and ranges from infinity ($\theta = -1$), which implies straight-line isoquants and perfect substitutability of factors, to zero ($\theta = \infty$) which implies rectangular isoquants and no substitutability of factors. This latter case corresponds to the Leontief [50] or Johansen [41] approach, and when $\theta = 0$, $\sigma = 1$, we have the Cobb–Douglas function. Furthermore, if

$$Y^{-\theta/\mu} = \gamma^{-\theta/\mu}(\delta K^{-\theta} + (1-\delta)L^{-\theta}), \tag{2.24}$$

the C.E.S. has returns to scale of μ (see [36]). Empirical work on this function has been carried out by a number of investigators using various estimation techniques. This has given rise to conflicting evidence about the elasticity of substitution with some concluding that it is zero, some that it lies between zero and unity and still others maintaining the view that the Cobb–Douglas function of unity best describes the data.

ESTIMATING THE C.E.S. FUNCTION

It should be noted that the function cannot easily be linearised as could the Cobb–Douglas function. The original investigators, Arrow et al. [3], used a stepwise estimation procedure beginning by estimating χ (which

TABLE 2.4

ISIC No.	Industry	Regression equations		Standard error S_b	Coefficient of determination $\bar{R}^2$	Degrees of freedom	Test of significance on b Confidence level for b different from 1 (per cent)
		log a	b†				
202	Dairy products	0·419	0·721	0·073	0·921	14	99
203	Fruit and vegetable canning	0·355	0·855	0·075	0·910	12	90
205	Grain and mill products	0·429	0·909	0·096	0·855	14	*
206	Bakery products	0·304	0·900	0·065	0·927	14	80
207	Sugar	0·431	0·781	0·115	0·790	11	90
220	Tobacco	0·564	0·753	0·151	0·629	13	80
231	Textile – spinning and weaving	0·296	0·809	0·068	0·892	16	98
232	Knitting mills	0·270	0·785	0·064	0·915	13	99
250	Lumber and wood	0·279	0·860	0·066	0·910	16	95
260	Furniture	0·226	0·894	0·042	0·952	14	95
271	Pulp and paper	0·478	0·965	0·101	0·858	14	*
280	Printing and publishing	0·284	0·868	0·056	0·940	14	95
291	Leather finishing	0·202	0·857	0·062	0·921	12	95
311	Basic chemicals	0·460	0·831	0·070	0·898	14	95
312	Fats and oils	0·515	0·839	0·090	0·869	12	90
319	Miscellaneous chemicals	0·483	0·895	0·059	0·938	14	90
331	Clay products	0·273	0·919	0·098	0·878	11	*
332	Glass	0·285	0·999	0·084	0·921	11	*
333	Ceramics	0·210	0·901	0·044	0·974	10	95
334	Cement	0·560	0·920	0·149	0·770	10	*
341	Iron and steel	0·363	0·811	0·051	0·936	11	99
342	Non-ferrous metals	0·370	1·011	0·120	0·886	18	*
350	Metal products	0·301	0·102	0·088	0·897	11	*
370	Electric machinery	0·344	0·870	0·118	0·804	12	*

* Not significant at 80 per cent or higher levels of confidence.
† b refers to χ in the text.
Source: Arrow et al. [3].

equals σ – see equation (2.23)) from equation (2.21) and computing θ from $\theta = (1/\chi) - 1$.

Tsurumi [71] using Canadian manufacturing data compares O.L.S. (stepwise estimation as used by Arrow *et al.*) with non-linear least squares and non-linear two-stage least squares. This last is applied to a six-equation model in which the exogenous variables are; expected values of output, labour input, the wage rate and the price level together with the interest rate, the unemployment rate and lagged profits. He also investigates the possibility of auto-correlated errors and posits an error term of the form

$$U_t = \xi U_{t-1} + \varepsilon_t,$$

where ε_t has the usual properties of finite variance, zero mean and serial independence. For total manufacturing they give estimates of σ, the elasticity of substitution, as 0·83 under O.L.S., 1·00 under non-linear least squares, and 1·00 under non-linear two-stage least squares. It seems that the stepwise procedure used by Arrow *et al.* may suggest that the Cobb–Douglas form is not appropriate but that non-linear estimates, whether single- or simultaneous-equations estimations, yields Cobb–Douglas functions.

Bodkin and Klein [9] using the same data as Arrow *et al.* use single-equation non-linear estimates with additive and multiplicative errors as well as simultaneous estimation (again with additive- and multiplicative-error terms). The simultaneous equations are carried out first using output, interest rate, wage rate and price level as exogenous with L and K endogenous, and secondly, specifying L and K as exogenous and output, interest rate, wage rate and price level as endogenous. This latter they call the least-preferred specification. Their results are shown in Table 2.5 (p. 50).

The single-equation, or 'straight' estimates give a very low elasticity of substitution with large standard errors suggesting that fixed-proportion functions are appropriate, but so large are the standard errors that the Cobb–Douglas function is not ruled out. Almost all output is due to capital since δ is insignificantly different from unity. Respecification of the error term has little effect on the estimates. If fixed proportions were assumed, then attributing all the output to capital is as unobjectionable as attributing it all to labour so that the estimate of $\delta = 1$ should not be taken as a reason for rejecting the estimate.

The simultaneous estimates with the preferred specification of the exogenous variables yield results similar to those of Arrow *et al.* with σ between zero and unity. The less-preferred specification yields Cobb–Douglas functions with the usual distribution of output between labour and capital. There seems to be no clear-cut case for assuming the elasticity of substitution is less than unity. Conversely, a number of investigations have found it to be between unity and zero.

The C.E.S. (that of Arrow *et al.*) function had been used previously by Dickinson [22] in an investigation of the possibility of changing factor

TABLE 2.5*

Estimates of the parameters of the C.E.S. production function

	A or log A (1)	ρ (2)	$\sigma = \dfrac{1}{1+\rho}$ (3)	δ (4)	μ (5)	λ (6)	10λ (7)	$\bar{R}^2$ S_u (8)	$\dfrac{\delta^2}{S^2}$ (9)
Straight regression, multiplicative error (1)	1·6466 (0·1083)	9·593 (7·591)	0·0944	0·9975 (0·0160)	1·210 (0·0456)	0·00675 (0·00036)	1·0157	0·9926 0·01346	1·395
Straight regression, additive error (2)	40·46 (9·37)	10·18 (8·713)	0·0894	0·9992 (0·0061)	1·220 (0·0625)	0·00663 (0·00048)	1·0154	0·9900 2·731	1·085
Simultaneous estimation, multiplicative errors[a] (3)	1·7340 (0·0252)	1·130 (0·4169)	0·4694	0·6037 (0·0958)	1·238 (0·058)	0·00643 (0·00041)	1·0149	0·9804 0·02186	0·477
Simultaneous estimation, additive errors[b] (4)	58·39 (1·62)	0·4750 (0·1891)	0·6780	0·4471 (0·0434)	1·362 (0·0905)	0·00589 (0·00061)	1·0137	0·9834 3·591	0·618
Simultaneous estimation, less preferred specification of endogenous variables, multiplicative errors[c] (5)	1·7997 (0·00814)	-0·0065 (0·145)	1·0065	0·3391 (0·0312)	1·250 (0·0896)	0·00583 (0·00052)	1·0135	0·9817 0·02114	0·523
Simultaneous estimation, less preferred specification of endogenous variables, additive errors[d] (6)	63·13 (1·22)	-0·0590 (0·142)	1·063	0·3287 (0·0302)	1·255 (0·0907)	0·00648 (0·00056)	1·0150	0·9835 3·585	0·534

* See notes 1–6 on pp. 63–4.

[a] $r_{uxo} = -0\cdot7524$.

[b] $r_{uxo} = -0\cdot3575$.

[c] $r_{uxo} = -0\cdot1974$.

[d] $r_{uxo} = -0\cdot0983$.

Source: Bodkin and Klein [9].

shares. It was used by Arrow *et al.* [3] to investigate the Leontief paradox that the United States seemed to export labour-intensive products. It has also been extensively applied to neoclassical growth models, for example Swan [68]. In general terms, it suffers from the same criticisms as does the Cobb–Douglas production function (see [36]).

FIXED PROPORTIONS

The C.E.S. function admits the possibility of complementary factors rather than substitutable factors. If this is so then employment can only be increased in the short run if there is idle capital which can be activated as new labour appears. When all the capital is in use, employment cannot be further increased. The cost (or aggregate supply) function of the Keynesian model therefore depends upon the returns to scale of the process rather than diminishing returns to any one factor.

In order to calculate the aggregate supply curve it is necessary to know the cost of using each unit of capital, r, the capital–output ratio, v (fixed by assumption), the wage rate and the labour–output ratio, ρ (again fixed by assumption). This would yield (1) total cost $= WL + rK = W\rho Y + rvY$, and (2) unit costs $= W\rho + rv$. If W and r are fixed, then unit costs are independent of the level of output and hence equal marginal costs. If we assume that suppliers equate marginal cost to price, then this yields a perfectly elastic supply curve up to full employment of the scarce factor of production.

The profit identity becomes

$$\pi \equiv YP - rK - WL$$
$$= Y(P - rv - W\rho). \qquad (2.25)$$

Therefore
$$\frac{\partial \pi}{\partial y} = P - rv - w\rho = 0$$

$$\Rightarrow P = rv + w\rho. \qquad (2.26)$$

Putting equation (2.26) into equation (2.25) yields zero profits at every level of output, and hence output cannot be determined if all the markets are perfectly competitive. The demand for labour function necessary for the determination of output in the classical model cannot be derived.

Abandoning the notion of factor substitution involves the loss of the marginal-productivity theory of distribution besides the loss of simple theories of labour demand, aggregate supply, investment and hence output.

There are a number of objections to the aggregate production function, some arising from the problems of aggregation; others, of a more practical kind, concern the lack of homogeneity of factors and the implausibility of substituting labour for capital in a developed technology. Empirical evidence, however, seems to confirm the existence of such functions. But no attempt to estimate the inputs of capital services has proved satisfactory, and hence what is being estimated is the substitution of labour services for capital stock. Once this is recognised, then the imposition of diminishing returns to labour, for example, is no longer tenable.

There are debates of a more theoretical kind concerning the nature of capital and the existence (or at any rate the usefulness of assuming the existence) of an aggregate production function. We have tried to concentrate on a fairly simple task of underlining the significance of the assumptions which typically are made in macroeconomic models and to present some of the empirical evidence.

No commentary on macroeconomic applications of production functions would be complete without mentioning a somewhat different approach to production.

INPUT–OUTPUT MODELS

The development of the Marshallian type of production, or supply, theory, with its somewhat unsatisfactory application to macroeconomic models, has been paralleled by the development of the rather less influential general-equilibrium or 'Austrian' theory of supply.

The theoretical basis of the general-equilibrium model derives from Quesnay's *Tableau Économie* by way of Walras's *Elements of Pure Economics; or the Theory of Social Wealth* [76]. It differs from the Marshallian theory in that national aggregates are not used, and it does not rely on the marginal-productivity theory for a basis of income distribution. In a sense, the resulting model is more mechanical and less behavioural than the Marshallian approach to supply.

The system stresses the existence of numerous products and production processes, and focuses attention on the interdependence of those processes. The nature and extent of the disaggregation is to some extent a matter of choice; if too many separate processes are distinguished, the model becomes too large to handle but, alternatively, if too few are distinguished, then the advantages of disaggregation are lost. It was perhaps the difficulty of treating such large systems of interdependent equations which held up the application of general-equilibrium models.

The interdependence between processes derives from the fact that some commodities are employed in the production of others. Some inputs are not produced (for example labour and raw materials), others are produced but are durable (fixed capital), and others are produced and perishable (single-use intermediates). Not all types of products are used in the production of other commodities (for example cigarettes) and not all that is produced of every product is used up in the production of commodities. The theoretical significance of this view of production is clearly set out by Sraffa [66], although the implications for economic analysis of adopting this view rather than the Marshallian view have yet to be fully spelt out.

The practical significance of the general-equilibrium view must be due to Leontief whose scheme of disaggregation followed the Standard Industrial Classification (S.I.C.) and gave rise to the Inter-Industry Input–Output Table [50, 51] evolving at about the same time as Keynes's *The General Theory*.

Obviously, the preparation of such tables requires a great deal of information about individual industries and these are collected at intervals in censuses of production [10]. For some general comments on their construction, see [11, 72, 73].

In order to endow this purely descriptive device with some analytical power it is necessary either to assume or to demonstrate a certain predictability in these interrelationships. If this was so, then the predicted levels of final demands (export, investment and consumer goods) could be translated into demands made on each sector both directly, if the sector produces final goods, and indirectly, if the sector supplies other sectors which in turn produce consumer goods. Thus it is possible to derive demands for labour, capital and raw materials. Hence the production function has been used to translate a predicted pattern of final demands into a pattern of factor demands, and we have the kernel of a multi-sector macroeconomic model (see Tables 2.6, 2.7 and 2.8 on pp. 54–59). What we have not got is a simple amoral method of generating supply and price decisions by each sector.

There are a number of ways of imposing predictability on the inter-industry relationships. The simplest, and that adopted by Leontief, is to assume that the inputs required by each sector depends solely upon the output of that sector. Thus, if each element of a column of the input–output matrix were divided by the output of the industry buying those inputs, then the result would be a column of input–output coefficients which were constant. This is tantamount to assuming constant returns to scale, a fixed-proportion production function and no technical progress. The last two assumptions may be justifiable if the model is limited to the short run, but the first is a very strong assumption. A less strong assumption would be that the marginal input–output coefficients, rather than the average input–output coefficients, are constant.

There is some evidence to suggest that coefficients do change over time [1, 4, 6, 14, 15, 59, 70, 74, 78]. The changes seem to be largely trends, in which case two observations of each coefficient is sufficient to predict their changes (see Table 2.9 on pp. 60–2).

A rather less naive method of investigating changes in coefficients requires fairly detailed knowledge of each sector so that changes in the physical production function may be understood and so may the economic influences on the choice of available technique. This has been done for the fuel sector of the United Kingdom and is reported by Wigley [78].

In view of the large quantities of data necessary to construct input–output tables, the number of observations of input–output coefficients are

TABLE

INDUSTRIAL INPUT AND OUTPUT

Summary input–output

Purchases by		Agri- culture, forestry and fishing	Coal mining	Other mining and quarry- ing	Food, drink and tobacco	Mineral oil refining	Other chemi- cals and allied indus- tries	Metal manu- facture	Vehicles (including aircraft) and ship- building	Other engin- eering	Textiles, leather and clothing
Sales by		1	2	3	4	5	6	7	8	9	10
Agriculture, forestry and fishing	1	—	5	—	571	—	—	—	—	—	28
Coal mining	2	1	—	1	14	—	156	12	5	9	16
Other mining and quarrying	3	—	—	—	3	2	9	19	—	19	—
Food, drink and tobacco	4	315	—	—	—	—	35	—	—	—	2
Mineral oil refining	5	19	1	1	9	—	78	20·	6	14	7
Other chemicals and allied industries	6	91	9	12	156	48	—	95	69	140	34
Metal manufacture	7	—	48	—	8	—	23	—	374	781	2
Vehicles (including aircraft) and shipbuilding	8	10	1	1	4	—	3	8	—	41	2
Other engineering	9	26	42	14	100	2	83	98	545	—	40
Textiles, leather and clothing	10	10	8	—	10	—	8	1	21	27	—
Other manufacturing	11	42	49	7	143	12	83	21	198	289	28
Construction	12	30	18	—	12	—	11	8	11	22	7
Gas, electricity and water	13	16	25	3	42	5	60	60	40	93	35
Services	14	281	40	51	404	84	232	212	247	510	148
Public administration, etc[1]	15	—	—	—	—	—	—	—	—	—	—
Imports of goods and services	16	151	5	1	507	284	284	315	107	221	436
Sales by final buyers to one another	17	—	—	1	8	—	5	66	22	22	8
Goods and services (1–17)	18	992	251	92	1,991	437	1,070	935	1,545	2,188	793
Taxes on expenditure *less* subsidies	19	−252	9	10	59	7	32	37	28	73	28
Income from employment	20	353	535	47	546	25	388	502	890	1,877	771
Gross profits and other trading income[2]	21	601	117	34	473	29	312	249	244	714	286
Total input (18–21)	22	1,694	912	183	3,069	498	1,802	1,723	2,807	4,852	1,878

often rather limited – too limited for any extensive investigation of their movements. In order to moderate this some techniques for generating input–output coefficients in the absence of a full census have been developed.

Perhaps the best known of these is the R.A.S. method (see Stone [67]). This method requires knowledge of one set of coefficients and of the row and column totals of another time period. The original coefficients are multiplied by the new gross outputs to yield an inter-sector flow matrix. These row sums can then be compared with the known row sums and any difference between these two is spread back along the row in proportion

2.6

transactions matrix, 1963   £ million

Other manufacturing	Construction	Gas, electricity and water	Services	Public administration, etc.[1]	Total intermediate output (1-15)	Final buyers					Total final output (17-21)	Total output (16 plus 22)	
						Current expenditure		Gross domestic capital formation					
						Personal sector	Public authorities	Fixed	Stocks	Exports			
11	12	13	14	15	16	17	18	19	20	21	22	23	
9	—	—	4	—	617	987	14	9	24	43	1,077	1,694	1
51	—	345	37	—	647	208	26	21	-23	33	265	912	2
58	54	—	2	—	166	—	—	—	—	17	17	183	3
3	—	—	76	—	431	2,290	49	—	56	243	2,638	3,069	4
18	20	30	64	—	287	61	15	8	2	125	211	498	5
156	96	22	124	—	1,052	244	135	—	-19	390	750	1,802	6
18	127	29	14	—	1,424	—	5	40	-27	281	299	1,723	7
7	9	2	313	—	401	484	598	437	67	820	2,406	2,807	8
128	192	68	217	—	1,555	353	284	1,322	81	1,257	3,297	4,852	9
76	5	—	42	—	208	1,145	37	—	15	473	1,670	1,878	10
—	465	25	647	—	2,009	631	151	42	13	318	1,155	3,164	11
14	—	8	118	—	259	387	303	2,170	21	10	2,891	3,150	12
83	9	—	236	—	707	653	81	158	—	4	896	1,603	13
410	202	160	—	—	2,981	6,787	742	437	2	1,473	9,441	12,422	14
—	—	—	—	—	—	1,440	2,732	—	—	—	4,172	4,172	15
451	143	17	680	—	3,602	1,656	186	242	16	262	2,362	5,964	16
13	—	—	74	—	219	167	-366	-95	—	75	-219	—	17
1,495	1,322	706	2,648	—	16,565	17,493	4,992	4,791	228	5,824	33,328	49,893	18
70	55	69	412	—	637	2,648	91	112	—	—	2,851	3,488	19
1,169	1,364	373	6,242	3,063	18,145	—	—	—	—	—	—	18,145	20
430	409	455	3,120[3]	1,109	8,582	—	—	—	—	—	—	8,582	21
3,164	3,150	1,603	12,422	4,172	43,929	20,141	5,083	4,903	228	5,824	36,179	80,108	22

[1] Public administration and defence, public health and educational services, ownership of dwellings, domestic services to households and services to private non-profit-making bodies serving persons.
[2] Before providing for depreciation but after providing for stock appreciation.
[3] Including the residual error.
Source: National Income and Expenditure, Blue Book (1967) [16].

to the size of each element. The column sums are then compared with known column sums, and again any difference is allocated up the column in proportion to the size of each element. The exercise is repeated for the rows and then again for the columns until the differences become acceptably small.

There are many variations on this method (see [5, 49]). It has the advantage of preserving the signs and zeros of the original matrix and to

TABLE 2.7

INDUSTRIAL INPUT AND OUTPUT

Total requirements per £100 of final industrial output in terms of gross output, 1963[1]

£

	Agriculture, forestry and fishing	Coal mining	Other mining and quarrying	Food, drink and tobacco	Mineral oil refining	Other chemicals and allied industries	Metal manu-facture
	1	2	3	4	5	6	7
Agriculture, forestry and fishing	1	104	1	—	19	—	—	—
Coal mining	2	1	101	2	2	1	10	2
Other mining and quarrying	3	—	—	100	—	1	1	1
Food, drink and tobacco	4	20	—	—	104	—	2	—
Mineral oil refining	5	2	—	1	1	101	5	2
Other chemicals and allied industries	6	8	2	8	7	10	102	7
Metal manufacture	7	1	7	2	2	1	3	102
Vehicles (including aircraft) and shipbuilding	8	1	—	1	1	1	1	1
Other engineering	9	.4	6	10	5	2	6	7
Textiles, leather and clothing	10	1	1	—	1	—	1	—
Other manufacturing	11	6	7	7	8	4	7	3
Construction	12	2	2	1	1	—	1	1
Gas, electricity and water	13	2	4	3	3	2	5	4
Services	14	23	8	32	21	20	18	16

	Vehicles (including aircraft) and shipbuilding	Other engineering	Textiles, leather and clothing	Other manufacturing	Construction	Gas, electricity and water	Services
	8	9	10	11	12	13	14
1 Agriculture, forestry and fishing	—	—	2	—	—	—	—
2 Coal mining	2	2	2	3	1	22	1
3 Other mining and quarrying	1	1	—	2	2	—	—
4 Food, drink and tobacco	—	—	1	—	.	—	1
5 Mineral oil refining	1	1	1	1	1	2	1
6 Other chemicals and allied industries	5	5	2	6	5	3	2
7 Metal manufacture	17	17	1	2	6	4	1
8 Vehicles (including aircraft) and shipbuilding	101	1	—	1	1	1	3
9 Other engineering	22	102	3	6	8	6	3
10 Textiles, leather and clothing	1	1	100	3	1	—	1
11 Other manufacturing	10	8	3	102	16	4	6
12 Construction	1	1	1	1	100	1	1
13 Gas, electricity and water	3	3	2	4	2	101	2
14 Services	16	16	10	16	12	14	102

[1] Each entry represents the value of the gross output of the 'row' industry required to produce £100 of final output by the 'column' industry.
Source: *National Income and Expenditure*, Blue Book (1967) [16].

TABLE 2.8

INDUSTRIAL INPUT AND OUTPUT

Total requirements per £100 of final industrial output in terms of net output, 1963[1]

£

		Agriculture, forestry and fishing	Coal mining	Other mining and quarrying	Food drink and tobacco	Mineral oil refining	Other chemicals and allied industries	Metal manufacture
		1	2	3	4	5	6	7
Agriculture, forestry and fishing	1	58	—	—	11	—	—	—
Coal mining	2	1	72	2	1	1	7	2
Other mining and quarrying	3	—	—	44	—	—	—	1
Food, drink and tobacco	4	7	—	—	35	—	1	—
Mineral oil refining	5	—	—	—	—	11	1	—
Other chemicals and allied industries	6	3	1	3	3	4	40	3
Metal manufacture	7	1	3	1	1	1	1	44
Vehicles (including aircraft) and shipbuilding	8	1	—	1	—	—	—	—
Other engineering	9	2	3	5	3	1	3	4
Textiles, leather and clothing	10	1	1	—	—	—	1	—
Other manufacturing	11	3	4	4	4	2	4	2
Construction	12	1	2	—	1	—	1	1
Gas, electricity and water	13	1	6	2	1	1	2	2
Services	14	17	—	25	15	15	13	12
Sales by final buyers	15	—	—	—	1	—	1	4
Imports of goods and services	16	18	5	6	24	61	22	22
Taxes on expenditure less subsidies	17	-14	2	7	—	3	3	3
Total	18	100	100	100	100	100	100	100

		8 Vehicles (including aircraft) and shipbuilding	9 Other engineering	10 Textiles, leather and clothing	11 Other manufacturing	12 Construction	13 Gas, electricity and water	14 Services
Agriculture, forestry and fishing	1	—	—	1	—	—	—	—
Coal mining	2	1	1	1	2	1	16	1
Other mining and quarrying	3	—	—	—	1	1	—	—
Food, drink and tobacco	4	—	—	⋮	—	—	—	—
Mineral oil refining	5	—	—	—	—	—	1	—
Other chemicals and allied industries	6	2	2	1	2	2	1	1
Metal manufacture	7	7	7	—	1	3	2	—
Vehicles (including aircraft) and shipbuilding	8	41	1	—	—	—	—	1
Other engineering	9	12	55	2	3	4	3	2
Textiles, leather and clothing	10	1	1	56	2	—	—	—
Other manufacturing	11	5	4	1	52	8	2	3
Construction	12	—	—	—	—	57	1	1
Gas, electricity and water	13	2	2	1	2	—	53	1
Services	14	12	12	8	12	9	11	77
Sales by final buyers	15	2	1	1	1	—	—	1
Imports of goods and services	16	12	11	26	19	11	6	8
Taxes on expenditure *less* subsidies	17	3	3	2	3	3	5	4
Total	18	100	100	100	100	100	100	100

[1] Each entry represents the value of the net output (including depreciation) of the 'row' industry required to produce £100 of final output by the 'column' industry.

Source: *National Income and Expenditure, Blue Book* (1967) [16].

TABLE 2.9*

Annual rate of change in requirements to produce ten sub-vectors of 1962 final demand 1947–58 technology

	Change in gross domestic outputs required		Per cent change per year		(1) Food and tobacco	(2) Textiles and clothing	(3) Drugs, cleaning preparations, paper	(4) Furniture	(5) Consumers' appliances automobiles	(6) Construction	(7) Non-electrical producers' durables	(8) Electrical machinery	(9) Transportation equipment	(10) Services excluding utilities
	1958–47 (a) (Millions of dollars)	1962–58 (b)	1947–58 (c)	1958–62 (d)										
I General inputs														
A Services and allied industries														
Business services, Advertising	8,457	4,903	3	4	5	2	1	1	9	6	8	5	9	1
Communications	3,245	267	3	0	8	5	10	7	8	7	9	5	8	1
Finance, insurance, Real estate and rentals	10,574	−1,674	1	0	2	3	7	4	7	3	9	4	7	6
Wholesale and retail trade	5,088	−716	1	0	1	0	5	7	8	3	8	6	9	0
Other services	1,439	−575	0	0	0	3	4	3	6	−1	7	6	6	0
Transportation and warehousing	−1,887	637	0	0	−1	0	−1	−1	1	0	3	1	1	−1
Printing and publishing	618	754	0	1	3	3	0	3	7	5	6	2	8	−2
Maintenance construction	−5,063	−561	−3	−1	0	−3	0	−1	1	0	1	−2	1	−4
B Energy														
Utilities	5,645	−63	2	0	5	5	6	7	6	7	6	5	6	4
Petroleum refining	743	652	0	1	2	0	3	2	0	3	3	0	0	1
Coal mining	−2,218	−648	−5	−6	−6	−6	−5	−4	−3	−3	−3	−5	−3	−10

C Packaging														
Paper products and containers	850	−693	1	−1	1	2	0	8	4	4	1	2	3	−2
Metal containers	−121	−78	0	−1	2	−2	3	3	−5	−3	−2	−5	−4	−7
Wooden containers	−500	−57	−6	−3	−6	−8	−10	−7	−6	−4	−10	−10	−10	−3
II Chemicals and paints, excluding plastics														
Basic chemicals	3,276	1,201	2	2	2	4	3	4	2	6	3	2	3	1
Drug, cleaning, and toilet items	891	0	1	0	5	−1	0	4	5	7	6	2	7	5
Paint and allied products	−477	92	−2	1	0	−5	−4	0	−3	−1	−1	−6	−3	−2
III Materials														
Plastics and synthetics	1,505	607	3	3	2	4	5	6	0	6	3	0	3	3
Stone and clay products	1,734	76	2	0	1	3	3	1	0	3	4	0	3	0
Rubber and plastic products	608	690	1	2	2	6	8	9	−3	5	1	−3	−3	1
Livestock	425	−626	0	−1	1	−7	−6	0	1	1	5	4	4	−3
Glass and glass products	−326	139	−1	1	−2	3	−6	6	4	−3	−2	5	4	−2
Crops	−5,382	−1,534	−2	−2	−1	−3	−8	1	1	5	3	1	1	−3
Non-ferrous metals	−3,278	794	−2	2	−3	−3	−4	0	−3	−2	1	−3	−1	−4
Lumber and products, except containers	−2,934	173	−3	0	−3	−2	2	−1	−4	−2	−4	−6	−1	−5
Iron and steel	−8,571	−1,105	−3	−2	−3	−4	−3	−2	−2	−1	−2	−4	−2	−5

TABLE 2.9 (continued)

IV Intermediate metalworking														
Electronic components	1,858	110	5	1	12	14	13	14	8	13	15	4	13	11
Instruments and clocks	602	223	1	1	5	9	0	-11	4	7	0	10	1	1
Hardware, plating, valves and wire products	538	-473	1	-2	2	3	-1	2	2	0	0	-1	3	-3
Heating, plumbing, structural metal products	81	336	0	1	-3	-5	-3	3	-2	2	-2	-5	1	-6
Electrical apparatus and motors	-511	-49	-1	-2	4	0	5	5	-1	5	2	0	4	-1
Batteries, X-ray, engine electric equipment	-334	123	-1	2	-2	-2	-1	0	1	-1	2	0	2	-5
Electric lighting and wiring equipment	-649	80	-2	1	-1	1	3	7	2	1	2	0	7	-3
Stampings, screw machine products	-1,446	-361	-2	-2	-3	-1	0	-2	-3	-2	-3	-3	-1	-5
Per cent absolute change per year (1947–58) in all input requirements to produce each sub-vector of final demand (P_j).				1·1	1·2	1·5	1·6	1·9	1·5	1·9	2·2	1·7	1·3
Per cent negative change (reduction in requirements) of total absolute change, 1947–58.				30	33	40	22	35	21	22	42	23	63

* See note 7 on p. 64.

Source: Carter [14].

yield results compatible with the known elements of national accounts. Obviously, negative signs are impossible as are coefficients which imply that the system consumes more of an output (directly or indirectly) in its production than it produces. This latter is the so-called Hawkins–Simons condition.

R.A.S. projections have been compared with actual coefficients by Paelinck and Waelbroeck [59] who found R.A.S. to be an improvement over the assumption of constant coefficients but, nevertheless, some discrepancies persisted.

Attempts to introduce this kind of approach to macro models have been done by Goodwin [30], Jorgenson [44] and Lovell [52]. They became principally mechanical models presumably because the decision rules became too complicated once substitution and single-goods models are abandoned.

CONCLUSION

We have tried to make more explicit the diverse and often incompatible roles asked of the aggregate production function in Keynesian and classical macroeconomic models. Two well-known forms of aggregate production functions were looked at together with some of the empirical evidence regarding their parameters. Some of the more basic objections to the notion of aggregate production functions were reinforced by the introduction of embodied technical progress. Some evidence on the size of the residual factor and the unsatisfactory methods of measuring inputs was presented. Aggregate production functions having fixed coefficients seem to introduce as many problems as they solve, particularly regarding the determination of national output.

Multi-sector macro models were discussed together with various methods of predicting input–output coefficients. The predictability of these coefficients was stressed and some evidence of their variability was presented. The R.A.S. method of generating coefficients from minimum industrial data (which provides a valuable data-generating device) was compared with some actual outcomes and was found wanting.

Notes on Tables 2.1–2.9

1. Standard errors in parentheses.
2. $\bar{R}^2$ (the coefficient of multiple correlation) and $\bar{S}_u$ (the estimated standard deviation of the residuals) are both corrected for degrees of freedom.
3. The last column is the von Neuman–Hart statistic where $\partial^2 =$ mean square successive differences of residuals. No auto-correlation would imply a 1·55 value of V.N.H. for this model.
4. r_{uv} is the correlation coefficient between the residuals of the production function and those of the marginal-productivity equations.

5. Simultaneity occurs because the behavioural equations of the entrepreneur also imply relations between output, labour and capital. See
equations (2.6) and (2.7) of the main text.
6. In rows (5) and (6) of Table 2.5 labour and capital inputs are
regarded as exogenous, and output and capital and labour costs are
regarded as endogenous.
7. The first four columns of Table 2.9 compare the industrial output
levels required to produce the 1962 bill of goods using 1947, 1958
and 1962 technologies:

(*a*) is the change in gross output required if 1947 coefficients are
used in place of 1958 coefficients; and

(*b*) is the change in gross output required if 1962 coefficients are
used in place of 1958 coefficients.

(*c*) and (*d*) are the changes described by (*a*) and (*b*) expressed in
annual percentage changes.

BIBLIOGRAPHY

[1]   A. G. Armstrong and D. C. Upton, 'A Review of Input–Output
      Applications', a paper presented at the 37th Session of the Interna-
      tional Statistical Institute (London, 1969).
[2]   K. J. Arrow, 'The Economic Implications of Learning by Doing',
      Review of Economic Studies, xxxix (1962).
[3]   —, H. S. Chenery, B. S. Minhas and R. M. Solow, 'Capital and
      Labour   Substitution   and   Economic   Efficiency',   *Review   of
      Economics and Statistics*, xliii (1961).
[4]   — and M. Hoffenberg, *A Time Series Analysis of Inter Industry
      Demands* (Amsterdam: North-Holland, 1959).
[5]   M. O. L. Bacharach, *Biproportional Matrices and Input–Output
      Change*, Department of Applied Economics (Cambridge University
      Press, 1970).
[6]   T. Barna, 'The Interdependence of the British Economy', *Journal
      of the Royal Statistical Society*, Series A, General, cxv, 1 (1952).
[7]   —, 'The Replacement Cost of Fixed Assets in British Manufactur-
      ing Industry in 1955', *Journal of the Royal Statistical Society*, Series
      A, General, vol. 120, 1 (1957).
[8]   — (ed.), *Structural Interdependence and Economic Growth* (Lon-
      don: Macmillan, 1963).
[9]   R. G. Bodkin and L. R. Klein, 'Nonlinear Estimation of Aggregate
      Production Function', *Review of Economics and Statistics*, xlix
      (1967).
[10] Board of Trade, *The Report on the Census of Production* (London:
      H.M.S.O., various).
[11] — and Central Statistical Office, *Input–Output Tables for the United
      Kingdom, 1954*, Studies in Official Statistics, no. 8 (London:
      H.M.S.O., 1961).

[12]   M. Brown (ed.), *The Theory and Empirical Analysis of Production*, Studies in Income and Wealth, vol. 31, National Bureau of Economic Research (New York: Columbia University Press, 1967).

[13]   — and A. M. Conrad, 'The Influence of Research and Education in C.E.S. Production Relations', in [11].

[14]   A. Carter, 'Incremental Flow Coefficients for a Dynamic Input–Output Model with Changing Technology', in [6].

[15]   —, 'Changes in the Structure of the American Economy 1947 to 1958 and 1962', *Review of Economics and Statistics*, XLIX (1967).

[16]   Central Statistical Office, *National Income and Expenditure*, Blue Book (London: H.M.S.O., various).

[17]   —, *Index of Industrial Production: Method of Compilation*, Studies in Official Statistics, no. 7 (London: H.M.S.O., 1957).

[18]   H. B. Chenery and P. G. Clark, *Inter Industry Economics* (New York: Wiley, 1959).

[19]   C. W. Cobb and P. H. Douglas, 'A Theory of Production', *American Economic Review*, supplement, XVIII (1928).

[20]   P. Daly and P. H. Douglas, 'Production Function for Canadian Manufacturers', *Journal of the American Statistical Association*, XXXVIII (1943).

[21]   E. F. Denison, *Sources of Economic Growth in the U.S.*, Supplementary Paper of the Committee for Economic Development (New York, 1962).

[22]   H. D. Dickinson, 'A Note on Dynamic Economics', *Review of Economic Studies* (1954).

[23]   W. E. Diewert, 'Hicks' Aggregation Theorem and the Existence of a Real Value Added Function', *Technical Report*, no. 84, Institute for Mathematical Studies in the Social Sciences (California: Stanford, 1973).

[24]   R. Dorfman, P. A. Samuelson and R. M. Solow, *Linear Programming and Economic Analysis* (New York: McGraw-Hill, 1955).

[25]   P. H. Douglas, *The Theory of Wages* (New York: Macmillan, 1934).

[26]   J. S. Duensenberry *et al.*, *The Brookings Quarterly Econometric Model of the United States* (Chicago: Rand McNally, 1965).

[27]   D. Durand, 'Some Thoughts of Marginal Productivity with Special Reference to Professor Douglas' Analysis', *Journal of Policitical Economy*, XLV (1937).

[28]   M. Frankel, 'The Production Function in Allocation and Growth', *American Economic Review*, LII, no. 7 (Dec. 1962).

[29]   A. Goldberger, 'The Interpretation and Estimation of Cobb–Douglas Functions', *Econometrica*, 35, no. 34 (1968).

[30]   R. M. Goodwin, 'The Multiplier as a Matrix', *Economic Journal*, LIX (Dec 1949).

[31]   W. Gossling (ed.), *Input–Output in the United Kingdom*, Proceedings of the 1968 Manchester Conference (London: Cass, 1970).

[32] G. Gunn, 'A Production Function for American Manufacturing in 1919', *American Economic Review*, xxxi (1941).

[33] — and P. H. Douglas, 'The Production Function for Australian Manufacturing', *Quarterly Journal of Economics*, lvi (1941).

[34] —, 'Production Function for American Manufacturing in 1914', *Journal of Political Economy*, l (1942).

[35] G. C. Harcourt, 'Some Cambridge Controversies in the Theory of Capital', *Journal of Economic Literature*, vii (1969).

[36] D. F. Heathfield, *Production Functions* (London: Macmillan, 1971).

[37] —, 'The Measurement of Capital Usage Using Electricity Consumption Data for the U.K.', *Journal of the Royal Statistical Society*, Series A, General, vol. 134, pt 2 (1972).

[38] J. R. Hicks, *The Theory of Wages* (London: Macmillan, 1967).

[39] K. Hilton and H. Dolphin, 'Capacity and Capital Utilisation in the U.K.: their measurement and reconciliation', *Bulletin Oxford Univ. Inst. Econ. Statist*, 32, no. 3 (1970).

[40] J. Houthakker, 'The Pareto Distribution and the Cobb–Douglas Production Function in Activity Analysis', *Review of Economic Studies*, xxii (1955–6).

[41] L. Johansen, 'Substitution versus Fixed Production Coefficients in the Theory of Growth: A Synthesis', *Econometrica*, xxvii (1959).

[42] —, *Production Functions* (Amsterdam: North-Holland, 1972).

[43] D. W. Jorgenson, 'Economic Studies of Investment Behavior', *Journal of Economic Literature*, xi, no. 4 (Dec 1971).

[44] —, 'The Stability of a Dynamic Input–Output System', *Review of Economic Studies*, xxviii (1960–1).

[45] — and Z. Griliches, 'The Explanation of Productivity Change', *Review of Economic Studies*, 34 (1967).

[46] J. M. Keynes, *The General Theory of Employment, Interest and Money* (London: Macmillan, 1936).

[47] L. R. Klein, 'Remarks on the Theory of Aggregation', *Econometrica*, xiv (1946).

[48] J. Kmenta and M. E. Joseph, 'A Monte Carlo Study of Alternative Estimates of the Cobb–Douglas Reduction Function', *Econometrica*, 37, no. 3 (July 1963).

[49] J. R. C. Lecomber, 'A Critique of Methods of Adapting, Updating and Projecting Matrices', mimeo. (Cambridge, 1970).

[50] W. W. Leontief, *The Structure of the American Economy 1919–1939: An Empirical Application of Equilibrium Analysis* (New York: Oxford University Press, 1951).

[51] — et al., *Studies in the Structure of the American Economy* (New York: Oxford University Press, 1953).

[52] M. C. Lovell, 'Buffer Stocks, Sales Expectations and Stability: A Multisector Analysis of the Inventory Cycle', *Econometrica*, 30, no. 2 (Apr 1962).

[53] J. Marshak and W. H. Andrews, 'Random Simultaneous Equations and the Theory of Production', *Econometrica*, XII, no. 34 (July–Oct. 1944).

[54] R. Maurice, *National Accounts Statistics: Sources and Methods* (London: H.M.S.O., 1968).

[55] J. E. Meade, *A Neoclassical Theory of Economic Growth* (London: Allen & Unwin, 1961).

[56] H. Menderhausen, 'On the Significance of Professor Douglas' Productive Function', *Econometrica*, 1 (1938).

[57] M. Nerlove, 'Recent Empirical Studies of the CES and Related Production Functions', in [11].

[58] O.E.C.D., *The Residual Factor and Economic Growth* (Paris, 1964).

[59] J. Paelinck and J. Waelbroeck, 'Etude Empirique sur l'Evolution de Coefficients Input–Output', *Economique Appliquee* (1963).

[60] I. F. Pearce, *International Trade* (London: Macmillan, 1970) pp. 457–75.

[61] J. Robinson, 'Euler's Theorem and the Problem of Distribution', *Economic Journal* (1934).

[62] —, 'Production Functions and the Theory of Capital', *Review of Economic Studies* (1954).

[63] W. E. G. Salter, *Productivity and Technical Change*, Department of Applied Economics, Monograph no. 6 (Cambridge University Press, 1969).

[64] R. M. Solow, 'Heterogeneous Capital and Smooth Production Functions: an Experimental Study', *Econometrica*, 31, no. 4 (Oct 1963).

[65] —, 'A Contribution to the Theory of Economic Growth', *Quarterly Journal of Economics* (1956).

[66] P. Sraffa, *Production of Commodities by Means of Commodities: Prelude to a Critique of Economic Theory* (Cambridge University Press, 1960).

[67] R. Stone, 'Multiple Classification in Social Accounting', *Bulletin of the International Statistical Institute*, XXXIX (1962).

[68] T. W. Swan, 'Economic Growth and Capital Accumulation', *Economic Record* (1956).

[69] J. Taylor, 'Hidden Unemployment, Hoarded Labour and the Phillips Curve', *Southern Economic Journal* (July 1970).

[70] C. B. Tilanus, *Input–Output Experiments* (Rotterdam University Press, 1966).

[71] H. Tsurumi, 'Non-Linear Two Stage, Least Squares Estimation of CES Production Functions', *Review of Economics and Statistics* (1970).

[72] United Nations, Input–Output Bibliography: (i) 1955–61; (ii) 1960–63; (iii) 1963–66. Statistical Paper Series *m*. (New York: United Nations).

[73]   —, *Problems of Input–Output Tables and Analysis* (New York: United Nations, 1966).

[74]   B. N. Vaccara and H. Simon, 'Factors Affecting the Post War Industrial Composition of Real Production', in *Studies in Income and Wealth*, 32 (National Bureau of Economic Research, 1968).

[75]   A. Vazquez, 'Homogeneous Production Functions with Constant or Variable Elasticity of Substitution', *Zeitschrift Fur Die Gesamte Staatswissennschaft* (Jan 1971).

[76]   L. Walras, *Elements of Pure Economics; or the Theory of Social Wealth* (London: Allen & Unwin, 1954).

[77]   P. Wicksteed, 'Coordination of the Laws of Distribution', *Economic Journal* (June 1894).

[78]   K. Wigley, *The Demand for Fuel: A Sub-Model for the British Fuel Economy* (London: Chapman & Hall, 1968).

[79]   G. C. Winston, 'The Reasons for Idle Capital', *Williams College Research Memorandum*, no. 52 (May 1971).

[80]   — and T. O. McCoy, 'Investment and the Optimal Idleman of Capital', *Review of Economic Studies*, XLI (3) no. 127 (July 1974).

3

The Supply of Labour

J. D. Byers

University College Aberystwyth

INTRODUCTION

Economic theorists have not been much concerned to examine the fundamentals of the labour-supply decision with the result that empirical investigations, which, in accordance with the current methodology, draw their inspiration from theoretical behavioural models, have been rather sparse compared to the amount of work expended on other parts of the standard macroeconomic model, such as the demand for money. A good part of the reason for this is the shift of focus introduced by Keynes in *The General Theory* [21] which emphasised the importance of the demand for labour in determining the level of employment, and led later writers to neglect the supply side of the market. Many writers (for example Patinkin [26] chs x–xii) have felt themselves free to make the assumption that the labour market is constantly in full-employment equilibrium (due to perfectly flexible wages) and so supply could safely be ignored. More recently, however, the neoclassical attack on Keynes's conclusion about the possibility of involuntary unemployment has involved a reconsideration of the labour-supply decisions of individuals in the light of optimal employment decisions over time and their effect on perceived wealth, as opposed to the idea that workers simply look at the current level of wages. Thus, whereas unemployment in Keynes's sense constitutes a welfare loss to society, the new approach asserts that under-utilisation of resources may be freely chosen. (On this see Phelps *et al.* [27] and Hutt [20].)

While the whole area is subject to much controversy, and appears likely to be so for some time, it does seem possible to derive some lessons of relevance to the interpretation of observations taken in the labour market to aid in the assessment of empirical investigations of the supply of labour, for it is clear that, in general, we do not observe equilibrium configurations of the market. What we see are results of decisions taken in the past in the light of the (almost certainly insufficient) information available, decisions which may, in the present, be revealed as mistaken, and this effect is reinforced if, as seems very likely, individuals do not react immediately to new developments but rather take time to adjust their behaviour. In consequence, labour-market observations are more likely to be of positions off demand and supply curves than on, with the result that it becomes difficult to accept econometric labour-supply curves with any great degree of confidence. However, this is not to say that we can learn nothing from such investigations; though opinions may differ as to how much.

THEORETICAL BACKGROUND

Most studies of the supply of labour have been concerned with the determinants of the aggregate amount of labour available in the economy, whereas the basic theory refers to the decisions taken by individual units. This, however, is not a problem so long as we accept the neoclassical methodology that macroeconomic functions should be derived by a process of aggregation from microeconomic behaviour, although aggregation problems are often conveniently forgotten. In particular, simple summation of micro functions depends on the assumption that labour is homogeneous, which is obviously not the case. Keynes tried to get around this problem ([21] p. 41) by assuming that different grades of labour enjoyed a fixed relative remuneration so that relative wages provided a weighting system. This, unfortunately, is reasonable only if relative wages reflect relative marginal products, an assumption which is somewhat at variance with Keynes's general thesis.

The simplest theory of the labour-supply decision takes the individual as deriving utility from quantities of some all-purpose consumption good and from leisure, and maximising his utility subject to a budget (time) constraint. The well-known result is that relative consumptions of goods-in-general and leisure will depend on relative prices (see, for example, Green [18] p. 71). A rise in the wage rate represents an increase in the opportunity cost of leisure and results in a decreased demand for leisure, that is an increased supply of labour. As usual we may divide the total effect of a price change into a substitution effect, which will be negative, and an income effect, which will depend on whether leisure is a normal or an inferior good. This latter leads to the oft-mentioned possibility that the supply curve of hours of labour may become backward-bending as a result of the income effect dominating the substitution effect at higher levels of wages. This argument has been used to explain the observation that as real wages have risen over long periods of time the average number of hours worked per week has steadily declined. However, whether a series of observations taken over many years can be taken to represent the backward-bending supply curve of economic theory is a matter for doubt. Such a supply curve implies that the individual in question will offer to supply the same number of hours of labour at two widely divergent wage rates. It is unlikely that the *ceteris paribus* assumptions required are valid for time-series observations.

The above theory has the attraction of simplicity but is open to the fundamental objection that it fails to take proper account both of the interrelationships between time and production and consumption, and also of the environment in which decisions about the use of time are taken. In particular, the analysis, by posing the problem as a choice between consumption and leisure, ignores the fact that time is required for the act of consumption as well as for production. One might also point out that an elementary principle of consumer theory is that decisions are taken by households, and although it is possible to interpret the foregoing analysis in terms of a household utility function, we can gain knowledge only about the total number of hours per time period that the household decides to supply. What we are not told is how this aggregate is divided between the individuals comprising the household. This constitutes a serious deficiency, for there would seem to be little doubt that the decisions of different groups of people to participate in the labour force are affected by different things. While our society is such that heads of households are expected to work, there is more leeway in the labour-force-participation decisions of other members of the family. We may, for instance, regard the household as possessing a technology with which to produce commodities which the members wish to consume, but productive processes can be labour or capital intensive so that at high wage rates the opportunity cost of work at home may become high enough to induce a more capital-intensive technology in the home and a greater quantity of labour supplied to the market. Decisions must also be taken about such things as the number of years of education that children undergo, and clearly forgone earnings will be important here also. This latter example is instructive in another sense, because the decision may well be taken with regard to the expected future earnings of the child. By taking account of perceived or expected household wealth we are again led to consider longer-run aspects of labour-participation behaviour.

Leaving to one side explicit account of wealth we proceed to a summary of a theory of the allocation of time (Becker [2]) which has provided a set of propositions which recent studies of labour supply (for example Bowen and Finegan [8]) have sought to test. As implied above, households are regarded as producing the fundamental utility-yielding commodities which they consume by combining inputs of goods and time according to the cost-minimisation rules familiar from the traditional theory of the firm. If the production of a unit of some fundamental commodity requires both an input of some good and of time, each of which has a price, then it is intuitively obvious that utility maximisation will yield the result that the marginal rate of substitution between two fundamental commodities will equal their relative 'full costs', that is the sum of the cost of the good (or goods) and of time, rather than simply the ratio of the prices of the goods. Under such circumstances an increase in non-labour income will tend to increase the consumption of all fundamental commodities and, since consumption requires time, we would expect the hours spent on work in the market to decrease. If we impose a uniform percentage rise in earnings for all allocations of time, then this must change relative commodity prices since time will be more important in some than in others. Thus households will be induced to shift away from commodities which have relatively large forgone earnings and to substitute goods-intensive for time-intensive commodities. The effect of a pure rise in earnings is to increase hours of market work. These two results are, of course, also provided by the standard labour–leisure analysis. This should not be surprising as that analysis is simply a special case of the Becker approach, a special case in which the cost of leisure consists entirely of forgone earnings and the costs of other commodities entirely of goods. The advantage of the Becker approach is that it leads us beyond simply looking at wage rates in searching for the determinants of the labour supply.

DETERMINANTS OF LABOUR-FORCE
PARTICIPATION

Empirical studies of the supply of labour have been almost completely concerned with the decision about whether to participate in the labour force or not. Very little attention has been given to the other dimension of labour supply, that is the number of hours worked (but see Finegan [15]). Accordingly it is the former aspect with which we shall be concerned and we begin with a look at cross-sectional studies of labour-force participation. These studies utilise census data to regress the labour-force-participation rates of various groups on variables suggested by the sort of analysis outlined in the introduction. Unfortunately, data on household production and consumption technologies and utility functions are not readily available so investigators have had to make do with proxy variables which, it is hoped, reflect the underlying influences on behaviour. In addition, a further strand of analysis has often been grafted on to take account of 'life-cycle' and 'permanent-income' considerations. Thus it might be expected that the participation rates of married women will be affected not only by the level of the household's permanent income, but also by the circumstance of current income being above or below that level. The total potential labour force is normally subdivided into those people who are expected to have a high degree of attachment to market work (for example heads of households) and those whose devotion to regular employment is at a lower level. These, respectively, are termed 'primary' and 'secondary' workers.

As might be expected it is somewhat easier to explain the participation rates of primary rather than those of secondary workers so we can illustrate the approach by reference to the most important group of primary workers, prime-age males (aged between 25–54 years) as analysed in Bowen and Finegan's massive study of labour-force participation [8]. Factors determining the labour-force status of prime-age males were divided into personal characteristics and variables reflecting market conditions. The procedure used to estimate the effect of personal characteristics was to take data derived from the U.S. Census of 1960 to arrive at the proportion of men with a given characteristic who were also in the labour force (that is those employed or unemployed but looking for a job) and then to utilise the results of a regression of the participation rate of prime-age males on the various personal characteristics in order to adjust the original proportions for differences in characteristics. The most important factor in predicting a man's labour-force status turned out to be his marital position. On the basis of the unadjusted figures, 98·1 per cent of married men, with wife present, were in the labour force, while those who were divorced, widowed, separated or who had never married had a labour-force-participation rate of 89·8 per cent. An adjustment was then carried out to allow for differences in schooling, colour, other (that is non-labour) income and age to arrive at the proposition that, *ceteris paribus*, the probability of finding a married man in the labour force was 98 per cent while that of finding an unmarried man was 90.2 per cent. In other words, given that one man was married and another was not, there is a higher probability that the former will be in the labour force than the latter. In fact, the adjustments in this case have made very little difference, the gap narrowing from 8·3 to 7·8 per cent.

As mentioned earlier all variables used are, to varying extents, proxies for true influences on behaviour, so that a problem frequently arises as to exactly what underlying factor a particular proxy is representing, and this is a case in point. One possible explanation for the importance of the marital-status variable is that marriage, by increasing financial responsibilities, increases the 'taste' for income, and therefore results in a higher propensity for labour-force participation. There may be psychic costs involved, in that society expects a married man to be participating in the labour force while an unmarried man is freer from these pressures. Again, men who prefer liberty from regular work may also prefer not to marry. The alternative explanation is that expected market earnings (that is money income plus psychic income) may well be smaller for those men who exhibit physical and mental characteristics leading to difficulty in finding and keeping a wife. Thus defects in body or mind lower a man's potential earnings and therefore the strength of his attachment to the labour force, and also inhibit his chances of finding a wife. There is, unfortunately, no unambiguous evidence to support either of these alternatives over the other, though Bowen and Finegan come down on the side of the personal-traits explanation as being of primary importance. No doubt part of the difficulty is that the two explanations are not completely independent. If marriage increases the psychic costs of not working, then a married man is bound to have a higher net rate of expected market earnings than an exactly similar unmarried man.

The second most important determinant of labour-force participation from the U.S. data is the colour of a man's skin. Bowen and Finegan found the unadjusted participation rate for blacks was 93·1 per cent as opposed to 98·1 per cent for whites. After adjustment for educational background, other income and marital status the rates closed to 95·1 and 96·9 per cent respectively. Presumably the rest is racial discrimination. This difference might not seem very large until one notes that it seems likely that the number of black males completely missed by the 1960 census was *30 per cent larger* than their reported unemployment and non-participation totals combined.

The other variables considered by Bowen and Finegan as determining the labour-force participation of males were years of schooling, amount of other income and age. One might easily expect greater labour-force participation by men with more years of schooling since education can be taken as increasing expected market earnings (in the sense of finding a more pleasant job, if not a better paid one, and perhaps by increasing the probability of finding a job) so that the opportunity cost of staying out of the market is higher. And so it turned out. Educational achievement was found to be strongly associated with labour-force participation. Even after adjustment for other variables, the rates rose steadily with the number of years of schooling, from 90·3 per cent for 0–4 years to 99·1 per cent for 17 years or more. Economic theory predicts that the higher the level of non-labour income the lower will be the participation rate and, again, a negative relation emerged from the data, even for low levels of other income. This latter appears to be the result of an identification problem, that is it was not that the men abstained from work as a result of receiving other income but that they received this income precisely because they had been unable to find work. In other words, it was unemployment benefit. Increasing age appeared to have some effect in lowering labour-force-participation rates but the effect was small, and smaller still when adjustments for other influences were made.

Turning to the effect of labour-market conditions Bowen and Finegan examined differences in the prime-age male labour-force-participation rate among standard metropolitan statistical areas (S.M.S.A.s) using as independent variables the unemployment rate in the local market, the ratio of male jobs to total jobs in the area – an industry-mix variable which reflects job opportunities for men – and a measure of the average wage in the local markets.

Since the simple average male participation rate of the hundred largest

S.M.S.A.s in 1960 was 96·4, with a standard deviation of 1·2, one might initially expect that variations in labour-market conditions would have little effect on the participation rates of primary workers. However, this turned out not to be the case. Bowen and Finegan calculated that, *ceteris paribus*, an area with an unemployment rate one per cent above the all-S.M.S.A. average would have a prime-male participation rate of about 0·3 per cent below the average. Here the rate of unemployment serves as an indicator of the probability that a potential labour-force entrant will be able to find a job in the area in a given period of time, so that the greater the unemployment rate the lower the probability of finding a job in the area in a given period of time, and hence the lower expected market earnings and hence the lower the participation rate. Use of the industry-mix variable turned up another significant relationship, a one per cent difference between otherwise similar S.M.S.A.s being associated with a difference of about 0·2 per cent in the prime-age male participation rate. Obviously this variable also serves as an indicator of the chances of finding a job. The third variable considered was a measure of potential earnings from employment in a given region. This, also, was found to be significant but at a lower level of importance than the former two variables, apparently reflecting the fact that prime-age males are expected to work and so are not very responsive to fairly small differences in wages.

In many ways this last is a disappointing result because this is the first time that we have come across a variable (*the* variable) which enters into the normal textbook 'supply curve' (as opposed to factors determining its position) and that variable (wage) has not performed all that well. Two problems arise here. One is that variables such as the unemployment rate and the industry mix may reflect interactions between the supply and demand sides so that one cannot be sure that one is not estimating some hybrid demand–supply function which is the result of the market process. The second problem emerges when a reconciliation is attempted by claiming that the quantity variables affect expected market earnings. We then have three different factors all of which are proxies for expected market earnings, which is a somewhat peculiar state of affairs. Differences in labour-market tightness between areas may be reflected in different levels of earnings as well as different employment rates.

A further difficulty in the interpretation of the relationships between participation rates and job opportunities is the possibility (Mincer [25] pp. 79–81) that migration to areas with easier markets is an alternative to leaving the labour force. Thus a negative relationship could be obtained if the better workers left the area to find jobs elsewhere, leaving behind those men whose attachment to the labour force was, by reason of their personal characteristics, much less strong. However, when Bowen and Finegan tested for this by including a variable to measure migration, its coefficient turned out to be insignificantly different from zero. One might argue that, in recessions, it will be the better workers who hang on to their jobs for longer while others become unemployed but who, by reason of their personal characteristics, are unable or unwilling to migrate. The problem here is that while some variables (for example expected market earnings) in cross-section studies are to be taken to be at equilibrium values, others (such as unemployment and migration rates) presumably are the result of transitory phenomena and there is no guarantee that full adjustment has taken place.

It was this distinction between permanent and transitory components that formed part of the basis of Mincer's study of the labour-force participation of married women [24]. Married women are the most important group of 'secondary workers', and have therefore attracted a considerable amount of attention. Interest in them has been heightened by an apparent contradiction in their labour-market behaviour, for their rate of participation has risen quite dramatically in the last few decades despite the fact that the real wages of their husbands have also been increasing. This conflicts with the reasonable presupposition that, there being less need for them to work, they would have worked less. The confusion becomes deeper when evidence derived from cross-sectional studies is brought to bear, for these have usually shown that the higher *per capita* income in an area the lower is the female labour-force-participation rate.

Mincer's basic model concerned the making of decisions in the household context about the three-way division of time between market work, leisure and household work. Family income, as a whole, affects the total amount of work supplied while market wage rates determine each individual's allocation of hours between the different sorts of activities. The second strand in the analysis was derived from considerations arising from Friedman's 'permanent income hypothesis' [16], since it was argued that the labour-force response of married women to changes in income would depend on whether such changes were in transitory or permanent income. The hypothesis to be tested was that the labour-force-participation rates of wives would be higher, (a) the smaller is the permanent income of the husband, and (b) the lower is current income in relation to the permanent income of the husband, where permanent income is, in some sense, that income which the family regards as normal, and transitory income represents deviations from this norm. Naturally other factors, such as age, education and number of children, would also be expected to influence decisions about labour-force participation and Mincer allowed for these, partly by judicious choice of data, and partly by including extra variables in the regression equations. Again empirical proxies had to be used for some variables which were directly unobservable, for example median income of male family heads was used to represent permanent income in some regressions. The hypothesis, which basically comes down to a test of the relative importance of (permanent) income and substitution effects, was tested against a variety of data derived from cross-sectional and budget studies.

The results obtained provided reasonable confirmation for the hypotheses. It was found that the labour-force participation of wives was inversely related to husbands' income but positively related to female wage rates, and that the elasticity of the former was about one-half that of the latter, so that the higher the husbands' income the less wives tended to work, while the more the wife was able to earn the more likely she was to work, and if both types of income were increasing then wives' labour-force-participation rates should be observed to be increasing. The response of wives to transitory decreases in earnings was found to be more than twice their response to changes in permanent income. When transitory effects were not present, the positive elasticity with respect to wives' earnings was more than sufficient to overcome the negative elasticity with respect to husbands' permanent income. When the results were used to predict changes in labour-force-participation rates of wives over time the model was able to resolve the apparent contradiction between cross-sectional and time-series observations by predicting increased rates. It should be noted however that the model did not predict decade-to-decade movements in the participation ratio particularly accurately.

Bowen and Finegan, in their massively researched book on the economics of labour-force participation [8], attempted to assess the influence of almost every conceivable factor which might determine the labour-market behaviour of married women. The list of variables in the category entitled 'Individual Characteristics' included colour, number and age of children, size of house, age, education, other family income and employment status of husband. Forces at work in the labour market included wages of domestic servants, earnings possibilities, the number of female-type jobs available in comparison to the number of females available to fill them and the rate of unemployment. Some of these pull in both directions at once. Thus the number of children might be expected to decrease the labour-force-participation rate of married women by increasing the amount of work to be done in the house, while, on the other hand, the effect might be to increase participation because of the greater need for money income to provide for larger families. The resultant appears to depend on the ages of the children involved: labour-force participation of married women is reduced by the presence of children under fourteen years of age and especially of children under six. Housing is a similar variable in that one might expect that the larger the house the more money would be required to run it and therefore the greater the degree of labour-force participation. However, larger houses also need more time for cleaning etc. which would indicate a decreased labour-force-participation ratio. Moreover, there is a problem in that the size of house may reflect family income leading to a possible confounding of the effects of two different explanatory variables. Whether or not the two opposing tendencies cancelled out is impossible to say, but housing turned out to be an insignificant variable, in fact the only insignificant variable of the set under consideration. The relationship of age to

participation rates was found to follow an inverted U-shape, the rates for
teenagers and older women, when adjusted for other influences, being
significantly below the rates for women between the ages of twenty and
forty-four. The effect of education should be to increase expected market
earnings as the number of years of education increases and this should
cause a substitution of time devoted to labour-market activities for work
in the house. However, education itself may well change preferences in
favour of market work whereas the test is supposed to be about the effect
of education on the 'budget constraint', and thus the finding that participation increases with years of education must be treated with some
caution. The expected inverse relationship between participation rates
and other family income was also discovered.

Turning to labour-market conditions, the factors that we would expect
to influence the participation decision of married women are potential
earnings and some measure(s) of job availability. *A priori*, areas in which
female earnings are above the national average should have above-
average female participation rates because the opportunity cost of working at home is greater. Bowen and Finegan found that not only did this
substitution effect exist but that it was much larger than the equivalent
effect on male participation, perhaps reflecting the greater choice available to women as between market work and work in the home. Participation rates are also positively associated with the proportion of 'female
jobs' in an area relative to the number of females potentially available for
filling them, that is the lowering of the search costs incurred in finding a
job more than offsets the increased competition for jobs brought about by
a larger number of females in a given area. The participation decision
should also be affected by the rate of unemployment but here there are
two influences working in different directions. The existence of unemployment among primary workers may cause additional (secondary) workers to appear in the market, and so the participation rate of married
women should vary positively with the rate of employment. However, the
discouraged-worker effect will be operating in the other direction and so
the net effect will depend on the relative strengths of the two forces. The
results derived by Bowen and Finegan showed that, on average, the
discouraged-worker effect prevails (this is discussed below).

LABOUR-FORCE PARTICIPATION AND UNEMPLOYMENT:
TIME-SERIES STUDIES

The major question which time-series studies of labour-force participation have attempted to answer was first posed in the 1930s with the
emergence of two apparently conflicting hypotheses concerning the reactions of members of the labour force to variations in the availability of
employment opportunities. The 'discouraged-worker' hypothesis argued
that, in times of recession, people who became unemployed would, when
faced with the difficulty of finding a new job, tend to drop out of the

labour force altogether. On the other hand, the 'additional-worker' hypothesis claimed that labour-force participation increased at low levels of economic activity since pressure would be exerted on 'secondary workers' (for example housewives and elder children) to enter the labour force in order to supplement the family income which had declined due to the 'primary worker' losing his job. While the additional-worker hypothesis refers particularly to secondary workers, either primary or secondary workers could become 'discouraged', though the effect on secondary workers may be expected to be greater since their labour-market attachment will be weaker. It should be emphasised that the hypotheses refer to cyclical movements in and out of the labour force; the test of labour-force membership being whether the individual in question is looking for a job or not.

Clearly the propositions are not mutually exclusive. There is no reason why both effects should not be observed. The problem then is to discover which of the two is the stronger. This is, in fact, an issue of some practical importance for economic policy, since if the discouraged-worker hypothesis dominates, then measured unemployment will understate the amount of actual unemployment. Policies designed to increase employment, which depend on the official figures, will not be sufficient to provide jobs for everyone who will be attempting to find work when the economy is on the upswing again. If, alternatively, the additional-worker effect is more important, expansionist policies will overshoot the target since additional workers will drop out of the labour force as the economy expands. Early work on this problem by Clarence Long [22] suggested that these effects tended to balance out, though later researchers have produced different conclusions.

Strand and Dernburg [31] hypothesised that the net rate of defection from the labour force declined during a cyclical downswing as the entry of additional workers into the labour force offset the losses due to the discouraged-worker effect. They estimated the equation,

$$\left(\frac{L}{P}\right)_t = a_m + a_1\left(\frac{E}{P}\right)_t + a_2\left(\frac{X}{P}\right)_{t+2} + a_3\left(\frac{1}{P}\right)_t,$$

where P is the total adult civilian non-institutional population, L and E are the subsets of P (the labour force and employed) respectively, and X is the number of unemployment-compensation exhaustions. The employment ratio enters the equation as a proxy for the degree of tightness of the labour market (earlier studies had used indices of industrial production and gross national product), and might be taken as representing the probability of obtaining a job, though such an interpretation is somewhat easier in cross-sectional studies. Accordingly, the value of its coefficient will be an estimate of the discouraged-worker effect, while the coefficient on the exhaustions ratio will measure the additional-worker effect. This is so because the prospect that unemployment compensation will soon be exhausted (hence the two-period lead) is taken to cause the entry of secondary workers into the labour force. The population variable enters partly to lessen the chances of spurious correlation due to the common-population denominator, and partly to pick up the direction and magnitude of secular trends in the labour-force-participation ratio.

Since the discouraged-worker hypothesis implies that labour-force participation increases (decreases) with increases (decreases) in the employment rate, the coefficient a_1 is expected to be positive. Similarly, a rise in the exhaustion ratio is taken to represent increased pressure on secondary workers to enter the labour force and thus the additional-worker hypothesis leads us to expect a positive value for the coefficient a_2. The results of the regression seemed to provide striking confirmation of both the discouraged- and the additional-worker hypotheses.

The equation appeared to explain about 80 per cent of the variation in labour-force participation, allowance having been made for seasonal factors. All variables were found to be significant at the 1 per cent level and the coefficients on E/P and X/P had the right sign, although the size of the coefficient on the exhaustions ratio (12·347) led Mincer [25] to wonder why, other things being equal, the prospect of one additional exhaustion of unemployment benefit should result in the additional participation of 12 (!) secondary workers. Mincer suspected that the exhaustions ratio was acting as a proxy for the unemployment–population ratio U/P since the labour force is equal to the sum of those employed and those looking for employment. Strand and Dernburg would then be exploiting an identity. However, a regression excluding the exhaustions ratio still produced a net discouraged-worker effect.

Two studies by Tella [34, 35] also provided support for the hypothesis that the labour force reacts to short-term demand changes. Here again the ratio of employment to population of working age is used as a measure of changing manpower demands. This, and a trend term, Tella concluded, explained a large proportion of annual movements in the labour force in the post-war period. In addition, by regressing average annual participation rates for males and females aged fourteen or more separately, he took a step towards answering the important question of who are the discouraged and additional workers. He found that the female labour force reacts more readily than the male to changing job opportunities, females revealing a stronger tendency to leave, or not to enter, the labour force in times of recession and to enter it in periods of rising employment. The second article is an attempt at a more sophisticated analysis by disaggregating the population into 14 age–sex groups. For no good reason that is apparent, Tella also included members of the armed forces in the labour force. Thus, letting A be armed forces and the subscript i stand for the population group concerned, Tella's representative equation can be written as

$$\left(\frac{L+A}{P}\right)_{it} = a_0 + a_i\left(\frac{E+A}{P}\right)_{it-1} + a_2 \log T_t.$$

(Note that the employment variable is lagged one quarter to minimise the danger of correlated sampling errors in E and L.) Again the results seemed to provide ample support for the discouraged-worker hypothesis. All the net regression coefficients for the employment ratios came out positive and, with the exception only of males aged 35–44, each was easily significant at the 10 per cent level.

Although there is no exhaustions ratio here to attract criticism, doubts can still be raised about the validity of the employment ratio as a measure of job opportunities and the applicability of the time trend. The main difficulty had already been faced by Strand and Dernburg. It is simply that since E_i is such a large fraction of L_i, there is a good chance of a spurious positive correlation between $(L/P)_i$ and $(E/P)_i$ when L_i changes for reasons not to do with the demand for manpower. This is precisely why a time trend was introduced, and no doubt this reduces the size of the problem by picking up trends in participation and employment. Unfortunately, trends are somewhat different from autonomous short-term changes, and that is where the difficulty of an upward bias in the group regression coefficients arises. Tella [34] justified his regression of (L/P) on (E/P) by arguing that the alternative regression of (L/P) on (E/L) would, by introducing the same variable in both the numerator of the dependent variable and the denominator of the independent variable, result in a negative correlation and that (E/P) is a superior choice since then (L/P) and (E/P) are only positively related. This, however, is the whole problem and the difficulty is even more serious when group ratios are used, since some groups will be more open to short-term autonomous changes than others.

Dernburg and Strand [14], answer questions as to who are the discouraged and additional workers by examining the participation behaviour of the same fourteen age–sex groups that Tella studied, and attempting to determine the relationship between employment and labour-force participation in these groups. They estimated the equation,

$$\left(\frac{L_i}{P}\right)_t = a_{mi} + a_{1i}\left(\frac{E}{P}\right)_t + a_{2i}\left(\frac{X}{P}\right)_{t+2} + a_{3i}\left(\frac{1}{P}\right)_t + a_{4i}\left(\frac{P_i}{P}\right)_t.$$

The ratio of group to total population is included because of the peculiar way in which the participation ratios have been defined, which means that rates will vary with the proportion of the total population in any group. The aggregate exhaustions ratio remains since additional workers are additional because of the exhaustion of compensation by members of other groups. Similarly, the aggregate employment ratio is used because the discouraged-worker effect relates to the over-all degree of market tightness, so that a statistical correlation between E_i and L_i would not be a sufficient test of the discouraged-worker hypothesis. In addition, the inclusion of (E/P) instead of (E_i/P) goes some way to getting over the already noted problem of group employment being a large proportion of group labour force, and hence the chance that, if the sample value of employment in a group is larger than the true value, the sample value of the group labour force is also likely to be over-estimated. There is less reason to suppose that sampling errors in a particular subgroup are correlated with sampling errors in the population as a whole.

Estimation of this equation gave general support to the existence of a widespread discouraged-worker effect, except in the case of prime-age males, and indicated decreasing male, and increasing female, participation rates over time. Dernburg and Strand also repeated an exercise performed in their previous paper [31] to find the net effect of a rise in total unemployment on the participation rates. This further work becomes necessary because, since the exhaustions ratio is a function of previous levels of employment, the coefficient on the employment ratio does not tell the whole story if we want to derive estimates of the stationary effect of a given increase in unemployment. The results here showed that, for all groups combined, an increase in employment by 1000 jobs would cause an expansion of the total labour force by 454 persons and a fall in unemployment of 546, most of the increased participation being by females and most of the fall in unemployment being experienced by men. If all this seems in danger of generating a certain amount of confidence in the conclusions, it should be pointed out that the summation of the coefficients for the additional-worker effect indicates that, other things being equal, the imminent prospect of one additional exhaustion of unemployment benefit would result in *nine* additional workers entering the labour force, an estimate that might be thought to be a little on the high side.

Barth [1] attempted to test the Dernburg and Strand [14] thesis with an equation of the form

$$\left(\frac{L}{P}\right)_{it} = a + b\left(\frac{U}{L}\right)_{t-1} + c\left(\frac{X}{U}\right)_{t+1} + dT + \text{seasonal dummies},$$

where U is total unemployment. Estimating this equation for twenty-one age–sex groups, Barth found support for the discouraged-worker effect among the male groups, but neither the discouraged- nor the additional-worker effects were evident for most of the female groups. He concluded that he had found some support for the Strand–Dernburg thesis, but not sufficient to get even moderately excited about. He then estimated the equation without the exhaustions variable, partly on the grounds that it had turned out to be insignificant and partly on the grounds that some multi-collinearity existed between this variable and the unemployment rate. Positive correlation between the participation rate and the unemployment rate is possible for reasons which we have already gone into, though this danger is lessened by taking the data from different quarters. (This may go some way towards explaining the low values obtained for the coefficients.) Now the discouraged-worker effect showed up significantly amongst male categories, and the coefficients always had the right

sign. However, they remained small. The females were again less predictable and Barth suggests several reasons for this: first, an increase in the
unemployment rate in a given quarter affects the participation rate only
gradually (which is the original Strand–Dernburg thesis and the reason
why they introduced the exhaustions variable); secondly, there is the
possibility that an increase in unemployment in the present period could
cause both a flow of females into, and a flow of females out of, the labour
force, and these two flows might cancel each other out (which *is* a denial
of the Strand–Dernburg thesis which posited an initial discouragement
effect with the additional-worker effect becoming operative after some
time lag); and thirdly, that 'unlike males, possibly most females in the
labour force and out of it do not respond in a systematic fashion to
changes in the unemployment rate' ([1] p. 380).

Bowen and Finegan [8] estimated an equation of the form,

$$\left(\frac{L}{P}\right)_{it} = a + b\left(\frac{U}{L}\right)_{t-1} + c\left(\frac{E_m}{E}\right)_{t-1} + \text{time trends,}$$

where, as usual, the unemployment rate is taken to measure the over-all
degree of market tightness and is lagged for one period for three reasons:
(1) on economic grounds – it is expected that some time elapses between
a change in unemployment and decisions to change participation; (2)
for statistical reasons – the lag permits the distinction between cause and
effect and lessens the risk of spurious correlations between the unemployment rate and participation rates; and (3) because a one-quarter lag gave
as good or better results than did more complicated lags or no lags at all.
The lagged ratio of manufacturing employment to total employment was
included to take account of changes in labour-market conditions which
have differential effects on primary and secondary workers. On the
presumption that prime-age males are largely employed in manufacturing
industry, a fall in this ratio, *ceteris paribus*, would signify an expansion in
the employment opportunities of the secondary groups (younger and
older workers and all females) relative to those of prime-age males.
Although the inclusion of this industry-mix variable is definitely a step in
the right direction it causes problems. One can no longer simply take the
partial regression coefficient on the unemployment rate as showing the
net effect of a cyclical change in unemployment on labour-force participation, since E_m/E will vary inversely with U/L over the cycle. Consequently, an adjustment is necessary on the coefficient of U/L to correct
for changes in E_m/E and its effect on participation.

Despite running regressions for different periods and different
variables no definite conclusions could be formed. Cyclical changes in
labour-market conditions emerged as having scarcely any effect on
the rate of labour-force participation. When the regression coefficient
on employment was significant it had a negative sign, but it was often
insignificant. Furthermore, the results obtained appeared to be very
sensitive to the time period under consideration. The only groups for

which the rate of unemployment appeared to exert a large impact on participation rates were those of teenagers and males over the age of sixty-five. This result is at variance with those of most other time-series studies. Bowen and Finegan's time-series results also conflict markedly with the conclusions of their cross-sectional studies. In these the influence of the employment status of the husband provides a test of the additional-worker effect. It was found that, *ceteris paribus*, the participation rate for women whose husbands were 'not in the labour force' were significantly lower than those for women whose husbands were simply 'unemployed'. If one is prepared to regard these two cases as showing permanent and transitory effects, it would provide further support for the idea that transitory decreases in family income lead to larger increases in the wives' participation rate than do permanent decreases. However, the discouraged-worker effect presents a difficulty here by indicating that being out of the labour force is not necessarily a 'permanent' state of affairs.

This section began with a question about the relative sizes of the additional- and discouraged-worker effects, and it must be said that on the basis of empirical studies we are not in a position to give a definite answer. The general impression is that the discouraged-worker effect dominates, if only because a rise in unemployment affects all workers either in employment or those looking for work but only those wives whose husbands have lost their jobs, and because investigators have been unwilling to accept the estimated size of additional-worker effects. Even if a recession continues for some time, it seems unlikely that additional workers will enter the labour force faster than discouraged workers are leaving it. It could well be that the data available are simply not sufficiently sensitive to the timing problems involved to come to an accurate conclusion. Suffice it to say that the labour force appears to contract when the economy does.

HIDDEN UNEMPLOYMENT

Since the extent of labour-force participation of any given group of workers appears to respond to the availability of employment opportunities, which in turn depend on the level of economic activity, it follows that the observed degree of unemployment at any time is unlikely to be an accurate guide to the number of jobs required if the whole of the labour force is to be employed. In particular, since recorded labour-force participation is lower in recessions than in periods of full employment, it follows that observed unemployment under-estimates the actual man-power loss. The term 'hidden (or disguised) unemployment' refers to those who, at a specified time, are counted as not in the labour force but who would be in the labour force if jobs were easier to find. Thus, if hidden unemployment exists, simple comparisons of the actual rate of unemployment with some target rate of full employment will tend to under-estimate the social and economic losses involved in under-utilising resources.

The problem is to decide which rate of unemployment shall be taken as corresponding to 'full employment'. Since nothing can be derived from the concept itself to help us, the 'full-employment' rate of unemployment will have to be imported from other economic considerations, for example that rate of unemployment which is consistent with price stability or with that level of aggregate demand beyond which employment cannot be further increased. However, one is still left with problems arising from the existence of frictional and structural unemployment and so decisions about what constitutes 'full employment' is liable to be essentially arbitrary. A figure of 4 per cent unemployment has commonly been used in U.S. studies. The rate for the United Kingdom would be somewhat lower.

Calculations of hidden unemployment have typically proceeded by using regression equations relating labour-force-participation rates to employment (or unemployment) ratios in conjunction with a postulated rate of 'full-employment' unemployment to construct estimates of what the 'real' size of the labour force would have been had full employment been obtained. The difference between the estimated and the recorded labour force then provides an estimate of hidden unemployment. Using this one can go on to estimate the total manpower loss at any given time as the sum of hidden and observed unemployment, as long as a correction is made for the fact that the observed figure reflects cyclical, not total, levels of unemployment. In other words, simply taking the cyclical component as it stands assumes implicitly that full employment corresponds to zero unemployment. It should be noted that not all studies make this correction. A further problem arises as to whether considerations of output forgone and social welfare indicate that the two kinds of unemployment can be compared and added together, since hidden unemployment largely occurs amongst secondary (mostly female) workers, while being cyclically unemployed is mainly a masculine preserve. This has led Mincer to argue that differences in the level of economic activity, and therefore in the availability of employment opportunities, will produce effects on the (optimal and voluntary) timing of movements in and out of the labour force by secondary workers, and thus produce the illusion of hidden unemployment [25]. He does not, however, deny the existence of 'involuntary' labour-force withdrawal (that is, pure discouragement). However, since we lack hard evidence on the importance and frequency of such movements the issue is unresolved.

Many studies of the determinants of labour-force participation (for example Tella [35], Dernburg and Strand [14], Bowen and Finegan [8]) have used the results gained to estimate the degree of hidden unemployment by the procedure mentioned above. By and large, the figures arrived at have been somewhat greater than might have been expected, but much of this can be explained by the technique used. For instance, Tella used the ratio of employment to population which biased the regression coefficient. Dernburg and Strand concluded that hidden unemployment had increased during the period under consideration, particularly during the latter part, but they assumed that there had been a pronounced upward trend in the labour-force-participation rate, and this, in fact, accounts for most of the estimated increase in hidden unemployment. In general, estimates based on the regression method are very sensitive to the labour-market variable used.

A second way of measuring hidden unemployment was used by Taylor in his regional analysis of hidden unemployment in Britain between 1951 and 1966 [33]. His procedure was to examine the time series of female participation rates and to identify cyclical peaks as points at which the labour force has reached its short-run maximum, that is zero unemployment, and then join them up with straight lines. Hidden unemployment could then be calculated from the ratio of actual participation to 'full-employment' participation. The hidden unemployment estimates of the regression method depend strongly on the chosen unemployment rate but the 'trends through peaks' method requires the assumption that the full-employment peaks in participation are of equal strength. The interest in Taylor's paper derives from the distinction drawn between hidden *cyclical* and hidden *structural* unemployment, for if hidden structural unemployment exists then there will still be disguised unemployment when aggregate demand is such that hidden cyclical unemployment is zero. The policy implications of this are clear; whereas hidden cyclical unemployment can be removed by increasing the level of demand, the alleviation of hidden structural unemployment requires different measures such as, for example, regional policies. Taylor found that there had been significant hidden cyclical unemployment of secondary workers in the regions of Britain during the time period that he studies, and that hidden structural unemployment in the North-West region was such that the 'rates of recorded unemployment give us no indication at all of the relative incidence of hidden structural unemployment across a region's localities' ([33] p. 299). As in many studies of labour-supply behaviour the principal lesson to be derived is that recorded unemployment rates, either national or local, provide a very poor guide to the actual situation.

CONCLUSIONS?

If one is prepared to accept the procedures followed, then empirical studies of the determinants of the labour-supply decision lend some broad support to some predictions of economic theory. Whether that theory is adequately developed is another question. Even at the present time, theory requires knowledge of such things as household technologies and expectations which are not directly observable. Consequently, investigators have, by and large, restricted themselves to studying the effects of only a small number of influences, in particular wage rates and unemployment. Attention has been concentrated on the participation aspect to the neglect of the number of hours worked which households decide upon simultaneously for each of its members. In general, the distinction between these two has been fudged in empirical research. For instance, Mincer's theoretical model concerns the long-run equilibrium supply of labour hours, but for estimation purposes this becomes transformed into a determination of participation rates. Again, there is no guarantee that the data available may safely be construed as preserving the distinction between permanent and transitory influences. Cross-sectional observations may well be interpreted as representing differences in equilibrium labour supplies resulting from differences in equilibrium income and wage rates, but that still leaves unspecified the dynamic process by which we get from one position to another, and it is arguable whether time-series observations of reactions to changes in wages and income can fill this gap. Moreover, it is likely that even cross-sectional observations will also reflect some transitory influences.

There remains the problem of whether supply functions have actually been observed or not. Almost all results derived from empirical studies of the supply of labour have been estimated from single-equation models (but cf. Black and Kelejian [4]). In so far as unemployment variables have been included in the estimation function no explicit attention has been

TABLE 3.1
Some results

Variable → Class ↓	Tella [35] $\left(\frac{E}{P}\right)_t$	Dernburg and Strand [14] $\left(\frac{E}{P}\right)_t$	$\left(\frac{X}{P}\right)_{t+2}$	Barth [1] $\left(\frac{U}{L}\right)_{t-1}$	$\left(\frac{X}{U}\right)_{t+1}$	Bowen and Finegan [8] $\left(\frac{U}{L}\right)_t$
Males						
14–19	0·36	0·23	1·05	—	—	—
20–4	0·46	0·03	0·35	−1·03	0·28	−0·41
25–34	0·20	0·00	0·04	−0·33	0·07	—
35–44	0·07	0·00	0·01	−0·12	0·61	—
45–54	0·14	0·02	0·34	−0·18	0·54	—
55–64	0·46	0·01	0·57	−0·31	0·17	—
65+	0·74	0·07	0·92	−0·01	−0·03	−0·49
Females						
14–19	0·40	0·11	0·91	—	—	—
20–4	0·44	0·03	0·60	0·25	−0·08	—
25–34	0·52	0·06	0·96	−0·18	−0·01	−0·25
35–44	0·51	0·10	1·40	−0·32	0·07	−0·25
45–54	0·69	0·09	1·10	−0·02	0·04	−0·18
55–64	0·63	0·07	0·43	0·21	−0·15	−0·41
65+	0·70	0·05	0·54	0·08	−0·30	−0·20

given to the fact that the demand for labour also helps to determine the observed pairs of observations of earnings and employment. In plain terms, there is an identification problem. Without specifying a complete model of the demand for and supply of labour we cannot say whether a supply curve has been estimated, or a demand curve, or a hybrid of the two. Since identification, in the absence of other restrictions on one or other of the functions, depends on one equation excluding variables that the other does not, it seems likely that more often than not a supply curve has not been estimated. Ideally one would like to see both demand and supply estimated as part of a complete macroeconomic model. However, the costs of doing this, in addition to the statistical problems involved, are substantial.

Until further improvements are made we are basically left with the propositions that the supply of labour responds to cyclical changes in aggregate demand, to changes in wage rates, both long and short run (though these adjustments may be made by different people) and that a large number of other demographic and environmental variables also exert an effect on labour-force participation.

BIBLIOGRAPHY

[1] P. S. Barth, 'Unemployment and Labour Force Participation', *Southern Economic Journal*, vol. 34 (1968).

[2] G. Becker, 'A Theory of the Allocation of Time', *Economic Journal*, vol. 75, (1965).

[3] Y. Ben-Porath, 'Labour Force Participation Rates and the Supply of Labour', *Journal of Political Economy*, vol. 81 (1971).

[4] S. W. Black and H. H. Kalejian, 'A Macro Model of the U.S. Labour Market', *Econometrica*, vol. 38 (1970).

[5] — and R. R. Russell, 'Participation Functions and Potential Labour Force', *Industrial and Labour Relations Review*, vol. 24 (1970).

[6] J. M. Bonin and W. Y. Davis, 'Labour Force Responsiveness to Short Run Variations in Economic Opportunity', *Southern Economic Journal*, vol. 38 (1971).

[7] W. G. Bowen and T. A. Finegan, 'Labour Force Participation and Unemployment' in *Employment Policy and the Labour Market*, ed. A. M. Ross (University of California Press, 1965).

[8] —, *The Economics of Labour Force Participation* (Princeton University Press, 1969).

[9] G. Cain, *Married Women in the Labour Force* (University of Chicago Press, 1966).

[10] —, 'Unemployment and the Labour Force Participation of Secondary Workers', *Industrial and Labour Relations Review*, vol. 20 (1966–7).

[11] M. S. Cohen, R. I. Lennan and S. A. Rea, 'Area Employment

Conditions and Labour Force Participation: A Micro Study', *Journal of Political Economy*, vol. 79 (1971).

[12] B. A. Corry and J. A. Roberts, 'Activity Rates and Unemployment: The Experience of the United Kingdom, 1951–66', *Applied Economics*, vol. 2 (1970).

[13] —, 'Some Further Results', *Applied Economics*, vol. 6 (1974).

[14] T. Dernburg and K. Strand, 'Hidden Unemployment 1953–62: A Quantitative Analysis by Age and Sex', *American Economic Review*, vol. 56 (1966).

[15] T. A. Finegan, 'Hours of Work in the United States: A Cross-Sectional Analysis', *Journal of Political Economy*, vol. 70 (1962).

[16] M. Friedman, *A Theory of the Consumption Function*, (Princeton: National Bureau of Economic Research, 1957).

[17] P. Galambos, 'Activity Rates of the Population of Great Britain 1951–64', *Scottish Journal of Political Economy*, vol. 20 (1967).

[18] H. A. J. Green, *Consumer Theory* (Harmondsworth: Penguin, 1971).

[19] L. C. Hunter, 'Some Problems in the Theory of the Labour Supply', *Scottish Journal of Political Economy*, vol. 17 (1970).

[20] W. H. Hutt, *The Theory of Idle Resources* (London: Jonathon Cape, 1939).

[21] J. M. Keynes, *The General Theory of Employment, Interest and Money* (London: Macmillan, 1936).

[22] C. D. Long, *The Labour Force under Changing Income and Employment* (Princeton: National Bureau of Economic Research, 1958).

[23] J. Mincer, 'Labour Supply, Family Income and Consumption', *American Economic Review*, vol. 50 (1960).

[24] —, 'Labour Force Participation of Married Women: A Study of Labour Supply', in *Aspects of Labour Economics*, ed. H. G. Lewis (Princeton: National Bureau of Economic Research, 1962).

[25] —, 'Labour Force Participation and Unemployment: A Review of the Recent Evidence', in *Prosperity and Unemployment*, ed. R. A. Gordon and M. S. Gordon, (New York: Wiley, 1966).

[26] D. Patinkin, *Money, Interest and Prices*, 2nd edn (New York: Harper & Row, 1965).

[27] E. S. Phelps *et al.*, *Microeconomic Foundations of Employment and Inflation Theory* (New York: Norton, 1970).

[28] G. L. Perry, 'Unemployment Flows in the U.S. Labour Market', *Brookings Papers in Economic Activity*, 2 (1972).

[29] L. Robbins, 'On the Elasticity of Demand for Income in Terms of Effort', *Economica* (1930).

[30] S. Rosen, 'On the Interindustry Wage and Hours Structure', *Journal of Political Economy*, vol. 77 (1969).

[31] K. Strand and T. Dernburg, 'Cyclical Variations in Civilian Labour Force Participation', *Review of Economics and Statistics*, vol. 46 (1964).

[32] J. Taylor, 'Hidden Employment, Hoarded Labour and the Phillips Curve', *Southern Economic Journal,* vol. 37 (1970).
[33] —, 'A Regional Analysis of Hidden Unemployment in Great Britain, 1951–66', *Applied Economics,* vol. 3 (1971).
[34] A. Tella, 'The Relation of Labour Force to Employment', *Industrial and Labour Relations Review,* vol. 17 (1964).
[35] —, 'Labour Force Sensitivity to Employment by Age, Sex', *Industrial Relations,* vol. 4 (1965).
[36] M. L. Wachter, 'A Labour Supply Model for Secondary Workers', *Review of Economics and Statistics,* vol. 54 (1972).
[37] G. C. Winston, 'An International Comparison of Income and Hours of Work', *Review of Economics and Statistics,* vol. 48 (1966).
[38] W. S. Woytinsky, *Employment and Wages in the United States,* (New York: Twentieth Century Fund, 1953).

4

Fixed Investment

E. Greenberg

Washington University
St. Louis

E. Greenberg

Washington University
St. Louis

I INTRODUCTION

For many years, and especially since the publication of Keynes's *The General Theory*, the study of fixed investment has been a central concern of economists. Keynes's contribution was to focus attention on changes in the level of income. In a simple Keynesian model

$$Y = C + I \quad \text{and} \quad C = a + bY,$$

where Y is income, C is consumption expenditure, I is investment, and a and b are parameters. It is easily established by substituting for C into the first equation that

$$Y = \frac{a}{1-b} + \frac{I}{1-b}.$$

The expression $1/(1-b)$ is called the multiplier. If b is close to unity, as Keynes believed, the multiplier will be large (for example if $b = 0.9$, $1/(1-b) = 10$) so that a small change in I leads to a much larger change in Y. Keynes's views on the determinants of I are considered below.

Investment was the subject of some of the earliest econometric work, for example that of Tinbergen [42] in the late 1930s. Designed to test empirically the business-cycle theories catalogued by Haberler [21], that empirical research was subsequently recognised in the first Nobel Prize in Economics (to Tinbergen and Frisch) in 1969.

This chapter will concentrate on plant and equipment expenditures. The remaining components of additions to the economy's capital stock, primarily agricultural investment and residential construction, are not explicitly considered. We first examine the micro investment decision under certainty in order to obtain insights for the development of macro investment models. We then extend this model to take uncertainty into account, consider macro aspects of the problem, and briefly review the major work.

II INVESTMENT AT THE MICRO LEVEL
UNDER CERTAINTY

The purpose of this section is to use micro theory to suggest those variables which might be important in an explanation of aggregate investment, or at least which should be considered in the construction of macro models. As we shall see, most of the existing investment models are incomplete or unsatisfactory in some respects; for this reason our approach is pragmatic. We select from each approach the insights it offers, and are not overly concerned with possible inconsistencies amongst the various models.

A.   *The Simplest Accelerator Model*

Consider a firm which produces an output, x, according to the production function

$$x = f(L, K),$$

where L is the amount of labour and K the flow of fixed capital services (plant and equipment), respectively, employed. For this model we assume that labour can be hired at constant unit cost, w, and that capital services can be rented at constant unit cost, q. The rental assumption is introduced at this point to avoid problems associated with ownership of capital; these are taken up below.

The firm desires to maximise profits subject to the production function constraint, that is

$$P = px - wL - qK - \lambda(x - f(L, K)),$$

where P is profits, p is the price of the product, and λ is a Lagrange multiplier. Under appropriate assumptions (for example p is a decreasing function of x, or the production function exhibits diminishing returns), this problem can be solved to yield the optimal values of x, L and K. If there is a change in p, w, q or in the underlying technology, we would expect the firm to select different values for x, L and K. Investment in period t, I_t, is

$$I_t = K_t - K_{t-1} + D_t,$$

where K_t and K_{t-1} are, respectively, the profit-maximising values of capital stock needed in periods t and $t-1$; and D_t represents depreciation (capital which has worn out during the period). These variables are defined in real terms, but, in practice, money values are used to aggregate the great variety of capital goods produced in the economy.

This result, however, is too general to be of much use; to obtain more definite relationships we need to add assumptions. One such set of assumptions leads to the *accelerator* model: It is assumed that $f(L, K)$ is of the fixed-coefficient variety (see Chapter 2); then,

$$x = \min(\alpha K, \beta L).$$

Assuming profit maximisation, output in period $t(x_t)$ will be produced with the minimum amount of K, and we have the relationship,

$$x_t = \alpha K_t$$

or

$$K_t = (1/\alpha)x_t.$$

Accelerator theorists generally ignore the fact that output for a competitive firm is indeterminate in this case.

If, for some reason, x_{t+1} is different from x_t there will be a change in K as well, that is if

$$K_{t+1} = (1/\alpha)x_{t+1}$$

then

$$I_t = K_{t+1} - K_t + D_t = (1/\alpha)(x_{t+1} - x_t) + D_t.$$

In this case we see that net investment, $I_t - D_t$, is proportional to the change in output, and is independent of w and q; this is the strongest version of the accelerator principle. Although strictly valid only in special cases, the accelerator model has been a starting point for much empirical work and also for theoretical models.

B. Durability of Capital and Irreversibility of Investment

One deficiency of the accelerator model is immediately obvious – capital equipment lasts longer than one production period, and may be difficult to sell. Unless equipment can be rented one period at a time at the same cost (that is there exists a perfect market for capital goods) it becomes necessary to consider the fact that purchase of an item of capital has implications for future, as well as current, profits. A pound received today is worth more than a pound received a year from today because it is possible to earn interest on the former. To make the two comparable, we ask what one would be willing to pay to receive £1 in a year. If it were possible to lend money at 5 per cent, an individual would be indifferent between receiving £1/(1·05) today or £1 a year from today. In general, an amount R_t, payable t years from today is worth $R_t/(1 + r)^t$ today (on the assumption that the interest rate, r, is constant).

In this context, it is customary, particularly in the business literature on the subject (see [38] for example) to conceive of an investment project as the purchase of an asset which yields a stream of returns (cash flows) over time, $(R_1, R_2, \ldots, R_n)$, where the last return includes the scrap value of the capital. If the firm can earn $100r$ per cent on alternative investment we can compute the present value of the project, V, as

$$V = \frac{R_1}{1+r} + \frac{R_2}{(1+r)^2} + \cdots + \frac{R_n}{(1+r)^n} - I,$$

where we have assumed that no revenue is received until the end of the first period and that all investment expenditures occur at the beginning of the project. If $V > 0$, the investment is worth making because it returns more than the alternative use of the funds (the cost of capital), r; otherwise, the project should be turned down.

There is another approach to the problem, which, under the assumed conditions, will lead to the same decision. Suppose we determine the value of ρ which equates I to the present value of the stream of returns when ρ is used as the discount rate; that is ρ equates the two sides of the equation,

$$I = \frac{R_1}{1+\rho} + \frac{R_2}{(1+\rho)^2} + \cdots + \frac{R_n}{(1+\rho)^n}.$$

In this expression, ρ is called the 'internal rate of return', and is compared to the interest rate. If $\rho > r$, the investment should be made; otherwise it should be rejected.

If it is assumed that at any given time there are many possible investment projects (additions to capital stock) which may be ranked by their internal rates of return, and that there are few projects yielding high returns and more yielding lower returns, we can graph the relationship between optimal capital stock and ρ as in Figure 4.1; this relationship is the 'marginal efficiency of capital' (m.e.c.) schedule. The firm should acquire all investment projects for which $\rho > r$, indicated by K_t^*. Investment is then determined as $K_t^* - K_{t-1} + D_t$.

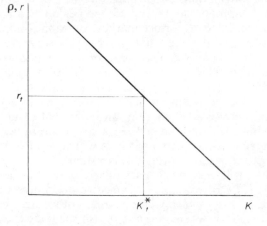

Fig. 4.1

From this view of investment, it is evident that the decision to invest depends on the stream of returns (which depends in turn on demand conditions, factor costs and tax laws), the cost of investment goods and the interest rate (or more generally, the marginal cost of funds). A project is more likely to be accepted if (1) the stream of returns increases (as a result of demand conditions or factor costs) or is redistributed over time so that more returns are available sooner, (2) if the price of capital goods falls, (3) or if there is a fall in the return on alternative uses for the funds.

Individual firms' m.e.c. schedules can be aggregated to obtain the relationship between the interest rate and aggregate investment. This is the type of investment function generally assumed in both classical and Keynesian models. The major difference between these has to do with the interest elasticity of the investment function. Many Keynesians believe this is small because the function is dominated by uncertain future cash flows, while economists in the classical tradition believe that investment is sensitive to interest rates. The issue is important for economic policy – if investment is not sensitive to interest rates the ability of monetary policy to affect investment through interest rates is restricted.

C. The Neoclassical Investment Model

In a series of papers Jorgenson and his associates [28] have developed a model which combines the capital–labour substitution possibilities of the general accelerator model of Section A with the present-value maximisation of Section B. The model assumes that capital equipment is purchased (not rented) at unit cost, q; that capital stock depreciates at constant rate per period, δ; and that the production function is of the Cobb–Douglas form. The last two assumptions can be written as

$$I_t = K_t - K_{t-1} + \delta K_{t-1}$$

and
$$x_t = AK_t^\alpha L_t^\beta.$$

Subject to these two constraints, the firm is assumed to maximise the present value of cash flows after taxes. Cash flows are given by

$$px - wL - qI,$$

and taxes can be expressed as

$$u\left[px - wL - qK\left(v\delta + yr - z\frac{\Delta q}{q}\right)\right],$$

where u = income-tax rate, v = tax allowance on depreciation, y = tax allowance on interest payments, and z = tax allowance for capital gains and losses. If, for example, there are no capital gains or losses, and depreciation and interest are fully deductible from taxes, the tax expression reduces to

$$u[px - wL - qK(\delta + r)].$$

Such features of the tax laws as special allowances can be incorporated into this framework (see, for example, [22]).

The present-value-maximisation problem can be solved for a time path of investment, I_t, given future values of p, w, q, u, v, y and z. The solution requires calculus of variation techniques [27], and yields the result,

$$K_t = \frac{\alpha p_t x_t}{c_t},$$

where

$$c_t = q_t \left[\frac{1-uv}{1-u} \delta + \frac{1-uy}{1-u} r - \frac{1-uz}{1-u} \frac{\Delta q}{q} \right].$$

Investment is thus given by

$$I_t = \alpha \left[\frac{p_t x_t}{c_t} - \frac{p_{t-1} x_{t-1}}{c_{t-1}} \right] + \delta K_{t-1}.$$

Jorgenson calls c_t the 'user cost of capital'; it is the net cost of holding a unit of capital stock for one period. As expected, the cost increases with q, δ and r. Further, an increase in the future price of capital goods, $\Delta q/q > 0$, reduces the cost of holding capital. An anticipated rise in q provides a 'speculative' motive for increasing capital-stock holdings.

It is instructive to examine the expression for K_t more closely. It is proportional to $(p_t/c_t)x_t$, the product of a relative price term and output. The assumptions employed by Jorgenson imply that the elasticity of investment with respect to p_t/c_t is equal to the elasticity with respect to x_t. This is crucial for policy purposes; it is inconsistent with Keynes's view that output changes exert considerably more effect than changes in interest rates (a component of c_t). Jorgenson, in his empirical work, assumes that these elasticities are equal, whereas others maintain that this assumption can, and should, be tested (see [13, 17]). A considerable portion of the debate between Jorgenson and his critics has been whether the Cobb–Douglas production function is a good description of production conditions, since the properties of this function are important for yielding the above form for capital stock. A related point has to do with the composite term, c_t. This term includes variables representing tax laws, interest rates and capital gains. It has been argued (see [17]) that one can test the assumption that these variables affect investment uniformly, rather than assume that they do by using the composite variable.

An important difference between Jorgenson's explicitly dynamic approach and the present-value model of Section B is that the former permits assets to be bought or sold as necessary for maximisation, while the latter generally assumes that an asset will be held for a fixed time period. Although the assumption of a fixed holding period appears unduly restrictive, the assumption of a perfect market for capital goods (unlimited investment or disinvestment at a constant price) is not altogether convincing either. Models which relax the assumption of a fixed rate are considered below.

In summary, the model relies on strong assumptions concerning the production function in order to obtain a simple, intuitively appealing functional form relating capital stock to its determinants. The effect of taxes, interest rates, depreciation, and prices of capital goods are contained in one variable, c_t, which enters the equation as a divisor of the value of output. Finally, Jorgenson's equation includes the effects of future changes in the price of capital goods.

D. Vintage-Capital Models

The Jorgenson model assumes that, in response to a change in factor prices, investment (or disinvestment) occurs in order to adjust the capital–labour ratio to the new factor price ratio. An alternative assumption regarding technology is that the capital–labour ratio for a unit of capital is variable before the capital is installed; once in place, however, it must be operated with a fixed amount of labour. This technology is of the 'putty–clay' variety in the sense that it is fully flexible up to installation (putty) and then fixed afterwards (clay) [25]. An implication of this assumption is that a change in factor prices alone does not stimulate investment as it does in the Jorgenson model; it is like the fixed-coefficient accelerator model of Section A in this respect. In contrast to the simple accelerator, a change in factor prices will change the ratio of factor inputs as output grows and as old capital is replaced. This occurs because capital wears out or because it becomes economically obsolete in the sense that operating costs using capital with the old factor ratios are greater than operating plus acquisition costs of new capital.

For macro models the time path of investment will depend on whether the vintage-capital model is more accurate than Jorgenson's original formulation. In particular, investment in the latter will respond to a change in factor prices holding output constant, whereas this is not true in the vintage-capital model.

E. Desired Capital Stock, Delivery Lags and Adjustment Costs

Many authors define a concept called 'desired capital stock', K^*, which represents the profit-maximising level of capital stock, given factor prices, technology, and product price. In their view, investment in a given period may not be equal to the difference between desired and actual stock; rather, investment is likely to be less than necessary to bring the firm to the point where it is employing optimal capital stock. Desired capital stock can be generated by any of the models discussed above, for example, in the Jorgenson case, $K_t^* = \alpha p_t x_t / c_t$, but

$$I_t \neq K_t^* - (1-\delta)K_{t-1}.$$

A justification for this view is that investment goods consist of items which are produced to specification and are not immediately available. A new plant, for example, may take several years to build, and special-purpose equipment may require a waiting period of several months.

Under this hypothesis the actual amount of investment goods delivered, measured by I_t, depends on previous orders for new plant and equipment. A common assumption is that a fraction of orders placed at time t is delivered in subsequent periods, as follows:

Time period	$t,$	$t+1, \ldots, t+i$
Fraction of orders placed in t delivered	$\mu_0,$	$\mu_1, \ldots, \mu_i$

The sum of the μ_i equals one, indicating that all orders are eventually delivered.

Jorgenson's assumption regarding the placing of orders is that orders are placed in each period so that the backlog of uncompleted projects is equal to the difference between desired and actual capital stock. In this case, orders placed in the tth period are equal to $K_t^* - K_{t-1}^*$; to see this, note that with no further changes in prices and technology, this ordering procedure will provide the firm with its optimal capital stock after the delivery lags have run their course. Thus, investment in any period is a distributed lag in $K_t^* - K_{t-1}^*$, that is

$$I_t = \mu_0(K_t^* - K_{t-1}^*) + \mu_1(K_{t-1}^* - K_{t-2}^*) + \cdots + \delta K_{t-1}.$$

Since $K_t^* = \alpha p_t x_t / c_t$, the main effect of this series of assumptions regarding delivery lags and ordering policies is to add lagged values of $p_t x_t / c_t$ to the equation for I_t. Moreover, the other optimum capital-stock models considered above can be modified in a similar way with analogous results: lagged values of the various explanatory variables are added to the original equation for investment.

The presence of time lags has important implications for macro models and macro policy. Such lags create difficult problems for the timing of fiscal and monetary policy designed to affect output and employment through investment; since these policies will have impacts over a period of time, it may happen that action designed to stimulate investment in a particular time period will continue to have effects long after they are desired.

Two problems with this approach might be noted. First, how much output should the firm produce in a period in which it has not yet attained its desired capital? As we saw in Section A, the usual theory of the firm tells us that inputs and the level of output are simultaneously determined by prices and technology. If one (or more) of the factors are not fully adjustable, the profit-maximising output is different from what it would be if all factors could be completely changed. Thus, the *observed* output, in this case, would not represent the output to which the firm is attempting to adjust. That is, if there is a constraint on how quickly K can be adjusted, current output will not be set at its equilibrium level, and it cannot be used to estimate K^*. (See Gould [19] for a detailed analysis of this and similar problems.)

Second, in a certainty model with a known structure of delivery lags μ_i, it is not clear why the firm does not anticipate the delays and set its ordering policy in such a way that it is always using its 'desired capital'. Since the Jorgenson and other accelerator-type models considered above permit unlimited investment or disinvestment in each period at a known price, it should be possible to make the adjustments as required. (See Nerlove [36] for related comments.)

A different assumption concerning the cost of obtaining a unit of capital may be used, in special cases, to derive a partial-adjustment model. Rather than assume the cost of a unit of capital is a constant, some authors have argued that a firm attempting to install large quantities of capital in a period will find the cost increasing more than proportionately. A simple specification which has this characteristic is the quadratic, $C(I) = q_0 I + q_1 I^2$; $q_0, q_1 > 0$. The increasing cost may be due to higher prices charged by suppliers or internal costs of absorbing large quantities of equipment in a short period of time. Gould's model [18] is a continuous formulation which has the firm maximising the present value of cash flows, V, over an infinite horizon such that

$$V = \int_0^\infty e^{-rt}[px - wL - c(I)]\, dt = \int_0^\infty H(K, L, \dot{K}, t)\, dt,$$

where $\dot{K} = \dfrac{dK}{dt}$. Gould assumes a constant depreciation rate, δ, so that we can define investment as

$$I = \dot{K} + \delta K,$$

and a production function which is homogeneous of degree one, $x = F(L, K)$. V is maximised by using the calculus of variations to find the optimal time path for L and K. The necessary conditions for a maximum are given by

$$\frac{\partial H}{\partial L} = e^{-rt}\left[p\frac{\partial F}{\partial L} - w \right] = 0,$$

and

$$\frac{\partial H}{\partial K} - \frac{d}{dt}\frac{\partial H}{\partial \dot{K}} = e^{-rt}\left[p\frac{\partial F}{\partial K} - (r+\delta)C' + (\ddot{K} + \delta\dot{K})C'' \right],$$

where

$$\ddot{K} = \frac{d}{dt}\dot{K}.$$

If it is further assumed that r, p and w are constant over time, it can be shown that the optimal policy is to invest at a constant rate, I^*. Since this rate of investment will be continued when no net investment is necessary, $I^* = \delta K^*$, where K^* is the ultimate maximising value of K. Combining this with the previous expression for I, we obtain

$$\dot{K} = \delta(K^* - K),$$

which is a type of partial-adjustment model.

Unfortunately, if the assumptions of fixed prices, wage rates and interest rates is abandoned, current investment is found to depend on the future time paths of these variables, and the simple partial-adjustment model no longer holds.

F. *Summary*

This section has emphasised the variables which should enter investment-demand equations as suggested by consideration of the theory of the individual firm under certainty. This theory indicates the importance of output price, factor prices, interest rates, and technology. As we have seen, the assumption that gaps between desired and actual capital stock are only partially filled during a particular time period imply that lagged values of the variables must be included in empirical work. Moreover, since investment generally involves the purchase of long-lived assets, decision-makers must be aware of future, as well as current, values of these variables.

III UNCERTAINTY AND INVESTMENT

There is no generally accepted theory of investment under uncertainty at this time. For empirical work, and the policy implications which follow, one possibility is to ignore uncertainty and, in effect, assume either that firms have accurately predicted future values during the sample period, or that the certainty model is a sufficiently good approximation to behaviour under uncertainty. Moreover, if one believes that there is no limit to the amount of investment or disinvestment which a firm can undertake in a particular period, the problem of uncertainty largely disappears (except for profits or losses on capital gains) since optimal capital-stock levels can be reached in any period. The problem becomes more complicated if adjustment costs or limits to changes in capital stock are present.

There are approaches which attempt to deal with uncertainty in a partial manner, emphasising one or another way in which it affects decisions. Several of these are reviewed in the following sections.

A. *Uncertainty Regarding Future Sales*

As was noted in the previous section, future demand conditions are part of the information required for investment decisions, particularly if ownership rather than rental of equipment is necessary. Estimates for future values of sales, for example, are probably developed by firms for their own decision-making, but such data are not generally available for research purposes. It has been argued that the observed values of sales are not satisfactory substitutes for expected sales since actual sales may be greatly affected by random variations during a particular time period. Borrowing a concept used in consumer theory, Eisner has suggested that firms attempt to separate 'permanent' from 'transitory' components of sales, and adjust their capital stock to permanent changes in the level of sales. In his empirical work [11] permanent sales are assumed equal to a distributed lag in past changes in sales.

A simple formal model, due to Koyck [30], will clarify the approach. Assume an accelerator model with $K_t = \alpha S_t^f$ where S_t^f is permanent (or forecasted) sales, ignoring depreciation and delivery lags for the sake of simplicity. It is further assumed that S_t^f is estimated by a weighted average of past sales with geometrically declining weights, that is we have

$$S_t^f = (1 - \lambda)[S_t + \lambda S_{t-1} + \lambda^2 S_{t-2} + \cdots],$$

where $0 < \lambda < 1$. A value of λ close to 0 indicates that relatively high weights are given to current and recent periods compared to those in the more distant past. Larger values of λ are associated with a more evenly distributed pattern of weights. Applying the same expression to S_{t-1}^f and substituting into the expression for K_{t-1}, we obtain

$$K_t - K_{t-1} = I_t = \alpha(1 - \lambda)[(S_t - S_{t-1}) + \lambda(S_{t-1} - S_{t-2}) + \cdots],$$

which is a distributed lag in changes of sales. Although the expression implies an infinite number of variables on the right-hand side, a transformation is possible which reduces the problem to manageable proportions. Lagging the expression for I_t by one period and multiplying by λ, we have

$$\lambda I_{t-1} = \lambda \alpha(1 - \lambda)[(S_{t-1} - S_{t-2}) + \lambda(S_{t-2} - S_{t-3}) + \cdots].$$

If this is subtracted from the expression for I_t and rearranged, the result is

$$I_t = \alpha(1 - \lambda)[S_{t-1} - S_{t-2}] + \lambda I_{t-1}.$$

Estimation of this expression is discussed in Chapter 1.

It should be noted that Eisner, the major proponent of the generalised or 'flexible' accelerator model, does not employ the geometric lag distribution. Instead, he includes a number of lagged sales changes and determines their coefficients directly by ordinary least squares (see Chapter 1). In addition, he includes depreciation and other variables in his equations.

B. *Financial Factors*

Duesenberry's approach [10] to investment decision-making under uncertainty emphasises financial considerations. In his model, the marginal efficiency of investment (m.e.i.) schedule (which relates investment expenditures to marginal rates of return on those expenditures) is combined with a marginal cost of funds schedule. The latter is not perfectly elastic at an opportunity interest rate as in the model presented earlier (see pp. 93–4), but rises with the amount of investment. The explanation for the rising cost is to be found in the firm's reluctance to incur debt in the presence of uncertainty. Debt creates a charge to the firm every period which must be met to avoid bankruptcy. In the event that sales revenues fall short of expectations, and if reserves of liquid assets are inadequate, then the firm may have to take extraordinary steps to cut expenditures. Such actions as releasing valuable employees or selling assets hurriedly may affect the firm adversely well into the future. On the other hand, if investment can be financed from internal funds (retained earnings and depreciation funds), additions to fixed commitments can be avoided. A third source of funds for investment is new equity, but because of tax laws this source is more costly than internal funds and usually is more costly than debt.

From these considerations, Duesenberry suggests that the marginal cost of funds schedule is as depicted in Figure 4.2. The initial elastic portion (at an interest rate which measures alternative opportunities) continues until internal funds are exhausted. The schedule rises as new debt is issued, reflecting management's concern over taking on new fixed commitments. Finally, the rate levels off as new equity sources are used. Investment and its associated financing is determined by the interaction of the m.e.i. and marginal cost of funds schedules.

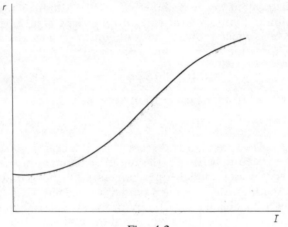

Fig. 4.2

This model adds a large set of variables for consideration as determinants of investment. These include the flow of retained earnings, variables representing the firm's level of fixed commitments, and variables measuring ability to meet such commitments.

It should be noted that, in Duesenberry's approach, the firm simultaneously determines the investment it will undertake and whether to finance the investment by internal funds, new debt, or new equity, or by some combination of these. Moreover, the marginal cost of funds schedule is a non-linear function of investment.

C.   Utility-Maximisation Models

In many areas of economics it has been found useful to apply the expected utility-maximisation model in the presence of uncertainty [2].

Briefly, from a set of axioms describing rational behaviour under uncertainty, the theory develops a utility function which can be used to rank probability distributions of wealth, W, that is W is a random variable. The probability that it takes on values in a given interval is given by its probability distribution. It may be defined for a particular time period, or, more generally, W may represent the joint distribution of future values of wealth in many time periods. Discussion here is limited to the single-period case. The function is denoted by $U(W)$, with $U'(W) > 0$ and $U''(W) < 0$ (the addition to utility of an additional pound of wealth increases at a decreasing rate). A decision-maker with this type of utility function is called a 'risk averter'. In typical applications of this theory it is assumed that the decision-maker can control some of the variables which affect the probability distribution of W, and values for those variables should be chosen so as to maximise the expected value of $U(W)$.

With respect to the investment decision, a typical model [40] assumes that the firm is subject to a random price, but can vary its output in reaction to that price; capital stock must be chosen before price is known so that output adjustment is achieved by varying labour input; and the utility function is characterised as above, with the additional property of 'decreasing absolute risk aversion', that is $-U''(W)/U'(W)$ is a decreasing function of wealth, W. This property can be interpreted to mean that the individual's willingness to take risks increases with his wealth. As discussed in [3, 4, 40, 41], it can be shown that output will be less than the output which would be produced if the random price were equal to its expected value with certainty; the greater the fixed costs (or the smaller the initial wealth) the less will be the output, and hence the amount of inputs; that with known factor costs the smaller production will be produced with the cost-minimising factor proportions; and if the resale price of capital is uncertain, the firm is likely to use relatively more labour. One implication of these results is that use of expected values of uncertain variables in certainty models (a 'certainty-equivalence' approach) is inappropriate for some utility functions. Although these results follow from rather special and restrictive cases, they support the idea that initial wealth positions, uncertainty about factor costs and attitudes toward risk are determinants of investment. We return to the latter two in a discussion of Minsky's model below.

D. *Mean-Variance Models*

A special case of the expected utility model which has been widely utilised in the theory of finance (see [16]) has interesting implications for investment decisions. The capital-asset pricing model assumes that investors are concerned with just two parameters of the probability distribution of their wealth – expected value and variance. An individual security contributes to that wealth through its expected value, variance, and covariance with other securities. In this model, the market for securities will determine a set of prices that clears the market; in other words, each

security will be priced so that investors are willing to hold the quantity of
that security which is in the market, given the expected value of that
security's return and its covariance with all securities in the market.

A decision to invest in fixed capital can be considered a choice of the
mean-covariance properties of the firm's securities, and we assume that
managers will undertake investment to the point that the firm's market
valuation is maximised. The contribution of this approach is that it
provides, albeit under strong assumptions concerning investors' preferences and businessmen's motivations, an explicit framework in which to
consider attitudes toward risk (aversion to positive covariance).

Specifically, with this approach, the market valuation of the jth firm, V_j,
is given by

$$V_j = (1/r)[E(\tilde{D}_j) - \lambda \sigma_{jm}],$$

where $\tilde{D}_j$ is the (random) cash flow generated by firm j's assets, $\tilde{D}_m$ is the
(random) cash flow generated by all firms, $E(\ )$ is the expected value
operator, σ_{jm} is the covariance between $\tilde{D}_j$ and $\tilde{D}_m$, $r = 1 + i$, where i is
the one-period riskless rate of interest, σ_m^2 is the variance of $\tilde{D}_m$, V_m is the
market value of all firms, and $\lambda = (E(\tilde{D}_m) - rV_m)/\sigma_m^2$. λ may be interpreted
as the 'market price of risk'; it represents investors' trade-offs between
expected return and variance of that return. Low values of λ imply a
willingness to bear risk, while high values imply a lesser desire for risky
assets.

To relate this model to the investment decision, consider a firm which
has the opportunity to invest in a project which offers a random rate of
return, $\tilde{\rho}$. This is assumed to have expectation $\bar{\rho}$, variance σ_ρ^2, covariance
with the remainder of the firm's activities of $\sigma_{\rho j}$ and covariance with the
market of $\sigma_{\rho m}$. We further assume constant stochastic returns to scale,
that is the returns from an investment of I are $\tilde{\rho}I$.

An investment should be undertaken if the market value of the firm is
increased. For comparison with an earlier model (see pp. 93–4) assume
first that a project is available which costs I_0. If the investment is made,
under the assumed conditions, the new market valuation is given by

$$V_j(I_0) = (1/r)\{E(\tilde{D}_j) + \bar{\rho}I_0 - \lambda[\sigma_{jm} + I_0(\sigma_{\rho m} + \sigma_{\rho j} + I_0\sigma_\rho^2)]\} - I_0.$$

The project should be undertaken if

$$V_j(I_0) > V_j(0),$$

or

$$(1/r)\{\bar{\rho}I_0 - \lambda I_0(\sigma_{\rho m} + \sigma_{\rho j} + I_0\sigma_\rho^2)\} > I_0,$$

which implies

$$\frac{\bar{\rho}I_0}{1 + i + \lambda(\sigma_{\rho m} + \sigma_{\rho j} + I_0\sigma_\rho^2)} > I_0.$$

The last expression is comparable to the present-value formulation presented above. Here $\bar{\rho}I_0$ is the (expected value of) returns available next
period, but the discounting factor now includes an explicit 'risk premium',

$\lambda(\sigma_{\rho m} + \sigma_{\rho j} + I_0 \sigma_\rho^2)$. As before, if the present value is greater than the cost of investment, the investment should be undertaken.

If we assume that investment can be varied continuously, we can solve for the value-maximising I. It is given by

$$I = (1/2\lambda\sigma_\rho^2)[(\bar{\rho} - r) - \lambda(\sigma_{\rho m} + \sigma_{\rho j})].$$

(For details see [24].) It can easily be seen from this expression that the amount of investment varies directly with $E(\bar{\rho})$ and inversely with r and λ. Thus attitudes toward risk may be expected to influence the quantity of investment undertaken by firms.

From another point of view, note that the attitude-toward-risk variable, λ, includes V_m, the security market's valuation of all firms, and it is easily seen that investment is an increasing function of V_m. This suggests that market values of corporate securities be included in investment equations.

E. *Summary*

Consideration of uncertainty adds further variables to the list begun in Section II. It is recognised that firms should act on the basis of anticipations of future sales or output, but that such data are not often available. If one is willing to assume that anticipations are based upon recent experience, lagged values of variables should be included. Moreover, since a decision to invest is a decision to reduce liquidity, the firm's ability to meet its fixed commitments and the degree of uncertainty may be expected to influence the extent to which a firm is willing to lose flexibility in order to increase expectations of profits. Finally, attitudes toward risk of investors or managers may play a role.

IV MACRO ASPECTS OF INVESTMENT MODELS

To this point, we have considered investment theory at the level of the individual firm, under certainty and uncertainty. This exercise has suggested a large number of variables which are likely to influence the level of investment spending during a particular time period. We now turn our attention to some problems which arise when macro investment is under consideration.

A. *Level of Aggregation*

The general problem of estimating equations at the macro level which are based on micro theory is discussed in Chapter 1. Briefly, in the context of investment decisions, the question is whether we can think of the economy as one firm, or whether the distribution of independent variables among firms or industries affects the level of investment. For example, suppose there is an increase in sales of £1 million. If this increase has the same effect on total investment whether the sales growth occurs in the aircraft industry, or the textile industry, or some other, then

TABLE 4.1
'*Preferred*' *manufacturing equations**

Food
$$I = 2 \cdot 35 \quad -0 \cdot 0408 K_{56} + 0 \cdot 0165 S_{56} + 0 \cdot 3322 L_{56} - 0 \cdot 176 i_{56}$$
$$\quad\quad\quad (0 \cdot 0117) \quad (0 \cdot 0078) \quad (0 \cdot 0892) \quad (0 \cdot 061)$$
$$\quad\quad\quad [1 \cdot 28] \quad\quad [0 \cdot 94] \quad\quad [0 \cdot 48] \quad\quad [0 \cdot 33]$$
0·396

Textiles
$$I = 0 \cdot 92 \quad +0 \cdot 0220 Cp_1 - 0 \cdot 0810 K_{56} + 0 \cdot 0288 S_{56} - 0 \cdot 204 i_{56}$$
$$\quad\quad\quad (0 \cdot 0035) \quad (0 \cdot 0080) \quad (0 \cdot 0077) \quad (0 \cdot 029)$$
$$\quad\quad\quad [1 \cdot 90] \quad\quad [1 \cdot 88] \quad\quad [0 \cdot 82] \quad\quad [0 \cdot 71]$$
0·717

Paper products
$$I = -2 \cdot 39 + 0 \cdot 0317 Cp_1 + 0 \cdot 0449 S_{56} + 0 \cdot 2492 L_{56} - 0 \cdot 188 i_{56}$$
$$\quad\quad\quad (0 \cdot 0046) \quad (0 \cdot 0122) \quad (0 \cdot 1192) \quad (0 \cdot 054)$$
$$\quad\quad\quad [2 \cdot 31] \quad\quad [0 \cdot 80] \quad\quad [0 \cdot 30] \quad\quad [0 \cdot 54]$$
0·775

Chemicals
$$I = -7 \cdot 13 + 0 \cdot 0928 Cp_1 - 0 \cdot 0610 K_{56} + 0 \cdot 1070 S_{56}$$
$$\quad\quad\quad (0 \cdot 0093) \quad (0 \cdot 0112) \quad (0 \cdot 0174)$$
$$\quad\quad\quad [2 \cdot 93] \quad\quad [1 \cdot 29] \quad\quad [1 \cdot 73]$$
0·689

Petroleum
$$I = -9 \cdot 72 + 0 \cdot 1512 Cp_1 - 0 \cdot 0250 K_{56} + 0 \cdot 1275 S_{56} + 0 \cdot 3098 L_{56} - 1 \cdot 261 i_{56}$$
$$\quad\quad\quad (0 \cdot 0271) \quad (0 \cdot 0117) \quad (0 \cdot 0416) \quad (0 \cdot 1456) \quad (0 \cdot 288)$$
$$\quad\quad\quad [2 \cdot 44] \quad\quad [0 \cdot 61] \quad\quad [1 \cdot 20] \quad\quad [0 \cdot 37] \quad\quad [0 \cdot 78]$$
0·657

Rubber
$$I = -0 \cdot 46 + 0 \cdot 0067 Cp_1 - 0 \cdot 0144 K_{56} + 0 \cdot 0192 S_{56} + 0 \cdot 1351 L_{56}$$
$$\quad\quad\quad (0 \cdot 0009) \quad (0 \cdot 0055) \quad (0 \cdot 0053) \quad (0 \cdot 0666)$$
$$\quad\quad\quad [1 \cdot 54] \quad\quad [0 \cdot 39] \quad\quad [0 \cdot 78] \quad\quad [0 \cdot 36]$$
0·731

Stone, clay and glass
$$I = -1 \cdot 96 + 0 \cdot 0271 Cp_1 + 0 \cdot 0609 S_{56} - 0 \cdot 134 i_{56}$$
$$\quad\quad\quad (0 \cdot 0032) \quad (0 \cdot 0094) \quad (0 \cdot 044)$$
$$\quad\quad\quad [2 \cdot 41] \quad\quad [0 \cdot 95] \quad\quad [0 \cdot 48]$$
0·781

Iron and steel
$$I = -0 \cdot 84 + 0 \cdot 0738 S_{12} + 0 \cdot 0553 S_{56} - 0 \cdot 0270 K_{56}$$
$$\quad\quad\quad (0 \cdot 0143) \quad (0 \cdot 0136) \quad (0 \cdot 0070)$$
$$\quad\quad\quad [1 \cdot 12] \quad\quad [0 \cdot 84] \quad\quad [0 \cdot 66]$$
0·403

Primary non-ferrous metals
$$I = -1 \cdot 45 + 0 \cdot 0129 Cp_1 - 0 \cdot 0364 K_{56} + 0 \cdot 1243 S_{56}$$
$$\quad\quad\quad (0 \cdot 0040) \quad (0 \cdot 0051) \quad (0 \cdot 0132)$$
$$\quad\quad\quad [1 \cdot 37] \quad\quad [1 \cdot 41] \quad\quad [2 \cdot 82]$$
0·604

Non-electrical machinery
$$I = -2 \cdot 45 + 0 \cdot 0310 Cp_1 + 0 \cdot 0331 S_{56}$$
$$\quad\quad\quad (0 \cdot 0036) \quad (0 \cdot 0035)$$
$$\quad\quad\quad [1 \cdot 37] \quad\quad [0 \cdot 85]$$
0·764

Electrical machinery
$$I = -1 \cdot 32 + 0 \cdot 0208 Cp_1 - 0 \cdot 0304 K_{56} + 0 \cdot 0220 S_{56} + 0 \cdot 1900 L_{56}$$
$$\quad\quad\quad (0 \cdot 0019) \quad (0 \cdot 0072) \quad (0 \cdot 0047) \quad (0 \cdot 0546)$$
$$\quad\quad\quad [1 \cdot 66] \quad\quad [0 \cdot 71] \quad\quad [0 \cdot 90] \quad\quad [0 \cdot 31]$$
0·873

Autos
$$I = 0 \cdot 56 \quad +0 \cdot 0159 Cp_1 + 0 \cdot 0723 S_{56} - 1 \cdot 005 i_{56}$$
$$\quad\quad\quad (0 \cdot 0052) \quad (0 \cdot 0074) \quad (0 \cdot 106)$$
$$\quad\quad\quad [0 \cdot 61] \quad\quad [1 \cdot 90] \quad\quad [1 \cdot 77]$$
0·663

Other transportation
$$I = -0 \cdot 22 + 0 \cdot 0035 Cp_1 + 0 \cdot 0297 K_{56} + 0 \cdot 4592 L_{56}$$
$$\quad\quad\quad (0 \cdot 0019) \quad (0 \cdot 0087) \quad (0 \cdot 1133)$$
$$\quad\quad\quad [0 \cdot 38] \quad\quad [0 \cdot 47] \quad\quad [0 \cdot 46]$$
0·680

* Figures in brackets are elasticities.
Source: Evans [14].

it is legitimate to aggregate. If different firms (or industries) react differently to changes in sales, we can expect to achieve less accuracy with the macro model.

As a compromise, some empirically estimated macro models allow different investment functions for each industry; this approach permits a certain amount of differential response without attempting to estimate investment functions for every decision-maker. Presumably, firms in the same industry are relatively homogeneous with respect to such characteristics as technology and uncertainty. Empirical studies conducted at the industry level have revealed quite different coefficients for various industries.

For example, Table 4.1 contains results obtained by Evans [14] using quarterly U.S. data for 1949–63 at the industry level. In the table, Cp_1 is the ratio of sales to full-capacity sales, K is capital stock, S is sales, L is a measure of cash flow, i is the interest rate, and the subscript '56' indicates a distributed lag in the first differences of the respective variables which begins five and six periods in the past. These are the 'preferred' equations for each industry – insignificant variables and those with the 'wrong' sign have been eliminated. Note the large differences in coefficients and the presence or absence of particular variables in the various equations. Evans was not completely successful in accounting for these differences on the basis of industry characteristics, such as differential variances in Cp_1 or in industry-concentration ratios (share of sales of the four largest firms).

B. *Supply of Capital Goods*

Although it may be reasonable to assume that an individual firm is able to obtain its capital equipment at the going market price, this assumption becomes less reasonable when the investment activity of the whole economy is being considered. In that case it becomes necessary to examine the supply side of the investment-goods market – the firms which produce capital goods. An interesting formulation which is concerned with this aspect of the problem is due to Witte [44]. He derives a downward-sloping demand for capital stock as a function of its price, with the position of the schedule depending on the interest rate, the price of labour and other variables. Together with the current capital stock, this demand curve establishes a price for capital goods which applies to the new, as well as to the existing capital stock. Witte postulates the existence of a second function which relates the production of new capital goods (investment) to the price determined above. This function has a positive slope, that is an increase in the price leads to increased production of capital goods because of short-run increasing costs for firms which produce capital goods. As noted above, new and old capital goods will sell for the same price. Witte's analysis is represented in Figure 4.3.

A somewhat different interpretation can be given to the model as well. The first stage can be taken to represent the valuation of firms through

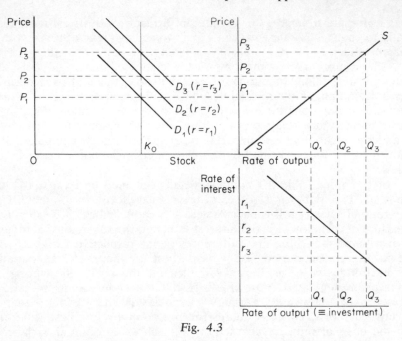

Fig. 4.3

the stock market which, in turn, places a value on the assets of firms. This interpretation suggests that stock-market valuations be included in investment equations.

Thus, an important distinction between micro and macro approaches to investment is that, with the latter, we must take into account the fact that the economy determines both the price and the quantity of capital goods. The micro theory of investment stresses the demand for capital goods as a function of its price and other variables; the macro theory reminds us that the price is itself determined by the economy, and serves to ration the existing stock as well as to induce production.

C. Uncertainty in Macro Models

Minsky has added financial factors and uncertainty to the type of model considered in the previous section (see [33, 34, 35]). In his model it is assumed that the price of capital stock is affected by the money supply – through portfolio considerations. Minsky's model emphasises firms' liquidity positions and their access to capital markets, particularly the tendency in a capitalist economy for moderate growth to turn into rapid growth due to changes in expectations about the future and in attitudes toward risk aversion which result from a period of steady growth. The financial system becomes increasingly fragile as the rate of economic activity increases, and becomes more and more vulnerable to a disturbance. Minsky stresses the value of capital assets in a resale market if it becomes necessary, because of financial commitments, to sell such assets. The price of these assets is determined both by their value in production and their value in raising funds through sale or use as collateral for loans; the weights shift according to the stage of the business cycle. This model is highly non-linear, and its empirical implementation poses challenging conceptual and econometric problems.

V EMPIRICAL STUDIES

A. *Difficulties*

Many of the same problems which arise in connection with empirical research in other areas of economics arise in research on investment as well. Two of these have been noted above. One was the problem caused by aggregating over firms or industries with possibly different coefficients. A second was the problem of simultaneity exemplified by Duesenberry's approach (which determines financing and investment simultaneously) and by Witte's model (which determines investment and the price of capital goods simultaneously). In addition, the lack of any anticipations data and estimation of distributed lags should be mentioned.

As we have seen, perhaps more than for any other economic decision, the decision to invest is a forward-looking one; it requires that the firm add to its portfolio assets which have uncertain resale values, apt to be low precisely at those times when the firm wishes to convert them into cash. In these circumstances we expect firms to invest only if they have good reason to believe that future cash flows will be available to meet commitments without the forced sale of assets. However, relatively small amounts of sales-anticipations data are collected, rarely for more than a few periods into the future. Thus, an important variable for such studies is simply not available to the econometrician, although the firms themselves may make such forecasts. As a proxy, researchers have often used past sales data on the assumption that expectations for the future depend on the past. Quite apart from the adequacy of the assumption that the firm does not have other sources of information about the future, there arise serious problems of estimation.

As noted in Chapter 1, the estimation of distributed lags is difficult. Indeed, many of the most widely used techniques for distributed-lag estimation were developed in connection with the estimation of investment models. For example, the techniques of Almon [1], Jorgenson [26] and Koyck [30] were all developed for investment studies.

B. *Comparison of Models*

Many authors have surveyed and compared the wide variety of investment models discussed above (particular reference should be made to Bridge [6] ch. 6, Evans [15] chs 4, 5, Lund [31], Jorgenson [28] and, in connection with the Jorgenson survey, Klein [29] and Eisner [12]). For

our purposes, an article by Bischoff [5] is the most useful since he
evaluates five different models using the same body of data. Bischoff uses
U.S. quarterly data for the period 1953–68 to estimate equations for
aggregate equipment expenditures and for aggregate construction expenditures. Distributed lags are estimated by Almon's technique and auto-
correlation is treated by jointly estimating the auto-correlation coefficient
and the other parameters (see Chapter 1 for explanation of these con-
cepts).

TABLE 4.2
Summary statistics for five investment models

Model	$\bar{R}^{2a}$	Standard error of estimate $\overline{SEE}^{a,b}$	Coefficient of autocor- relation ρ	Durbin– Watson statistic DW	Number of terms in Almon lag n
		Equipment expenditures			
Generalised accelerator	0·9901	957	0·706	1·86	23
Cash flow	0·9924	841	0·585	1·71	23
Securities value	0·9874	1016	1·000	1·98	13
Standard neoclassical	0·9893	995	0·801	1·74	13
Standard neoclassical (alternate)	0·9869	1099	0·864	1·70	15
Federal Reserve–M.I.T.– Penn	0·9931	800	0·251	2·06	21
		Construction expenditures			
Generalised accelerator	0·9611	553	0·849	2·15	23
Cash flow	0·9664	515	0·646	2·09	23
Securities value	0·9630	540	0·930	2·37	13
Standard neoclassical	0·9613	551	0·774	2·02	23
Standard neoclassical (alternate)	0·9579	576	0·885	2·07	15
Federal Reserve–M.I.T.– Penn	0·9733	459	0·663	2·41	17
Federal Reserve–M.I.T.– Penn (alternate)	0·9633	537	0·814	2·21	19

[a] The 'corrected' $\bar{R}^2$ and standard error of estimate are computed using more than the
normal correction factor to allow for biases due to (a) the 'data mining' involved in choosing
the best length of lag, n, and because ρ is estimated; (b) seasonal adjustment of the data;
and (c) the fact that several parameters used in deriving the F.M.P. model – parameters
affecting the rental variable and the price elasticity of demand – are approximated on the
basis of experience gained in previous non-linear estimation. For these reasons, five extra
degrees of freedom were subtracted for the generalised accelerator, cash-flow, standard
neoclassical, and securities value models; nine subtracted for the F.M.P. equipment equation; and eight for the F.M.P. construction equation. These bias adjustments are at best
crude approximations. SEE refers to the square root of the estimated variance of e (not u)
in the note to Table 1. $\bar{R}^2$ refers to $1 - \dfrac{\text{Variance estimated for } e}{\text{Variance estimated for } Y}$.
[b] Millions of 1958 dollars.
Source: Bischoff [5].

The models studied by Bischoff are:

(1)   a generalised accelerator model, in which investment depends on a distributed lag in output and on a beginning of period capital stock;

(2)   a cash-flow model, with investment depending upon a distributed lag in corporate internal funds divided by a price index for investment goods and capital stock at the beginning of the period;

(3)   a securities-value model, in which investment is a function of a distributed lag in the market value of corporate stocks and bonds in relation to the stock of capital,

(4)   the standard neoclassical model, described earlier (p. 95–7) – two variants are considered, one ignoring capital gains, the 'alternate' including them; and

(5)   the Federal Reserve–M.I.T.–Penn (F.M.P.) model, which is the one described above (p. 97) – the 'alternate' version of this model includes capital gains.

Bischoff's results are summarised in Table 4.2. Note that the $\bar{R}^2$ are uniformly high thus providing little basis for choosing between the equations. Estimated values of the auto-correlation coefficients are generally close to one; this means that lagged values of all the variables, including investment, are contained in the equations. Under these conditions, little confidence can be placed in predictions because the unknown future values of the dependent variable must be used to predict future values of the same variable. Errors in prediction occurring in one period thus will be fed back into the model for future predictions.

Although the $\bar{R}^2$ are similar, the models yield quite different estimates of the future. Table 4.3 indicates the response over time to changes in the independent variables indicated in the footnote to the table. Note the different patterns of response. Finally, Table 4.4 indicates the results of extrapolating outside the sample period. Bischoff remarks that the cash-flow equations perform poorly, but since U.S. financial conditions were rather unsettled in the extrapolation period, 1969–71, it may be that the equations did not do justice to the ideas behind the cash-flow model.

C.   *Other Variables*

In this section we consider a number of studies, mainly using relatively low levels of aggregation, which emphasise variables in addition to those considered already (pp. 109–11). These are discussed under two headings, financial factors and supply considerations.

Financial factors

Resek [39] attempted to allow for the non-linear marginal cost of funds schedule (see pp. 101–2), by examining the variable

$$\frac{1}{M-(D-F)/A},$$

TABLE 4.3

Estimated short- and long-run responses of capital expenditures to a given change in explanatory variables (millions of 1958 dollars, quarterly flows at annual rates)

Model	Quarters after change											
	0	1	2	3	4	5	6	7	8	9	10	100
Equipment expenditures												
Generalised accelerator[a]	0	63	110	144	166	180	186	188	187	183	179	91
Cash flow[b]	0	28	48	63	73	80	85	88	90	92	93	68
Securities value[a]	0	20	44	69	95	118	139	157	171	183	194	[d]
Standard neoclassical[a]	0	38	60	71	76	79	81	85	92	100	110	69
Federal Reserve–M.I.T.–Penn[a]	0	165	181	192	199	201	200	195	189	180	171	97
Construction expenditures												
Generalised accelerator[a]	0	26	45	59	68	73	75	74	71	66	60	23
Cash flow[b]	0	7	13	18	22	26	29	31	33	34	34	20
Securities value[a]	0	1	8	17	27	37	46	53	57	59	58	[d]
Standard neoclassical[a]	0	13	25	36	46	55	62	68	72	75	77	24
Federal Reserve–M.I.T.–Penn[a]	0	11	23	36	49	60	69	76	81	83	83	19

[a] Estimated response is based on $1 billion permanent change in business gross product. For all relative prices, estimated values for 1971:1 are used. In percentage terms, and at the 1971:1 value of variables, the changes given in notes b and c are equivalent to this change.

[b] Estimated response is based on $155 million permanent change in corporate cash flow.

[c] Estimated response is based on $1·26 billion permanent change in market valuation of U.S. corporations.

[d] Not computed, for reasons explained in text.

Source: Bischoff [5].

TABLE 4.4

Actual investment and simulation of six alternative investment models, 1969–70[a] (billions of 1958 dollars, at seasonally adjusted annual rates)

Year and quarter	Actual	Generalised accelerator	Cash flow	S.N.C.	S.N.C. (alternate)	F.M.P.	F.M.P. (alternate)
Equipment expenditures							
1969:1	55·4	54·4	52·3	54·3	56·1	55·5	b
2	57·0	54·8	52·6	54·7	57·5	56·6	b
3	57·3	55·2	52·8c	55·0	58·7	56·9	b
4	57·8a	55·4c	52·3	55·1c	60·1	57·4c	b
1970:1	56·5	55·3	51·7	54·9	61·1	56·5	b
2	56·7	54·5	50·5	54·0	62·3	54·8	b
3	56·9	53·8	49·5	53·6	63·4c	53·9	b
4	54·5	52·9d	46·6d	53·9d	62·6d	52·9d	b
Mean error[e,f]	—	2·0	5·1	2·3	-3·1	0·8	b
Root-mean-square error[e,g]	—	2·1	5·3	2·4	3·8	1·4	b
Construction expenditures							
1969:1	23·8	23·5	22·2	24·0	23·1	24·0c	23·2
2	23·1	23·7	21·9	24·1c	23·8	23·9	24·0
3	24·6c	23·8	21·6	24·0	24·4	23·7	24·9
4	24·3	23·9a	21·2	23·8	25·2	23·3	25·9
1970:1	24·4	23·8	20·8	23·5	25·8c	22·7	26·9c
2	23·5	23·5	20·3	23·1	24·7	21·8	25·6
3	22·6	23·2	19·8	22·6	24·0	20·5	24·2
4	21·8	23·1	19·4	21·9	23·6	19·4	23·4
Mean error[d]	—	0·0	2·6	0·1	-0·8	1·1	-1·2
Root-mean-square error[g]	—	0·7	2·7	0·5	1·1	1·5	1·6

a No corrections have been made for errors.
b No alternate is given for the F.M.P. equipment equations because the original equation includes price expectations.
c Peak. For the cash-flow construction-equation, the peak comes before 1969:1.
d No correction was made for the effect of the automobile strike.
e Mean and root-mean-square errors are calculated using only seven observations.
f Average of actual minus predicted values.
g Square root of average squared errors.
Source: Bischoff [5].

TABLE 4.5

Elasticities and t ratios of regression coefficients for the following investment function for U.S. industries*

$$\frac{I}{K} = a_1 + a_2 Q_2 + a_3 Q_3 + a_4 Q_4 + b_1 \frac{O}{K} + b_2 \frac{(\Delta O)}{K} + b_3 r + b_4 \left(\frac{1}{M - (D - F)/A} \right)$$

		b_1	b_2	b_3	b_4
Food	Elasticity	−0·34	3·24	0·13	0·18
	t	0·25	1·95	0·32	0·11
Textiles	Elasticity	4·30	−0·98	−1·86	−1·06
	t	5·55	1·89	3·41	2·93
Paper	Elasticity	−0·83	5·92	−0·64	−0·42
	t	0·89	7·83	3·35	2·22
Chemicals	Elasticity	1·50	1·68	−1·37	−2·82
	t	4·02	2·56	4·70	9·06
Petroleum	Elasticity	1·81	0·14	−1·31	−0·60
	t	3·64	0·22	−9·31	−1·91
Rubber	Elasticity	1·72	1·52	−1·30	−1·20
	t	1·74	2·05	2·58	2·57
Stone, clay and glass	Elasticity	−1·33	3·69	−1·97	0·71
	t	2·47	7·43	7·03	3·59
Iron and steel	Elasticity	0·56	0·94	0·06	−0·15
	t	0·52	1·39	0·12	0·54
Non-ferrous metals	Elasticity	8·14	−2·02	−1·07	13·73
	t	3·02	0·82	3·75	3·14
Non-electrical machinery	Elasticity	2·05	1·64	−0·50	−1·00
	t	4·27	6·46	2·46	3·05
Electrical machinery	Elasticity	−0·94	2·32	0·10	−0·38
	t	1·15	5·16	0·61	1·87
Motor vehicles	Elasticity	2·30	1·13	−3·02	0·41
	t	6·01	5·10	10·71	2·62
Other transportation	Elasticity	−1·05	−1·04	−1·99	0·04
	t	2·34	3·76	4·37	0·43
All manufacturing	Elasticity	0·81	1·73	−0·96	0·46
	t	1·10	3·14	−5·60	1·79

* The Q_i are seasonal dummy variables.
Source: Resek [39].

where D is beginning of period debt, F is retained earnings, A is assets and M is a constant larger than D/A. This variable is included in equations which also contain output, O, interest rates, r and stock-market prices, SP. (See Table 4.5 for an example of his results.) Note that for several industries the debt variable noted above has the correct sign and is significant. However, the table reveals considerable differences among industries, confirming the findings of Evans discussed above.

In one of the few investment studies to use simultaneous-equation estimation techniques (see Chapter 1) Dhrymes and Kurz [9] investigate three interrelated decisions: investment, dividends, and borrowing. With data for individual firms over a number of years, they find changes in the coefficients of particular variables from year to year, and attempt to associate these with changing business conditions. Similar instability of coefficients is noted by Meyer and Glauber [32], whose equations indicate different patterns in upswings and downswings. These results support Minsky's view that more complex non-linear models and cumulative processes of growth and contraction must be developed.

Another group of studies [7, 20, 23] argues that the main role of financial variables is as determinants of the rate at which a gap between desired and actual capital stock is closed. In other words, rather than assume a generalised accelerator model with constant coefficients, these authors assume that the coefficients are themselves determined by financial positions. Coen [7] concludes that variable-adjustment-speed models perform better than the analogous constant-adjustment-speed model.

Feldstein and Flemming [17] attempt to generalise the Jorgenson model in several directions. In particular, they disaggregate the variable representing the cost of capital to permit its various components to have different effects. As noted above, the aggregate variable forces uniform effects for each component of the variable. It is noteworthy that tax allowances are found to have a greater impact on investment than other components of Jorgenson's cost-of-capital variable. These results might be explained by considerations of uncertainty. Many tax policies designed to stimulate investment have the effect of increasing returns in the near future, for example credits or accelerated depreciation, and near-term expectations are likely to be held with relatively greater certainty than those far into the future. Eisner [13] interprets the effects of taxes as inter-temporal shifts in investment, rather than changes in levels, and argues that output is the main determinant of investment. His empirical work suggests little over-all effect from tax-law changes.

Supply considerations

Popkin [37] and Tinsley [43] have presented models in which investment depends on supply conditions in the capital-goods-producing industries. Their models are used to determine investment as a distributed lag in firms' appropriations for capital expenditures, the decision to place an order for new plant or equipment. To complete the explanation of investment it would be necessary to relate appropriations to more basic variables. The novel aspect of their studies is that the distributed-lag parameters are assumed to depend on the ratio of backlogs (unfilled orders in the capital-goods-producing industries) to deliveries. If the capital-goods producers are working to capacity this ratio will be high, and the delivery lag will be relatively long.

D.   The Investment Function in the F.M.P. Model [8]

The F.M.P. investment equation, part of a large-scale econometric model, is based on the 'putty–clay' variant of the Jorgenson model discussed earlier (p. 97). The basic model is applied to the estimation of orders for new plant and equipment; that is, the orders depend on a distributed lag in the relative price, p/c, and output variables. The formulation permits a differential response of investment to changes in p/c and output respectively, by estimating two separate lag distributions. The relation between expenditures and orders incorporates Tinsley's research concerning the importance of supply considerations by having the lag between orders and expenditures depend on the ratio of orders to shipments of the capital-goods suppliers. A high ratio implies longer delivery lags.

To complete the system of equations determining investment, the model determines the 'user cost of capital' variable, c, by generating a value for the cost of funds. The equation for the latter is discussed by Bischoff [5]; it is assumed to depend on the market long-term interest rate adjusted for anticipated growth in earnings (which affect equity values) and for risk. The ratio of dividends to stock prices is included to capture these two effects. In view of the complex way in which financial factors affect investment, Bischoff characterises this approach as a 'very rough approximation' ([5] p. 83).

Thus, the investment equation of one of the largest full-scale

TABLE 4.6
Estimated short- and long-run elasticities of capital expenditure in the F.M.P. model*

Quarters after change	Equipment		Construction	
	output	p/c	output	p/c
0	0·000	0·000	0·000	0·000
1	1·535	0·000	0·559	0·280
2	1·691	0·152	1·219	0·610
3	1·796	0·272	1·909	0·955
4	1·855	0·367	2·567	1·284
5	1·875	0·441	3·147	1·573
6	1·862	0·497	3·636	1·818
7	1·822	0·539	3·998	2·000
8	1·761	0·569	4·238	2·119
9	1·683	0·593	4·359	2·179
10	1·593	0·610	4·362	2·181
Long run	0·902	0·902	0·991	0·496†

* Elasticities are calculated using 1970:3 values of output, p/c and initial conditions.
† It was assumed that the long-run elasticity of construction expenditures with respect to p/c is one-half.
Source: Bischoff [5] p. 28.

econometric models ever constructed for the U.S. economy contains a large number of variables. Although it is basically an accelerator world, it permits relative factor prices to play a role, and also allows impacts from the financial sector through securities prices and interest rates. Added to this is a complex lag structure which depends on production conditions in a group of industries. The result is a very complex theory of investment which must be analysed in the context of the full model, since it contains a number of endogenous variables. However, the model has been modified as theory and experience indicate; and it cannot be considered a final product. In particular, additional work on the financial variables and uncertainty would seem warranted in view of Bischoff's comment.

It is of interest to see what this model implies for the response of investment to changes in the quantity and relative price variables. Table 4.6 presents the time path over ten quarters and in the long run of the vintage-capital model estimated by Bischoff [5], which was also discussed above. Although this formulation does not consider the supply side of investment, the general pattern of impacts is revealing. Note that the output elasticity is larger than the p/c elasticity for each quarter, although the p/c elasticity is not negligible. This model suggests a role for monetary policy although a one per cent change in interest rates, for example, leads in the short run to a smaller impact than a corresponding change in output.

BIBLIOGRAPHY

[1] S. Almon, 'The Distributed Lag Between Capital Appropriations and Expenditures', *Econometrica*, vol. 33, no. 1 (Jan 1965) pp. 178–96.

[2] K. J. Arrow, *Aspects of the Theory of Risk-Bearing* (Helsinki, 1965).

[3] R. N. Batra and A. Ullah, 'Competitive Firm and the Theory of Input Demand Under Price Uncertainty', *Journal of Political Economy*, vol. 82, no. 3 (May–June 1974) pp. 537–48.

[4] I. Bernhardt, 'Fixed Costs and the Competitive Firm Under Price Uncertainty: Comment', *American Economic Review*, vol. LXII, no. 1 (Mar 1972) p. 193.

[5] C. W. Bischoff, 'Business Investment in the 1970's: A Comparison of Models', *Brookings Papers on Economic Activity*, 1 (1971) pp. 13–58.

[6] J. L. Bridge, *Applied Econometrics* (Amsterdam: North-Holland, 1971).

[7] R. M. Coen, 'The Effect of Cash Flow on the Speed of Adjustment', in *Tax Incentives and Capital Spending*, ed. G. Fromm (Washington: Brookings Institution, 1971).

[8] Frank de Leeuw and Edward Gramlich, 'The Federal Reserve–M.I.T. Model', *Federal Reserve Bulletin* (Jan 1968).

[9]   P. J. Dhrymes and M. Kurz, 'Investment, Dividend, and External
      Finance Behavior of Firms', in *Determinants of Investment Be-
      havior*, ed. R. Ferber (New York: National Bureau of Economic
      Research, 1967).
[10] J. S. Duesenberry, *Business Cycles and Economic Growth* (New
      York: McGraw-Hill, 1958).
[11] R. Eisner, 'A Distributed Lag Investment Function', *Econometrica*,
      vol. 28 (Jan 1960) pp. 1–29.
[12] —, 'Econometric Studies of Investment Behavior: A Comment',
      Economic Inquiry, vol. xii, no. 1 (Mar 1974) pp. 91–104.
[13] —, 'Tax Policy and Investment Behavior: Comment', *American
      Economic Review*, 59, 2 (June 1969) pp. 378–87.
[14] M. K. Evans, 'A Study of Industry Investment Decisions', *Review
      of Economics and Statistics*, vol. 49, no. 2 (May 1967) pp. 151–64.
[15] —, *Macroeconomic Activity: Theory, Forecasting, and Control* (New
      York: Harper & Row, 1969).
[16] E. F. Fama and M. H. Miller, *The Theory of Finance* (New York:
      Holt, Rinehart & Winston, 1972).
[17] M. S. Feldstein and J. S. Flemming, 'Tax Policy, Corporate Saving,
      and Investment Behavior in Britain', *Review of Economic Studies*,
      38, 116 (Oct 1971) pp. 415–34.
[18] J. P. Gould, 'Adjustment Costs in the Theory of Investment of the
      Firm', *Review of Economic Studies*, vol. xxxv, no. 101 (Jan 1968)
      pp. 47–55.
[19] —, 'The Use of Endogenous Variables in Dynamic Models of
      Investment', *Quarterly Journal of Economics*, vol. lxxxiii, no. 4
      (Nov 1969) pp. 580–99.
[20] E. Greenberg, 'A Stock-Adjustment Investment Model',
      Econometrica, vol. 32 (July 1964) pp. 339–57.
[21] G. Haberler, *Prosperity and Depression* (Harvard University Press,
      1937).
[22] R. E. Hall and D. W. Jorgenson, 'Application of the Theory of
      Optimal Capital Accumulation', in *Tax Incentives and Capital
      Spending*, ed. G. Fromm (Washington: Brookings Institution, 1971).
[23] H. M. Hochman, 'Some Aggregative Implications of Depreciation
      Acceleration', *Yale Economic Essays*, vol. 6 (Spring 1966) pp.
      217–74.
[24] M. C. Jenson and J. B. Long Jr, 'Corporate Investment under
      Uncertainty and Pareto Optimality in the Capital Markets', *Bell
      Journal of Economics and Management Science*, vol. 5, no. 1
      (Spring 1972) pp. 125–44.
[25] L. Johansen, 'Substitution versus Fixed Production Coefficients in
      the Theory of Economic Growth: A Synthesis', *Econometrica*, vol.
      27 (Apr 1959) pp. 157–76.
[26] D. Jorgenson, 'Rational Distributed Lag Functions', *Econometrica*,
      vol. 32, no. 1 (Jan 1966) pp. 135–49.

[27] —, 'The Theory of Investment Behavior', in *Determinants of Investment Behavior*, ed. R. Ferber (New York: National Bureau of Economic Research, 1967).

[28] —, 'Econometric Studies of Investment Behavior: A Survey', *Journal of Economic Literature*, vol. IX, no. 4 (Dec 1971) pp. 1111–47.

[29] L. R. Klein, 'Issues in Econometric Studies of Investment Behavior', *Journal of Economic Literature*, vol. XII, no. 1 (Mar 1974) pp. 43–9.

[30] L. M. Koyck, *Distributed Lags and Investment Analysis* (Amsterdam: North-Holland, 1954).

[31] P. J. Lund, *Investment: The Study of an Economic Aggregate* (Edinburgh: Oliver & Boyd, 1971).

[32] J. R. Meyer and R. R. Glauber, *Investment Decisions, Economic Forecasting, and Public Policy* (Harvard University Press, 1964).

[33] H. P. Minsky, 'Private Sector Asset Management and the Effectiveness of Monetary Policy: Theory and Practice', *Journal of Finance*, vol. XXIV, no. 2 (May 1969) pp. 223–38.

[34] —, 'An Exposition of a Keynesian Theory of Investment', in *Mathematical Methods in Investment and Finance*, ed. G. P. Szego and K. Shell (Amsterdam: North-Holland, 1972).

[35] —, *John Maynard Keynes* (Columbia University Press, 1975).

[36] Marc Nerlove, 'Lags in Economic Behavior', *Econometrica*, vol. 40, no. 2 (Mar 1972) pp. 221–51.

[37] Joel Popkin, 'The Relationship Between New Orders and Shipment: An Analysis of the Machinery and Equipment Industries', *Survey of Current Business* (Mar 1965) pp. 24–32.

[38] G. D. Quirin, *The Capital Expenditure Decision* (New York: Irwin, 1967).

[39] R. W. Resek, 'Investment by Manufacturing Firms: A Quarterly Time Series Analysis of Industry Data', *Review of Economics and Statistics*, vol. 48, no. 3 (Aug 1966) pp. 322–33.

[40] A. Sandmo, 'On the Theory of the Competitive Firm Under Price Uncertainty', *American Economic Review*, vol. LXI, no. 1 (Mar 1971) pp. 65–73.

[41] —, 'Fixed Costs and the Competitive Firm under Price Uncertainty: Reply', *American Economic Review*, vol. LXII, no. 1 (Mar 1972) pp. 194–5.

[42] J. Tinbergen, *Statistical Testing of Business Cycle Theories*, I, *A Method and its Application to Investment Activity* (Geneva: League of Nations, 1939).

[43] P. A. Tinsley, 'An Application of Variable Weight Distributed Lags', *Journal of the American Statistical Association*, vol. 62 (1967) pp. 1277–89.

[44] J. G. Witte Jr, 'The Microfoundations of the Social Investment Function', *Journal of Political Economy*, vol. 71 (Oct 1963) pp. 441–56.

5

Inventory Investment

Kenneth Hilton
*University of Southampton**

Kenneth Hilton
*University of Southampton**

I INTRODUCTION

In the National Income accounts, inventory investment (or stockbuilding) is treated as a part of final demand. If we look at stockbuilding simply in terms of the mean contribution it makes to the final demand, it would be difficult to explain the existence of such an extensive literature on stockbuilding; it would also be difficult to explain why a chapter of this book is devoted to this topic.

On average, stockbuilding constitutes less than one-twentieth of final demand in developed countries. Even in years of high inventory investment, stockbuilding has not exceeded ten per cent of total final demand in any developed country for which data are available. None the less, inventory investment is subject to wide fluctuations, whether these are measured on a year-to-year, or on a quarter-to-quarter basis. In many countries the year-to-year changes in inventory investment are often found to be greater than those for fixed capital formation (which on average is five to twenty times the value of stockbuilding). These points are illustrated in Table 5.1, which shows the level of aggregate stockbuilding and of fixed capital formation as a percentage of gross national product (G.N.P.) in seven developed countries together with the average year-to-year change of these two components of G.N.P.

This volatility of the level of inventory investment is important in

* This chapter was completed whilst the author was Visiting Professor at the University of New South Wales.

TABLE 5.1
*Variability of stockbuilding and of fixed capital formation in selected countries
1960–70 (as percentage of G.N.P.)*

| | Aggregate stockbuilding | | Aggregate fixed capital formation | |
	Average level	*Average of year-on-year change*	*Average level*	*Average of year-on-year change*
Australia	1·6	1·5	26·3	0·4
Canada	1·2	0·9	22·0	1·1
France	2·6	0·8	23·4	0·5
West Germany	1·6	0·9	25·0	0·9
Japan	4·0	1·6	32·3	1·3
United Kingdom	1·0	0·6	18·0	0·5
United States	1·0	0·4	16·9	1·0

Source: Calculations based on United Nations, *Yearbook of National Accounts Statistics* (1972).

explaining any macroeconomic aggregates, for fluctuations in stockbuilding will have an impact on other sectors of the economy (see [15] ch. 1). But there is a further reason for our interest in stockbuilding. We observe that businessmen appear to regard the level of their inventories as an indicator, or signal, in the process whereby they take decisions about other variables which the manufacturers influence, such as prices and output. As a consequence there is the possibility of economists using such information in order to explain and predict businessmen's behaviour (see [13] and [24] ch. 8). For most of this chapter we will be referring to manufacturers', and to a lesser extent, distributors' stockbuilding policies. Other sectors are clearly important, and perhaps too little attention is paid to them in the literature; but stocks in those sectors do appear less volatile, data for them are less satisfactory, and many of the ideas and approaches discussed in relation to manufacturers' stocks are applicable to those other sectors. A summary distribution of stockbuilding in the United Kingdom is provided in Table 5.2.

II MOTIVES FOR STOCKBUILDING

Before we consider variations in stocks, we need to examine why businessmen hold stocks at all. Let us view the economic world as one without uncertainty. Even in such a world we could explain the existence of inventories by references to the lags between

(a) the delivery of raw materials or semi-finished inputs for use by a plant or by a company *and* the usage of these materials – this gives rise to *raw-material stocks;*
(b) the commencement of a particular piece of work within a plant or

TABLE 5.2
Distribution of stocks held in the United Kingdom, 1972

Industry	£m. thousand 1972 book value	£m. thousand 1972 book value	Percentage of total stocks
Manufacturing industry:			
Materials and fuel	3·8		
Work-in-progress	4·2		
Finished goods	2·8		
		10·8	57
Distributive trades:			
Wholesale	2·0		
Retail	1·9		
		3·9	20
Agriculture and forestry		2·3	12
Other industries (including mining, gas and electricity and government)		2·1	11
Total stocks		19·1	100

Source: Central Statistical Office, *National Income and Expenditure* (1973).

company *and* its completion so far as that plant or company is concerned – this gives rise to *work-in-progress;* and

(c) the completion of a piece of work so far as particular plant or company is concerned *and* its delivery to the next or final user – this gives rise to *finished-goods stocks.*

Notice that this classification, one commonly used by national-income statisticians, relates to stocks as seen from the viewpoint of the *holder* of those stocks. It does *not* relate to the *kind* of good involved: what may be a finished good to one producer (sheet steel to a steel producer) may be raw materials to another (sheet steel to a motor-vehicle manufacturer). The classification depends on who *holds* the stocks.

The proportion of inventories in each of these groups will also depend on the economic-unit basis used in the measurement (usually *either* business unit *or* plant unit) and the degree of integration of the producing processes of the producing organisations. For example, suppose information is collected on a business-unit (company) basis, and company *A* takes over from one of its suppliers, company *B*. The items that were previously finished-good stocks of the supplying company (destined for company *A*) and the raw-material stocks of the using company (derived from company *B*). These will both become work-in-progress of the new company (*A* + *B*). This integration may have some behavioural impact, and the classification may be justified on these grounds.

In this world without uncertainty, if a producer could obtain, without additional cost, supplies in such quantities and at such intervals that they could be immediately used in the productive process, without delaying the operation of that process, it would be sub-optimal for the producer to hold input stocks, given that there is a positive cost of holding stocks. Similarly, if the producer could sell his goods the instant he produced them, output stocks would be unnecessary. Work-in-progress may need to be held because of the technological characteristics of the production process, although much 'work-in-progress' is not *in* a process but *between* processes within a particular business or plant. Even in the absence of uncertainty there would in practice be costs involved in arranging very frequent deliveries and this would tend to raise costs of inputs; in most industries there are few customers who are prepared to wait for goods to be delivered and, even then, production costs are often higher for small output runs. As a result the producer has to weigh the costs of holding interest on capital tied up, warehouse space, storekeepers' wages, obsolescence and depreciation of the stock on hand, and so on, on the one hand, and the cost of procuring or producing goods in small quantities at frequent intervals on the other. Any expected market price rises in the value of stocks may be treated as a negative cost, and may provide positive (speculative or precautionary) reasons for the holding of either input or output stocks. Similarly, expected price falls may be treated as an additional cost of holding stocks. Some firms and some industries produce at least some of their goods to order rather than for stock. The analysis of the behaviour of such industries provides additional problems, some of which are considered below (see also Belsey [4] and Courchene [6]).

The optimal (profit-maximising) strategy for a manufacturer to follow in this hypothetical world without uncertainty will depend on the particular cost (and benefits) involved in each case. There is an extensive management-science literature on the subject but there are difficulties in utilising even the simplest of these management-science models in macroeconomic analysis, although they may provide some guidance as to the nature of the more important variables that ought to be considered. We illustrate this by reference to one of the more popular and simplest of these models. For a discussion of this model and its application to economics see Eisner and Strotz [10].

The Harris optimal-order quantity model supposes there are two sets of costs facing a manufacturer in relation to his purchases and holding of materials for input. (In the following discussion we consider the case of input stocks but the framework is adaptable so as to encompass output or finished-goods stocks.)

(i) *The cost of holding stocks* (JI p.a.): this is defined as being equal to the average level of stocks, J, multiplied by the carrying costs per unit of stock in each period of time, say a year, I p.a.;

(ii) *The cost of procuring goods* ($YS/2J$ p.a.): this is the number of orders required each year, multiplied by the (assumed fixed) cost of a single order, S. The number of orders each year is equal to the (assumed constant) usage of input materials per year, Y, divided by the quantity ordered on each occasion (given reasonable assumptions, this is twice the average level of stocks, $2J$). This second set of costs is thus S multiplied by $Y/2J$ p.a.

Cost minimisation involves consideration of both these costs, and it can be readily shown, either by calculus or diagrammatically, that the optimal level of J, say J^*, is such that

$$J^* = \sqrt{2YS/I,} \tag{5.1}$$

that is, if the usage of inputs (or output, given constant material input per unit of output) reaches a new higher level and persists at that level indefinitely, we would expect the optimal stock level to rise to a new higher level; but that the micro relationship between the stock level and output is not a proportionate one for, in this model, the elasticity of the average optimal-stock level with respect to output is 0.5. Similarly, if we consider carrying costs, we would expect that a higher level of interest costs would have a negative effect on the optimal-stock level, with an elasticity between zero and -0.5.

III THE EQUILIBRIUM LEVEL OF STOCKS

We cannot easily use a model such as the one described above to specify the equilibrium level of stocks, even at the company level. Because the model applies only to a single line or product in a particular plant or business, we have to consider the aggregation of function (5.1). Special assumptions are required to aggregate linear functions, and the provision of macro functions from micro decision rules provides even greater difficulties. Some work has been undertaken in this area, and there is some evidence to suggest that, in practice, aggregation tends to have the effect of raising the elasticity of stock levels with respect to output closer to unity. (See Hilton and Cornelius [14] for references and a further discussion of this and the following points.)

Apart from the question of aggregation, there are other doubts that can be raised about the use of the above model. It is unlikely to be applicable to work-in-process. It is not clear, after account is taken of the costs of managing inventory systems, how far rules such as the one described above are optimal in a global sense. Many managers appear to use a constant stock–sales or stock-usage ratio, which may be modified at infrequent intervals. Mack [18] goes further than this and argues that many changes in inventory levels go unnoticed by managers, and that 'passive' rather than 'actively determined' inventory changes are the norm rather than the exception.

For these and similar reasons there has been a tendency to suppose, without specifying the precise cost function involved, that optimal inventory levels are a positive function of output and expected price rises, and a negative function of interest rates. Any non-proportionate effects have tended to be ignored, or 'taken care of' by using a constant in the function. Some writers, for example Mills [19], do have precise cost functions but these studies have been concentrated in the micro field. There have also been attempts to introduce non-linearities and variabled coefficients into fitted equations (see, for example, Darling [7]). Again, these are the exception rather than the rule in macroeconomic analysis. Similarly, the problems arising from the potential feedbacks from inventories to output and sales in aggregate models have tended to be ignored, in the hope that the lags in these feedbacks are sufficiently long to permit the investigator reasonably to assume that the estimation procedure is sufficiently robust to warrant its use.

Even given we accept the 'broad-brush' approach outlined above, we have still not considered the incorporation of uncertainty into the model. The real world is an uncertain place, and managers need to take account of this uncertainty in formulating optimal policies. The recognition that uncertainty exists will tend to mean that the optimal level of stocks will be higher than in the hypothetical state of certainty. This will be so because, in general, there are believed to be greater costs arising from having *ex post* too low a level of inventories (that is running out of stock) than into having too high a level. None the less, we would expect *variations* in the level of stocks to arise from this uncertainty margin only if the costs of running out of, or of holding additional, inventories, changes or if the risk of running out of stock changes significantly.

A further, associated, aspect of the treatment of uncertainty we have already touched upon, that is the production of goods to order. Several writers argue that it is important to separate those industries that produce mainly or wholly to order from those that produce wholly or mainly for stock, particularly in relation to finished-goods stocks. In industries that produce wholly to order, finished-goods stocks may be expected to be almost random accidents, and so the emphasis of explanation should be on production in relation to orders rather than on stocks (see Belsley [4], Childs [5] and Courchene [6]).

Here we are largely concerned with aggregate stock changes for the economy, and we treat the rate of new orders and the level of unfilled orders as factors influencing the level of stocks on hand. Users may order their inputs in advance, and they will take account of these orders in reviewing the risks of running out of stock. Similarly, producers may be making goods to order and, depending on the penalties attached to a buyer's refusal to take up an order, he will take account of the level of orders in deciding on his optimal level of finished-goods stocks. We have not the space here to examine in detail the relationship between unfilled orders and stocks but, in brief, the level (and changes in that level) of unfilled orders is likely to have an impact on the level of stocks for at least three reasons. First, variations in unfilled orders may provide an indication to a purchaser or seller of the risks he runs in running out of stock since the level of unfilled orders is often regarded by businessmen as an indication of how readily alternative sources of supply, or alternative outlets for sales, are available. Secondly, the level of unfilled orders for inputs may, in part, be a substitute for the holding of stocks of those inputs, that is it may provide a measure of the shifting of the holding of stocks from the purchaser to the supplier or vice versa. Thirdly, the level of, or change in the level of, unfilled orders may provide an indication of the state of business confidence, and may thus influence producers' expectations of the future level of sales.

In applications of inventory models different writers have believed, or found, different variables to be important in the explanation of stock-building. This is hardly surprising, given the differences of time, institutions and countries with which various writers have been concerned. Variables such as those outlined above, and other similar variables, have usually been used, but the form in which they have been used has also varied. *For simplicity of exposition only* we assume that whichever variables are included in the determination of the long-run equilibrium stock level they can be represented by an expository variable, X, and when we consider particular empirical work we will then specify the precise variables that are represented by X. Hence

$$J_t^* = \alpha_0 + \alpha_1 X_t^e, \tag{5.2}$$

where J_t^* is the equilibrium level of stocks at the *end* of time period t for the particular economic unit or group of units under consideration, and X_t^e is representative of the expectational variables that enter into the determination of the equilibrium level of stocks at the end of time period t.

Equation (5.2) may be regarded as providing the long-run equilibrium, or desired, level of stocks for a manufacturer or industry. The kind of variables we would expect to enter the set we have called X_t^e are the expected level of output, Q^e or sales, Y^e, the expected interest-rate costs, R^e, the expected change in the price of stocks held, ΔP^e, besides other variables indicative of the general level of business confidence (or of the risk of running out of stock) such as the level of outstanding or new orders, U, or the rate of change of sales, ΔY. Notice that the problem of *timing* arises as soon as we consider any other than a static-equilibrium case. Stocks are measured at a *point* in time (usually the end or the beginning of a time period) and other variables such as sales relate to a flow over a *period* of time. The matching of stock and flow variables is always an approximate procedure. The one most commonly used, and one we follow here, is to denote stocks at the *end* of time period t by a t subscript (for example J_t) and relate this to the flow variables prevailing, or expected to prevail, during the time period t, again denoted by a t subscript (for example Y_t).

IV PLANNED STOCKBUILDING

Above we have listed some of the determinants of the equilibrium level of stocks. But even if a producer does follow inventory rules of the kind we have discussed, will he move or attempt to move immediately to a new equilibrium level of stocks if one or more of the variables determining the optimal level of stocks changes? The answer is, in general, that he will not. We thus distinguish between the long-run equilibrium level of stocks, and that level which producers *plan* to achieve by the end of a given period.

This difference could arise for several reasons. The existence of uncertainty means the producer has to consider expected values of variables. These expectations may be held with varying degrees of uncertainty, and, depending on his loss function, the producer may be slow to react to changes in the expected value of, say, sales. There will be costs associated with rapid changes in the level of inventories, and producers will be reluctant to incur these costs. Once we take the costs of adjustment into account, the long-run optimum situation may depend on the initial position. (See Eisner and Strotz [10] for a discussion of this approach.)

These costs may be associated with fluctuations in purchases from suppliers in the case of input stocks, or with fluctuations in production, or directly with fluctuations of stock levels (for example the costs in procuring more or less space and store personnel at short notice). In summary, a firm may proceed towards a new equilibrium situation at a slow rate because (*a*) it is not certain of the future, and (*b*) it wishes to engage in a *smoothing* of potential fluctuations in orders, production or inventories.

We have little prior knowledge on the speed with which producers will seek to achieve the new equilibrium level of stocks as they see it. We could postulate that it will depend on whether the adjustment is upwards or downwards, whether it is large or small, whether the industry finds it easy or difficult to vary production levels, and so on. One practice in empirical work that appears to have yielded sensible results is to assume that the *planned* size of the adjustment (that is planned stockbuilding) is a proportion (constant over time) of the discrepancy between the initial stock level and the equilibrium. If one believes that the major reasons for the lack of immediate adjustment arises from the desire on the part of manufacturers to smooth production rather than smooth inventories *per se*, the justification for a *constant* partial-adjustment model is rather more difficult to see. A discussion of this is contained in Hay [12] and Darling and Lovell [9]. Nevertheless, for simplicity we follow this assumption, and so, in symbolic terms

$$J_t^p - J_{t-1} = \delta(J_t^* - J_{t-1}) + u_t, \qquad (5.3)$$

that is

$$J_t^p = \delta J_t^* + (1-\delta)J_{t-1} + u_t, \qquad (5.3a)$$

where J_t^p is the level of stocks the producer plans (where plans are formulated at the beginning of the period) to have at the end of period t, u_t is a random term, and δ is a constant reaction or partial-adjustment coefficient.

In this and all equations in this chapter, to avoid complicated reduced or final forms of equations, the expression u_t is used to denote a random element. No attempt is made to manipulate this random element, but in particular cases the properties of the random element are discussed.

An alternative approach, used by Johnston [16], is to assume that producers plan to produce the *whole* of the difference between the equilibrium level of stocks at the beginning and at the end of the period, *less* a proportion, δ', of the difference between the actual and equilibrium stocks at the beginning of the period, that is

$$J_t^p - J_{t-1} = J_t^* - J_{t-1}^* + (1 - \delta')(J_{t-1}^* - J_{t-1}) + u_t, \tag{5.4}$$

or
$$J_t^p = J_t^* + \delta'(J_{t-1} - J_{t-1}^*) + u_t. \tag{5.4a}$$

Within the framework of equation (5.3) we could insert the variables entering the determination of J_t^*, the set we have typified by X_t^e, and so provide an equation for planned stockbuilding. Before considering this further we discuss the possibility that producers' plans may not be fulfilled, that is unplanned stockbuilding exists.

V UNPLANNED STOCKBUILDING

It is not only businessmen's plans with respect to stockbuilding that are susceptible to non-fulfilment. Other economic agents may be unable to fulfil their plans in relation to the economic variables that they influence – a consumer who plans to purchase an item from a shop may be frustrated by the absence of the good he desires on the retailer's premises. Similarly, a businessman's plans for fixed capital extensions may be frustrated by a failure of a supplier to deliver the capital goods within a given time period. But, often, on the grounds of plausibility, as well as of simplicity in model building, it is assumed that the principal area in which the unplanned elements of the economic system arise is that relating to inventory investment, and in particular that relating to inventory investment in output (finished-goods) stocks.

We consider in more detail the nature of this unplanned element in stockbuilding by recourse to a microeconomic illustration of the way in which unplanned stockbuilding arises.

Suppose that a producer has a particular planning period, say a year, and that only on the first day of that year does he take decisions with respect to his activities during the year. When he makes these plans he knows what his finished-goods inventory holdings are at the beginning of the year (F_{t-1}, that is at the end of the previous year, $t-1$). He makes forecasts of sales, S_t^e, for the period, and from this and information about carrying costs, order costs, adjustment lags, and so forth, decides on his plans for the level of inventories of finished goods at the end of the period, F_t. Given his plans are consistent, he will have then determined his planned level of output for the year, Q_t^p, for F_{t-1} (stocks at beginning of year) + Q_t (output during year) is identically equal to F_t (stocks at end of year) + S_t (sales during this year), or

$$F_t^p - F_{t-1} = Q_t^p - S_t^e. \tag{5.5}$$

Alternatively, one may regard the producer as first deciding his plans for output and, as a result, determining his plans for end-period inventories.

Given that the output level is predetermined by the producer and given the initial stock position, the only sense in which unplanned inventory changes may arise is when the producer is incorrect in his sales' forecasts (or when he is unable to bring actual sales in line with the expected level of sales). If we add unplanned inventory changes (that is $S_t^e - S_t$) to planned inventory changes we will have a total inventory change. Adding this to each side of equation (5.5) we have

$$F_t - F_{t-1} = (F_t^p - F_{t-1}) + (S_t^e - S_t) = Q_t^p - S_t^e + (S_t^e - S_t). \tag{5.5a}$$

If producers' plans with respect to output are always fulfilled then equation (5.5a) becomes

$$(F_t^p - F_{t-1}) + (S_t^e - S_t) = Q_t - S_t. \tag{5.6}$$

Suppose that producers are able to modify their plans with respect to output during the year in the light of realised sales; then equation (5.6) could be modified as

$$(F_t^p - F_{t-1}) + (S_t^e - S_t) - (Q_t^p - Q_t) = Q_t - S_t, \tag{5.7}$$

and unplanned stockbuilding is then $(S_t^e - S_t) - (Q_t^p - Q_t)$. This means that the unplanned element in stockbuilding, the discrepancy between forecasted and actual sales, is modified by the difference between the output initially planned for the period, and the actual output. The introduction of this second (inventory-smoothing) term may be regarded as illegitimate given our initial framework in which a manufacturer is assumed to take decisions only once in a particular time period; and, as we will see, the introduction of this latter term provides some difficulties in interpreting empirical results. Ideally, we need to choose the time period, from which we take observations, to coincide with the producers' planning period, but, in practice, data are often not available for particular time periods, and all economic decision-takers do not choose the same planning period.

In empirical analysis an assumption is sometimes made that the extent to which producers are able, and willing, to adjust their production is in proportion to the unplanned stock change that would have occurred in the absence of modifications in the production plans, that is

$$(Q_t^p - Q_t) = (1 - \rho)(S_t^e - S_t) + u_t, \tag{5.8}$$

so that if $\rho = 0$, then $Q_t^p - Q_t = S_t^e - S_t$ and unplanned stockbuilding would not exist as producers would always be adjusting their actual output to their actual sales. If, on the other hand, $\rho = 1$, then $Q_t^p - Q_t = 0$ and the original production plans are always realised.

Introducing $Q_t^p - Q_t$ from equation (5.8), and rearranging terms, equation (5.7) becomes

$$F_t - F_{t-1} = (F_t^p - F_{t-1}) + \rho(S_t^e - S_t) + u_t, \tag{5.9}$$

where ρ is the output-adjustment coefficient.

VI THE ROLE OF EXPECTATIONS

If we join together the equations we have for optimal, planned and unplanned stockbuilding we obtain, from (5.2) (5.3) and (5.9), an equation for total stockbuilding. Thus

$$J_t - J_{t-1} = \delta([\alpha_0 + \alpha_1 X_t^e] - J_{t-1}) + \rho(S_t^e - S_t) + u_t. \tag{5.10}$$

Given data on businessmen's expectations at the beginning of the period with respect to their set of variables designated by X_t^e and for S_t^e, we could attempt to explain $J_t - J_{t-1}$ by the variables on the right-hand side of equation (5.10) and obtain values for the structural coefficients. Let us illustrate this with a simple case; suppose we assume that the only variable relevant to the long-run equilibrium level of stocks is expected sales (that is only S_t^e is included in the X_t^e set, and we have observed data for this variable) then

$$J_t - J_{t-1} = \alpha_0 \delta + \alpha_2 \delta S_t^e - \delta J_{t-1} + \rho S_t^e - \rho S_t + u_t \tag{5.11}$$

or $\qquad J_t - J_{t-1} = \alpha_0 \delta + (\alpha_2 \delta + \rho)S_t^e - \delta J_{t-1} - \rho S_t + u_t. \tag{5.11a}$

Suppose we then fit equation (5.11a) to the data by an appropriate statistical technique and we obtain regression coefficients a_0, a_1, a_2 and a_3 on each of the variables. Thus

$$J_t - J_{t-1} = a_0 + a_1 S_t^e + a_2 J_{t-1} + a_3 S_t + u_t. \tag{5.12}$$

We could then provide estimates for the structural coefficients thus:

the partial-accelerator coefficient, $\delta = a_2$;
the output-adjustment coefficient, $\rho = a_3$; and
the marginal equilibrium-stock-sales coefficient, $\alpha_2 = (a_1 - a_3)/a_1$.

More complex models can, in principle, be treated in the same kind of way, given the appropriate expectational data are available. But such data are not normally available. There have been some studies, principally in relation to the U.S. economy, that use expectations or anticipation data, collected by asking businessmen their intentions. The results, reported below, from such studies are encouraging. In the United Kingdom similar data have not been available, and are only available on a limited basis for the United States. There is the further problem with such data, that we do not know how such anticipations arise, and so although models including such data may 'explain' variations in stockbuilding quite well, they may not add a great deal either to our understanding or to our potential control of the economic system as a whole.

As a result, in many studies the expectational data are generated from actual observations, in the belief that businessmen form their expectations of the future by reference to the past or that businessmen's expectations are 'consistent' in relation to the realised data. Various possibilities have been tried: the simplest is to suppose that businessmen's expectations are based on the assumption that there will be no change from the existing state of the world when

$$X_t^e = X_{t-1} + u_t. \tag{5.13}$$

This may be regarded as a special case of two other approaches:

(i) Nerlove's adaptive-expectations model [21]:

$$X_t^e = X_{t-1} + \lambda(X_{t-1}^e - X_{t-1}) + u_t, \tag{5.14}$$

with $0 < \lambda < 1$. This can also be written as

$$X_t^e = (1 - \lambda) \sum_{i=0}^{\infty} \lambda^i X_{t-i-1} + u_t, \tag{5.14a}$$

and λ is usually assumed to be the same for all expectational variables. This implies that businessmen modify their expectations of no change by some proportion 'λ' of the error they made in the last period when they had formed their expectations in a similar way.

(ii) Lovell's constant-proportionate-error approach [17]:

$$X_t^e = X_{t-1} + \Phi(X_t - X_{t-1}) + u_t, \tag{5.15}$$

where $0 < \Phi < 1$. This model supposes that, by some means or other, businessmen's expectations or forecasts with respect to a particular variable differ from the realised outcome by a constant proportion, Φ, of the change that has taken place in that variable since the last time period. As with λ, Φ is usually assumed to be the same for all expectational variables.

How can we make use of the models portrayed by equations (5.14) and (5.15)? If we had information about λ or Φ, then we could use (5.14) or (5.15) to generate expected values for X_t variables in equation (5.10) and use this model in the way indicated above. The difficulty lies in obtaining values for λ or Φ and in choosing between the alternative methods of generating expectations. Extraneous information can be found to help us in this respect: comparisons may be made between anticipations data and the above models: other empirical work in which expectational data has been satisfactorily generated, and used, could also provide information in this respect. But, in the absence of satisfactory anticipations data, the usual approach has been to generate the expectations data at the same time as the estimation of the other coefficients in equation (5.10). Effectively, this involves choosing a value for Φ or λ so as to provide the best 'fit' in econometric terms. This procedure is not without problems.

We illustrate the procedure and some of the difficulties below by considering the application of (5.15), Lovell's approach, to (5.11a). We start from a rearranged form of (11a), that is

$$J_t = \alpha_0\,\delta - \rho S_t + (\alpha_2\,\delta + \rho)S_t^e + (1-\delta)J_{t-1} + u_t \qquad (5.11b)$$

Using, from (5.15),

$$S_t^e = S_t + (\Phi-1)(S_t - S_{t-1}) + u_t, \qquad (5.15a)$$

we have

$$J_t = \alpha_0\,\delta + \alpha_2\,\delta S_t + (\Phi-1)(\alpha_2\,\delta+\rho)(S_t - S_{t-1}) + (1-\delta)J_{t-1} + u_t. \qquad (5.16)$$

If we fit a regression equation of the form,

$$J_t = b_0 + b_1 S_t + b_2(S_t - S_{t-1}) + b_3 J_{t-1} + u_t, \qquad (5.17)$$

and find estimates for b_0, b_1, b_2, b_3 then we have

$$\alpha_0\,\delta = b_0$$
$$\alpha_2\,\delta = b_1$$
$$(\Phi-1)(\alpha_2\,\delta+\rho) = b_3$$
$$(1-\delta) = b_4.$$

From this we can find the partial-adjustment coefficient $\delta = (1-b_4)$, $\alpha_0 = b_0/(1-b_4)$, $\alpha_2 = b_1/(1-b_4)$ the marginal equilibrium stock–sales ratio, but we can find Φ and ρ only as functions of each other, that is $\Phi = (b_3/(b_1+\rho))+1$, the forecasting coefficient, and $\rho = (b_3/(\Phi-1))-b_1$, the output-adjustment coefficient.

This situation arises basically because we are trying to extract from our observations of the world more information than exists.

None the less, we may still learn something further about the nature of the world if we have prior beliefs about, at least, the *range* of values for the coefficients. Our prior beliefs will often be dependent on the time interval of the observations. If we are using monthly data, and we believe producers plan on a monthly basis, we may assume that output is inflexible within the planning period. On the other hand, if we deal with annual time periods, then we may expect that output plans will be varied during the time period. In the first case, we would expect ρ to be close to 1, and in the second, closer to zero. In this example consider the likely range of Φ and of ρ; when we can obtain a range estimate for ρ and Φ

respectively. We expect both ρ and Φ to lie in the range 0 to 1; consider then the limiting cases:

if $\rho = 1$ (output plans are inflexible), $\Phi = (b_3/(b_1+1))+1$;
if $\rho = 0$ (output is completely flexible), $\Phi = (b_3/b_1)+1$;
if $\Phi = 0$ (forecasts always assume no change), $\rho = -(b_3+b_1)$; and
if $\Phi = 1$ (forecasts are always exact) ρ is undefined (output adjustment in this case is unnecessary).

The above is illustrative of a whole class of cases that arise in inventory, and other, model building.

VII DATA AND ESTIMATION PROCEDURES

Before reviewing some empirical results, it is necessary to comment on the data used, and the estimation procedures.

Not much economic data are designed and collected for a specific purpose, and to that extent all economic model building has to 'make do' with imperfect data. In the case of stocks and stockbuilding, the data are typically of very poor quality. This arises because most inventory data used in macro models are collected from companies whose accountants have prepared valuations of stocks for tax or reporting purposes, the estimates of which are often based on fairly casual inspection of the stocks on hand. The method of valuation is not clear, it can vary from year to year even in the same company, and practices vary wildly across companies.

The 'book' value of the stocks is then subjected to a revaluation process by national-income statisticians, based upon their guess of the methods used by accountants, and the structure of the inventories. Estimates of National Income are often revised quite extensively some years after the first estimates have appeared. The above is not intended as a counsel of despair, but a warning that it is important to understand the derivation of the data used in each study, and the possibility of revisions in that data. Nevile [22] found that his inventory model provided better estimates of the revised estimates of Australian inventory changes than those derived from government statisticians' first estimates of the same inventory changes.

A second set of difficulties relates to the estimation procedure. In many instances students of inventory changes have used ordinary least-squares estimators. Some investigators acknowledge that this is unsatisfactory for many of the models, and recent econometric work has shown that the estimates derived from ordinary least squares can be subject to substantial bias especially in models involving a partial-adjustment or adaptative-expectations approach. The results should therefore be treated with caution. Trivedi's [27] study is one of the few not liable to this criticism.

The difficulties that arise with respect to the estimation procedure are exacerbated if one is interested in the structural parameters of the model.

These structural parameters are often very sensitive to small changes in the regression coefficients; few studies provide any indication of the standard errors associated with the structural coefficients, and one is often left with only the standard errors associated with the regression coefficients. These need careful interpretation if they are to tell us anything about the reliability of the structural coefficients.

VIII AN EXAMPLE OF AN ESTIMATED MODEL:
LOVELL [17]

To illustrate how the kind of model we have been discussing is used in practice, we consider briefly one of the best-known analyses of quarterly inventory changes: that by Lovell for the U.S. economy in the period 1948–55.

Lovell set out to explain the behaviour of constant price, seasonally adjusted manufacturing inventories, by industry and by stage of production. Here we consider only the models for total manufacturing: one for stocks of purchased materials and goods-in-process; one for finished-goods stocks.

For stocks of purchased materials and goods-in-process, M, Lovell postulated a model that assumed that, with respect to these stocks, producers' plans are fulfilled, that is $M_t^p = M_t$. He used a partial-adjustment model as in equation (5.3a), that is

$$M_t = M_t^p = \delta M_t^* + (1 - \delta)M_{t-1} + u_t. \tag{5.18}$$

He specified the variables relevant to the equilibrium level of stocks at the end of period t as the *following* period's output, Q_{t+1}, the change in output from the current period to the following period, $Q_{t+1} - Q_t$, the level of unfilled orders at the end of period t, U_t, and the proportionate price change, $(P_{t+1} - P_t)/P_{t+1}$.

The equilibrium equation is thus

$$M_t^* = \beta_0 + \beta_1 Q_{t+1} + \beta_2(Q_{t+1} - Q_t) + \beta_3((P_{t+1} - P_t)/P_{t+1}) + \beta_4 U_t + u_t. \tag{5.19}$$

Combining (5.18) and (5.19) yields

$$M_t = \delta\beta_0 + \delta\beta_1 Q_{t+1} + \delta\beta_2(Q_{t+1} - Q_t) + \delta\beta_3((P_{t+1} - P_t)/P_{t+1}) + \delta\beta_4 U_t + (1 - \delta)M_{t-1} + u_t.$$

This equation was then estimated by ordinary least squares and the following results are shown (standard errors in brackets):

$$M_t = 4004 + 0 \cdot 062 Q_{t+1} - 0 \cdot 100(Q_{t+1} - Q_t) - 0 \cdot 320(P_{t+1} - P_t)/P_{t+1})$$
$$\quad\quad (0 \cdot 016) \quad\quad (0 \cdot 030) \quad\quad\quad\quad (0 \cdot 206)$$

$$+ 0 \cdot 061 U_t + 0 \cdot 542 M_{t-1} \quad (5.20)$$
$$(0 \cdot 005) \quad (0 \cdot 046)$$

$$R^2 = 0 \cdot 993.$$

From this, it is possible to derive an estimate for $\delta(0\cdot458)$ and so for β_1, β_2, β_3 and β_4. In terms of Lovell's prior beliefs as specified in his paper, the coefficient on output ($\beta_1 = 0\cdot135$) and on unfilled orders ($\beta_4 = 0\cdot133$) are both consistent with his expectations. The results suggest that both following-period output and unfilled orders have a role to play in determining the equilibrium level of material stocks and work-in-progress. The partial-adjustment coefficient, δ, implies that producers plan to remove about half the difference between the equilibrium stock level and the level of stocks at the beginning of a quarter. Within a year, with stable levels of the variables determining equilibrium stocks, about 93 per cent $(1-(1-\delta)^4)$ of the adjustment towards equilibrium would have taken place.

The variable $Q_{t+1} - Q_t$ was intended to capture effects on the equilibrium level arising from rapid changes in output, so that when output is rising it is postulated that one would expect producers to increase their stocks in anticipation of further rises. Lovell concludes that there is no evidence to support this in view of the negative coefficient on $Q_{t+1} - Q_t$. An alternative interpretation can be derived by rearranging the terms, $\delta\beta_1 Q_{t+1} + \delta\beta_2(Q_{t+1} - Q_t)$ as $(\delta\beta_1 + \delta\beta_2)Q_{t+1} - \delta\beta_2 Q_t$, and in this form the following-period output is negative $(-0\cdot83)$ and the current-period output positive $(0\cdot22)$. Some of the problems of interpretation appear to arise from Lovell's use of following-period output, which would not be known to the decision-taker at the time these (end-) period stocks were determined.

The price variable was intended to consider a joint hypothesis: (*a*) that producers forecast price changes with complete precision; and (*b*) that producers take account of this expected price change in deciding on the appropriate level of stocks. The 'wrong' sign and non-significance of the coefficient on the price-change variable can be interpreted as denying support to either or to both these hypotheses.

In relation to stocks of finished goods, Lovell used a model of the following form: for equilibrium stocks,

$$F_t^* = \beta_0 + \beta_1 S_t^e + u_t; \tag{5.21}$$

for anticipated sales (using (5.15)),

$$S_t^e = \Phi S_{t-1} + (1 - \Phi)S_t + u_t; \tag{5.22}$$

for planned stocks (using (5.3a)),

$$F_t^p = \delta F_t^* + (1 - \delta)F_{t-1} + u_t; \tag{5.23}$$

for unplanned stocks (using (5.9));

$$F_t^u = \rho(S_t^e - S_t) + u_t. \tag{5.24}$$

Hence by adding (5.23) and (5.24), and substituting (5.22) for S_t^e in (5.21) and (5.23) and substituting (5.21) for F_t^* in (5.23) we obtain

$$F_t = \delta\beta_0 + (\delta\beta_1 + \rho)\Phi(S_t - S_{t-1}) + \delta\beta_1 S_t + (1 - \delta)F_{t-1} + u_t. \qquad (5.25)$$

Estimating this by ordinary least squares, Lovell found

$$F_t = -258 + 0 \cdot 132(S_t - S_{t-1}) + 0 \cdot 042 S_t + 0 \cdot 848 F_{t-1} \qquad (5.26)$$
$$(0 \cdot 042) \phantom{(S_t - S_{t-1}) + } (0 \cdot 020) \quad (0 \cdot 065)$$
$$R^2 = 0 \cdot 958.$$

From this we can derive $\delta(= 0 \cdot 152)$, $\beta_1(= 0 \cdot 276)$ and ρ and Φ in terms of each other, that is $\rho = (0 \cdot 132/\Phi) - 0 \cdot 042$, and $\Phi = (0 \cdot 132/(0 \cdot 042 + \rho))$. The adjustment coefficient here is rather smaller, implying a slower movement towards equilibrium; with a once and for all change in sales, after one year, less than half of the notional long-run adjustment that would have taken place.

Consider the output-adjustment and forecasting coefficients: if $\rho = 1$ (that is output plans are fixed) then the forecasting equation (5.22) becomes $S_t^e = S_{t-1} + 0 \cdot 874(S_t - S_{t-1})$, that is, on average, producers predict more than 87 per cent of changes in sales from one quarter to the next; if output plans are partially flexible, say $\rho = 0 \cdot 5$, then the forecast equation becomes $S_t^e = S_{t-1} + 0 \cdot 757(S_t - S_{t-1})$ and so even here, on average, producers appear to anticipate a large proportion of the sales change. The regressiveness of the forecasts seen here (that is with forecasters *under*-predicting any change) is typical of the results found in many studies.

Similarly, one could consider different possibilities with respect to forecasting, for example at the extreme of predicting, on average, no change in sales ($\Phi = 1$), $\rho = 0 \cdot 08$, that is output plans would need to have been very flexible indeed.

IX TYPICAL RESULTS

The kind of models we have been discussing do not represent the only possible approach to the study of inventories. Other approaches such as these of Abramovitz [1] and Stanback [25] have emphasised the careful inspection of time-series data. Time series of inventories or inventory–sales ratios are compared with other economic time-series data, and from these comparisons some conclusions about the behaviour of inventories may be drawn. If one is concerned to analyse the determinants of inventory investment it is normally more satisfactory to have a structural model, partly because unstructured comparisons tend to ignore many variables, and partly because it is easier to postulate the approximate size of parameters within a structure.

None the less, a structure *per se* can tell us little about the behaviour of the economic system under consideration. We need to have prior beliefs or estimated parameters before we can consider the behaviour of inventories in response to particular changes in other variables. The parameters estimated – and our beliefs – will vary according to the particular time and country we are considering. Hence little emphasis is placed in this chapter on the particular parameter estimates found. What we attempt to do here is to provide, by reference to a small number of studies, a flavour of the principal results. We consider the results in relation to (*a*) the equilibrium level of stocks, (*b*) the adjustment of planned towards equilibrium level of stocks, and (*c*) unplanned stocks and the formation of expectations.

A. *The Equilibrium Level of Stocks*

The dominant factor in the determination of the equilibrium level of stocks is, naturally, output (or sales). Sometimes the marginal stock–output ratio has been found similar to the average stock–output ratio, and this may be interpreted as providing (indirect) support for a proportionate relationship at the macro level between stocks and output. In other studies (for example Ball and Drake [3]) the authors' prior belief that the marginal and the average should be similar is used to discriminate between competing models. On the other hand, Trivedi's results [27] for U.K. manufacturing industry suggest an elasticity between stocks and sales (or output) substantially lower than one for both material and fuel and total stocks.

Other factors have also been considered. We have referred to Lovell's failure to find evidence of successful speculation by holders of input stocks. Trivedi [27], likewise, found no role for price changes in his model. Such results must be treated with caution. Producers could be speculating by varying the composition of their stocks on hand in antici-pation of price changes and this would not be revealed in this kind of models. It could even be that producers do attempt to raise their inventories of inputs when they anticipate price rises, but their suppliers, with similar expectations, may wish to delay deliveries. As a result the over-all effect may be so diffused as not to appear relevant in these models. The periods to which these models refer had by current (1975) standards very moderate rates of price increase. It could be that different results will be found by future investigators.

In view of its potential control by government authorities, a knowledge of the impact of the rate of interest may be regarded as particularly important. Until relatively recently few quantitative studies have dis-covered any statistically significant relationship between stockbuilding and the rate of interest. One of the earlier U.S. studies that found a significant relationship was that of Ando *et al.* [2] and, although the estimated long-run interest elasticity with respect to inventory levels was -0.4, the coefficients were not well determined. Trivedi [27] draws attention to the possibility that the difficulty in finding a significant role for the interest rate may have arisen from the estimation procedures used in many studies. He found, using quarterly U.K. data, that when he used ordinary least-squares estimators, the rate of interest did not appear as statistically significant, but when he used maximum likelihood estimators (to take account of a postulated error structure) for most industries, and for manufacturing industry in aggregate, the coefficient on the short-term interest-rate variable was statistically significant. The interest elasticity measured at the respective means was small, about $-1\cdot3$ in respect of inventory *investment;* this implies an interest elasticity with respect to inventory *levels* of rather less than $-0\cdot05$. This elasticity cannot be readily compared with the elasticity of $-0\cdot5$ implied by equation (5.1) for carrying costs, as the existence of carrying costs other than interest costs would reduce this elasticity for interest costs alone. Given a ratio of (marginal) non-interest-carrying costs to interest-carrying costs of 5 to 1, the elasticity that Trivedi found for material and fuel stocks of about $-0\cdot1$ is compatible with that implied by equation (5.1) for interest elasticity (again about $-0\cdot1$).

Courchene [6] in his study of Canadian inventories found that changes in interest rates appeared to affect work-in-progress (that is as interest rates rose so the time period of production fell), as well as having an impact, in some industries, on raw-material stocks. Courchene argues that, with more appropriate data, rather stronger relationships would have been found. For the Japanese economy, where monetary policy has been used extensively for some time, some evidence of negative elasticities have similarly been found by the government planning authorities.

The evidence on the interest elasticity of inventories is patchy. Yet although the elasticity tends to be low, the relative change in the rate of interest is often very large (for example 5–7 per cent represents about a 40 per cent change), and it could be that, given the higher interest rates of the recent past, future studies may reveal a greater effect on the equilibrium level of inventories arising from interest-rate changes.

A fourth set of factors considered in several studies is the level of orders outstanding or the rate of orders received. We have already referred to the difficulties of treating order variables in the same way as other variables, particularly in relation to industries that produce mainly to order. But, within the framework we have described, order variables do appear to have an effect, particularly in those industries that produce a significant proposition of their output to order (see Lovell [17] and Trivedi [27]). More recent U.S. studies, using anticipations data directly, have found that although businessmen's expectations appear to be influenced by the level of unfilled orders, the equilibrium level of stocks, given those expectations, do not appear to be so influenced. As a result the role of orders does appear to be rather uncertain.

B.   *Adjustment of Planned Stocks Towards Equilibrium*

As we have indicated, a variety of adjustment processes could be postulated, and different writers have used various structures in this respect. Ball and Drake [3] used both equations (5.3) and (5.4) to compare the results; but many writers have used the simple partial-adjustment model of the kind used by Lovell, and the results have been surprisingly uniform. In broad terms the quarterly studies suggest that nearly all the adjustment takes place within a year of any initial shock. Annual studies tend to suggest a slower adjustment, but these are not very different from the quarterly implications. (See, for example, Feinstein's U.K. estimates of 0·85, from annual data for 1951–61 [11] and Nevile's Australian estimate of 0·77, from annual data for 1955–73 [23]).

This conforms to what one might expect. But it is important to notice that, in quarterly models that use seasonally adjusted data, the smoothing of the data tends to reduce the estimated partial-adjustment time lag. Similarly, the use of ordinary least squares in inappropriate circumstances may yield eccentric estimates for the speed of adjustment.

C. · *Unplanned Stocks and the Formation of Expectations*

In the kinds of models described above we cannot, without anticipations data, find direct information on the formation of expectations, unless we are prepared to make prior judgements on the degree of output flexibility. Many researchers assume complete inflexibility of output during the decision observation period. The effect of this is to raise the estimate of the degree of accuracy in the producer's forecast of his sales. Lovell's results reported above are typical in this respect. Feinstein, using annual U.K. data, found that if output is assumed inflexible this implies that producers forecast 95 per cent of the change from one year to the next, while if 90 per cent adjustment is assumed ($\rho = 0·9$), the implied accuracy for producers' forecasts would be 80 per cent. Trivedi's quarterly analysis is more difficult to interpret but in broad terms with inflexible output the implied forecast accuracy is about 80 per cent, and with $\rho = 0·5$ it is still 65 per cent. Ball and Drake used two forecasting approaches in their study of quarterly U.K. stock changes. One was similar to Lovell's while the other assumed a variation of Nerlove's adaptive-expectations approach. With zero output flexibility (as they assumed) their results with Lovell's approach imply 99·3 per cent accuracy in forecasting quarterly sales changes. Using an adaptive-expectations approach, Ball and Drake found that their model implied that producers predicted by using the past values of variables as a measure of the expected value, with weights declining exponentially so that $\hat{S}_t = 0·5S_t + (0·5)^2 S_{t-1} + (0·5)^3 S_{t-2} \ldots$ It is difficult to choose between these two approaches on the basis of the reported results.

It will be clear from the above discussion that there are considerable obstacles in the way of interpretation of regression results. Part of these difficulties stem from the need to generate anticipations data within the model. If we have direct observations for businessmen's expectations and/or forecasts, the task of analysis becomes easier. For the United Kingdom there are no satisfactory anticipations data, but for the United States there have been several studies using anticipations data, and Hirsch and Lovell [15] in their extended analysis of the U.S. data have made comparisons of their results using anticipations data with results based on the use of models in which the anticipations are implicitly generated within the model. The use of the anticipation data directly had an effect on the significance of the parameter estimates of the models considered. In general terms the study found that the regression equations were more precisely determined using anticipations data, but that apart from an implied higher speed of adjustment towards the equilibrium level, δ, the remaining parameter estimates were not very different. Some other studies have in fact found 'better' results in a statistical sense by using 'proxy' anticipations rather than 'actual' anticipations. This can clearly arise if the anticipations data is subject to measurement error.

However, the use of the anticipations data does permit the discussion of the flexibility of output directly. Here the results were interesting. Production plans appeared to be revised very rapidly, and so the conclusions which imply that producers forecast very well may, in practice, simply reflect the fact that they are able, within the limits of the error of their forecast, to adjust their output–sales discrepancy very quickly. Adjustment of 80 per cent within a quarter is typical for the industries and time period Hirsch and Lovell studied, and the forecast accuracy implied by these direct results are accordingly lower.

X CONCLUSIONS AND APPRAISAL

We have attempted to develop one approach to the study of inventory behaviour and to discuss some of the empirical results. What conclusions emerge and how can we judge the empirical results obtained?

Because of the difficulties with data any study of inventories is necessarily heroic, and the results must accordingly be treated with some reserve. But within this framework some conclusions do emerge:

(1)   The dominant factor in determining the desired level of inventories is output (or sales);

(2)   Other factors that appear to be important include the cost of holding stocks, or the rate of interest;

(3)   There are time lags in adjusting to the equilibrium – partly these lags arise because of the *costs* of adjustment to this new equilibrium, and partly they arise from the failure of producers' expectations to match their realisations – the precise size of these lags is difficult to determine, and these could be crucial in examining the impact of inventory changes on the rest of the economy; and

(4)   This failure by producers to make perfect forecasts yields unplanned stock changes although adjustment of output within a quarter or a year appears to reduce some of the unplanned effects.

How successful has this approach been? Stekler [26] appraised eleven U.S. studies of the kind described above, and he concluded that all of them yielded superior results to a naive extrapolative procedure in terms of forecasting *real* inventory investment, although they were only a little better than some 'judgemental' forecast, and all were bad at forecasting the change in the *book value* of inventories. This is not strong praise even, simply, in terms of forecasting. How may the position improve in the future?

It could be argued that what is needed is more satisfactory data, particularly in relation to anticipations; certainly this is so for the United Kingdom. But then if we are to treat the world in a complete fashion we need to explain any 'observed' anticipations data. Another possible approach is to see how far cross-section or cross-industry analysis can provide stronger prior information for us to include in the models we have. Certainly without stronger prior beliefs the data currently available are unlikely to yield further insights into the analysis of inventory investment.

Yet, even so, much that has been achieved is doubtful in its validity. How far is it sensible to assume, in a macro system, that output is exogenous of inventory investment? If we look at a reduced form of the whole economic system one suspects that even the meagre advances that have been made will appear diminished.

All this makes the challenge of further work the greater – there is an enormous amount to be done here if we are to have a fuller understanding of the workings of the economic system as a whole.

BIBLIOGRAPHY

[1] M. Abramovitz, *Inventories and Business Cycles*, National Bureau of Economic Research, Studies in Business Cycles, no. 4 (Princeton University Press, 1950).

[2] A. Ando, E. C. Brown, J. Karaken and R. Solow, 'Lags in Fiscal and Monetary Policy' in *Stabilization Policies*, Commission on Money & Credit (Englewood Cliffs, N.J.: Prentice-Hall, 1963).

[3] R. J. Ball and P. S. Drake, 'Stock Adjustment Inventory Models of the U.K. Economy', *Manchester School*, 31 (May 1963) pp. 87–102.

[4] D. A. Belsley, *Industry Production Behaviour: The Order Stock Distinction* (Amsterdam; North-Holland, 1969).

[5] G. L. Childs, *Unfilled Orders and Inventories* (Amsterdam: North-Holland, 1967).

[6] T. J. Courchene, 'Inventory Behaviour and the Stock-Order Distinction', *Canadian Journal of Economics and Political Science*, 33 (Aug 1967) pp. 325–57.

[7] P. G. Darling, 'Manufacturers' Inventory Investment 1947–1958', *American Economic Review*, 49 (Dec 1959) pp. 950–62.

[8] — and M. C. Lovell, 'Factors Influencing Investment in Inventories', in the *Brookings Quarterly Econometric Model of the U.S.*, ed. J. S. Duesenberry *et al.* (Chicago: Rand McNally, 1965).

[9]   —, 'Inventories, Production Smoothing and the Flexible Accelerator', *Quarterly Journal of Economics*, 85 (May 1971) pp. 357–62.

[10] R. Eisner and R. H. Strotz, 'Determinants of Business Investment', in *Impacts of Monetary Policy*, Commission on Money and Credit (Englewood Cliffs, N.J.: Prentice-Hall, 1963).

[11] C. H. Feinstein, 'Stocks, Sales and Stockbuilding', *Times Review of Industry and Technology* (Mar 1963).

[12] G. A. Hay, 'Adjustment Costs and the Flexible Accelerator', *Quarterly Journal of Economics*, 84 (Feb 1970) pp. 140–3.

[13] D. F. Heathfield and I. F. Pearce, 'A View of the Southampton Econometric Model of the U.K. and its Trading Partners', in *Modeling the Economy*, ed. G. A. Renton (London: Heinemann, 1975).

[14] K. Hilton and D. J. Cornelius, 'Planned Stock Holding: Evidence from British Company Data', *Oxford Bulletin of Economics and Statistics*, vol. 56, no. 4 (Nov 1974).

[15] A. A. Hirsch and M. C. Lovell, *Sales Anticipations and Inventory Behaviour* (New York: Wiley, 1969).

[16] J. Johnston, 'An Econometric Study of the Production Decision', *Quarterly Journal of Economics*, 75 (May 1961) pp. 234–61.

[17] M. C. Lovell, 'Manufacturers' Inventories, Sales Expectations and the Acceleration Principle', *Econometrica*, 29 (July 1961) pp. 293–314.

[18] R. P. Mack, *Information, Expectations and Inventory Fluctuations* (New York: Columbia University Press, 1967).

[19] E. S. Mills, *Price Output and Inventory Policy* (New York: Wiley, 1962).

[20] F. Modigliani and O. H. Sauerland, 'Economic Expectations and Plans in Relation to Short Term Forecasting' in *Short-term Economic Forecasting*, National Bureau of Economic Research Studies in Income and Wealth, vol. 17 (Princeton University Press, 1955) pp. 261–351.

[21] M. Nerlove, 'Distributed Lags and Demand Analysis for Agriculture and Other Commodities', *Agricultural Handbook*, 141 (U.S. Department of Agriculture, 1958).

[22] J. W. Nevile, 'Forecasting Inventory Investment', *Economic Record*, 39, 2 (June 1963) pp. 238–42.

[23] —, *Fiscal Policy in Australia: Theory and Practice* (Melbourne: Cheshire, 1975).

[24] D. C. Rowan, *Output, Inflation and Growth* (London: Macmillan, 1968).

[25] T. J. Stanback, *Postwar Cycles in Manufacturers' Inventories* (New York: National Bureau of Economic Research, 1962).

[26] H. O. Stekler, 'Evaluation of Econometric Inventory Forecasts', *Review of Economic and Statistics*, 51, 1 (Feb 1969) pp. 77–83.

[27]   P. K. Trivedi, 'Inventory Behaviour in U.K. Manufacturing 1956–
       1967', *Review of Economic Studies*, 37, 4 (Oct 1970) pp. 517–36.
[28]   —, 'Retail Inventory Investment Behaviour', *Journal of Economet-
       rics*, 1, 1 (Mar 1973) pp. 61–80.
[29]   U.S. Congress Joint Economic Committee, *Inventory Fluctuations
       and Economic Stabilization*, U.S. Congress, 87th Congress, 1st
       Session (1961).

6

Imports and Exports

George McKenzie
University of Southampton

I INTRODUCTION

Over the past thirty years there has developed a large body of empirical work attempting to determine not only which variables influence international trade patterns but also their quantitative impact. The motivation for this work is clear: it is needed to form a basis for forecasting the effects of exchange-rate variations, changes in tariff structures and for tracing the international propagation of business cycles. The emphasis has been placed on determining the role of the international price mechanism on the one hand, and the effect of income changes throughout the world on the other.

Initial interest in this area arose near the end of the Second World War when it became necessary to determine whether exchange rates would have to be realigned during the period of reconstruction. Almost uniformly the studies revealed that trade patterns were highly insensitive to price changes, and therefore it was widely felt that exchange-rate variations would have little influence on the balance of trade. Indeed, it was thought by some that any effect might be perverse. The research which generated this 'elasticity pessimism' is surveyed in a useful article by Cheng [6].

Then, in 1950, Orcutt [17] showed that there were several important statistical reasons why the estimated price elasticities for traded goods might be biased towards zero. The impact of this article – parts of which we shall discuss in this chapter – was to put a damper on quantitative work in the field of international trade. A few brave souls continued to use the procedures criticised by Orcutt, presumably on the grounds that unless sufficient additional data were made available and the requisite statistical procedures became feasible, there was nothing else that could be done.

Work was progressing on the construction of national econometric models in a number of countries. Obviously, these would require equations explaining the level of imports and exports. Then, in 1968, Rhomberg proposed to the Social Science Research Council of the United States that research into the international transmission mechanism be initiated and that a useful procedure would be to link together existing econometric models. The project is now called *Link* (see [3, 20]).

The aim of this chapter is to examine the various approaches that international-trade economists have taken in their quantitative work and the problems they have faced. If there is any one lesson to be learned, it is that econometric work is something of an art, for what is theoretically the most desired approach must often be significantly modified in the light of the limitations of the data or of computational procedures used. Although the topics are obviously closely related, for convenience the chapter will be divided into three parts: data problems, theoretical methodology, and econometric procedures.

II DATA PROBLEMS

In a survey article in 1962, Prais [19] noted that international-trade economists were blessed with an abundance of data, perhaps more than any other area in economics. While his statement is true in *quantitative* terms, it is certainly not the case *qualitatively*. To see what is involved, let us note that there are basically three characteristics to any international-trade flow. First, it may be classified according to commodity or commodity grouping, second, by its place of origin, and third by its destination. If we are concerned with the construction of a multi-country model, all trade data must be calculated on comparable bases and in such a way that they can be related to statistics on domestic output and consumption. In addition, since an important part of the exercise will be to study the influence of price variations on trade flows, individual prices and/or price indices must be calculated according to the same breakdown as the data on trade flows.

Unfortunately, this is not the case. Aggregate data on imports and exports by direction are available. However, the value of imports is calculated so as to include the cost of carriage, insurance and freight (that is c.i.f.) whereas figures on exports do not include these charges. They are said to be calculated on a *free on board* (f.o.b.) basis. As a result U.S. imports from the United Kingdom will not equal U.K. figures for its exports to the United States. Thus adjustments must be made to ensure that imports and exports are measured on comparable bases.

Perhaps even more annoying is the fact that, at the level of commodities or commodity groupings, trade-flow data and import- or export-price indices are calculated on an entirely different basis from domestic-output and domestic-price indices. The trade data are compiled on the basis of the Standard International Trade Classification (S.I.T.C.) whereas domestic-output data are presented according to the Standard Industrial Classification (S.I.C.) scheme. The result is that it is difficult to relate the trade data to domestic supply and demand figures. And, of course, the price of domestic goods cannot be directly related to their counterparts which are imported or exported.

Then there is the problem of aggregation. Even if data are calculated according to the same classificatory scheme there may still be a difficulty. Suppose we are interested in comparing a price index for imports of chemicals from France with one for imports from West Germany. Now suppose that the price of a particular chemical goes up. If imports of this specific commodity from France are relatively small, its weighting in the first index will also be small, and hence the change in the over-all index will be negligible. However, if imports from West Germany are relatively large, this commodity will have a strong influence on the second index. Thus, it will appear as if the price of chemicals imported from West Germany has increased relative to chemical imports from France, even though the prices of individual chemicals are everywhere identical.

Finally, Orcutt has noted that errors in gathering and presenting the data may cause severe problems. In fact he supposed that the magnitude of the errors of observation is as large as the range of relevant price variation present in the statistical studies of import elasticities. Unfortunately, very little is really known about the magnitude or impact of such errors of observation.

III THEORETICAL METHODOLOGY

On the basis of the foregoing information, one might argue that no quantitative work can be undertaken until significant improvements in data availability occur. Alternatively, one can attempt to formulate an approach which utilises the available data to the greatest extent possible, albeit spelling out explicitly the simplifying assumptions underlying that work. In the next two sections we shall examine a number of approaches. However, let us begin with a basic discussion of some of the theoretical issues involved in studying international trade flows.

Consider a model involving only trade in final commodities and concentrating solely on final-equilibrium situations, as shown in Figure 6.1, which depicts the case of a small country engaged in international trade and facing a given terms of trade equal to the slope of *DH*. In terms of commodity prices, this slope equals

$$\frac{P_c}{P_w} = \frac{\text{price of cloth}}{\text{price of wine}}.$$

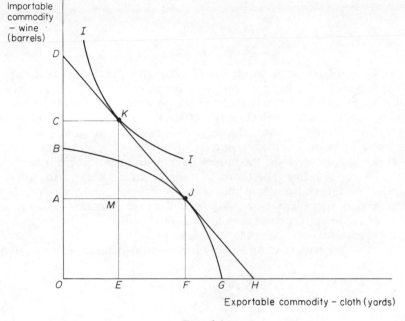

Fig. 6.1

Let us suppose that the preferences of consumers in this country can be aggregated together to obtain a community preference function. Then the indifference curve I determines the consumption pattern of these consumers at the point where it is tangent to the terms of trade line (that is at *K*). Under these circumstances, consumers will purchase *OC* barrels of wine and *OE* bales of cloth.

The terms of trade line is also tangent to the production-possibility frontier *BG* at point *J*, and as a result the pattern of production is *OA* barrels of wine and *OF* bales of cloth. The differences between the demand and supply of the two commodities is settled through international trade: there will be the importation of *AC* barrels of wine and the exportation of *EF* bales of cloth. Since the country is 'small' and faces a given terms of trade determined by the rest of the world, it is able to export any excess supply or import any excess demand without having an effect on those terms of trade.

The first lesson to be learned from this model is that we must be careful to distinguish between imports and importables on the one hand, and exports and exportables on the other. For example, the quantity of imports is the difference between the demand for and supply of importable wine. From consumer theory, we know that the demand for any product generally depends upon total income, Y, its own price and the prices of other commodities, whether they be substitutes or complements.

Thus

$$D_c = D_c(Y, p_w, p_c) \tag{6.1}$$

and

$$D_w = D_w(Y, p_w, p_c), \tag{6.2}$$

where D_c and D_w represents the total demand for the respective goods.

The factors determining supply are a bit more complicated. An examination of Figure 6.1 reveals that the supply of the two goods obviously depends upon relative prices. Given the production-possibility frontier, the higher the price of wine relative to the price of cloth (that is the flatter the terms of trade line) the greater will be the supply of wine and the lower the supply of cloth. Resources have been attracted from the latter to the former industry. The terms of trade is not the only factor affecting output. We must also know the amount of resources available. If we suppose that there are two basic factors of production, land, T, and labour, L, then any increase in their availability will cause the production-possibility frontier to shift out, and vice versa.

Therefore we can write the supply functions associated with our simple country as

$$S_c = S_c(T, L, p_w, p_c) \tag{6.3}$$

and

$$S_w = S_w(T, L, p_w, p_c). \tag{6.4}$$

And, as a result, we would write the import function as

$$M_w = D_w(Y, p_c, p_w) - S_w(T, L, p_c, p_w), \tag{6.5}$$

and the export function as

$$X_c = S_c(T, L, p_w, p_c) - D_c(Y, p_c, p_w). \tag{6.6}$$

Thus, if we are interested in forecasting these trade flows, we would first want to estimate the parameters associated with two demand and two supply functions. Imports and exports are 'residuals' within this system: there are no separate functions specifically explaining the behaviour of imports or exports.

This simple model can, in principle, be extended so as to include more than one country and more than two commodities thus yielding a complete international-trade model. Suppose that there exist n countries which produce and trade in m commodity groups. Then we shall have a total of n times m demand functions, that is

$$D_{ij} = D_{ij}(Y_i, p_1, \ldots, p_m), \qquad i = 1, \ldots, n; j = 1, \ldots, m, \tag{6.7}$$

where D_{ij} represents country i's demand for the jth commodity; and n times m supply functions, that is

$$S_{ij} = S_{ij}(\text{basic immobile factors}, p_1, \ldots, p_m),$$
$$i = 1, \ldots, n; j = 1, \ldots, m, \tag{6.8}$$

where S_{ij} represents country i's supply of the jth commodity; and m balance equations, that is

$$\sum_i D_{ij} = \sum_i S_{ij}, \qquad j = 1, \ldots, m, \tag{6.9}$$

which indicates that world demand for a product equals world supply. The unknowns in this system are the nm quantities demanded, the nm quantities supplied and the m prices. The variables, Y_i, T_i and L_i are treated as exogenous, although equations could be added to explain their behaviour. Thus there are $m(2n+1)$ unknowns. There is an equal number of equations with the result that the model is complete and capable of solution.

One of the implications of the above model is to punch some very serious holes in the underpinnings of previous research. Most of this work has, until recently, been undertaken without any formal, explicit model in mind. Basically, import or export demand functions were viewed as analogous to any commodity demand function. Total income and relative prices were the important determining factors and the functions themselves were assumed to be homogeneous of degree zero. The favourite functional forms were either linear, for example

$$M = a + b\frac{Y}{p_w} + c\frac{p_c}{p_w}, \tag{6.10}$$

or log-linear, for example

$$\log M = d + e \log \frac{Y}{p_w} + f \log \frac{p_c}{p_w}. \tag{6.11}$$

Other variables might be included, such as the degree of capacity utilisation to represent cyclical features. However equations (6.10) and (6.11) formed the basis for most work. A useful discussion of relevant variables appears in Leamer and Stern [13].

If we believe that the world is best described by the first approach discussed above, then the estimation of these forms poses an interesting methodological dilemma. In this case it is not possible to talk in any meaningful way about an elasticity of demand for imports or an elasticity of supply of exports. For example, let us suppose that we are interested in calculating an elasticity of the former type.

The own-price 'elasticity' of demand for imports E_w can be written as

$$E_w = \frac{p_w}{M_w} \frac{dM_w}{dp_w} = \frac{p_w}{M_w} \frac{\partial M_w}{\partial p_w}. \tag{6.12}$$

But, in fact, this is really a hodge-podge of demand and supply elasticities for the importable, since from equation (6.5) we know that

$$dM_w = \frac{\partial D_w}{\partial p_w} dp_w - \frac{\partial S_w}{\partial p_w} dp_w.$$

Therefore

$$E_w = \frac{p_w}{M_w}\left(\frac{\partial D_w}{\partial p_w} - \frac{\partial S_w}{\partial p_w}\right)$$

$$= \frac{D_w S_w}{M_w}\left[\left(\frac{p_w}{D_w}\frac{\partial D_w}{\partial p_w}\right)\frac{1}{S_w} - \left(\frac{p_w}{S_w}\frac{\partial S_w}{\partial p_w}\right)\frac{1}{D_w}\right]$$

$$= \frac{D_w}{M_w}(E_{ww}) - \frac{S_w}{M_w}(S_{ww}), \tag{6.13}$$

where E_{ww} is the elasticity of the demand for wine with respect to the price of wine and S_{ww} is the elasticity of the supply of wine with respect to the price of wine.

Thus, to obtain an accurate formulation of the elasticity of demand for imports, we must, in principle, not only know the two basic elasticities, E_{ww} and S_{ww}, but the level of total demand and supply, D_w and S_w respectively. Discussion of the elasticity of supply of exports is analogous. Performing the same calculations on equation (6.6), we find that this elasticity is a combination of the elasticities of demand and supply exportables.

It is interesting to note that an estimated elasticity of demand for imports should clearly be negative and quite large in value. In fact, in most circumstances, it should be larger than either of the two underlying structural elasticities. The reason for this is as follows. Normally, we would expect $E_{ww} < 0$ and $S_{ww} > 0$. Then if the value of imports is less than either home consumption or production, both elasticities will be multiplied by ratios which are greater than one. To utilise Orcutt's example, suppose that the quantity of imported wine, M_w, equals one-third of domestic supply. Then, since $D_w = S_w + M_w$, we learn that

$$E_w = 4E_{ww} - 3S_{ww}.$$

If E_{ww} equals minus one and S_{ww} is plus one, then the own-price elasticity of demand for imports will be minus seven.

IV SOME PRACTICAL PROBLEMS

So far it has been assumed that all goods are traded and that they are produced and consumed in all countries. In fact, certain importables are not domestically produced – these are often called *non-competing imports*. In addition, certain commodities produced at home may be *non-traded*. A full discussion of which category a particular commodity falls into is beyond the scope of this chapter. Suffice it to say that ultimate trading patterns depend upon the structure of both demand and production in each country. The more similar are countries, the fewer goods will be traded. In the extreme, no trade would occur if all countries were identical – all commodities would be non-traded. On the other hand, the more dissimilar countries are, the greater the opportunities for trade.

Again, in the extreme, if each country only had the productive capacity to produce one commodity specific to that country, and if all goods were demanded throughout the world, all would be traded. In general, the availability of basic factors in each country plays a crucial role in determining where commodities are produced and which are traded. And, of course, factor inputs as well as final commodities may be exchanged internationally. (For a further discussion of these and other important issues, the reader is referred to Pearce [18], especially ch. 12.)

A second problem arises when we attempt to study the determinants of international trade flows utilising aggregative data by commodity grouping. As Rhomberg [20] has noted, the framework outlined above explicitly assumes that a country may *either* import or export a particular commodity, *but not both*. However, in practice, it is the case that a country may import certain types of, say, chemical products and export others. In terms of the previous model, it appears as if the country is importing and exporting the same item, technically an impossibility. It would be possible to calculate the difference between exports and imports of a particular commodity category and then to examine the determinants of this variable. However, the task at hand is to explain gross and not net trade flows.

In an attempt to circumvent this dilemma, Armington [1, 2] has suggested that consumers not only differentiate between commodity categories alone, but also between the products of different regions. Thus pins imported by the United Kingdom from the United States are treated as being different from pins imported from West Germany even though the two are *technically* identical.

This procedure avoids two of the difficulties associated with the first approach. First, it circumvents the issue, raised by Pearce, and Orcutt before him, of whether the elasticities of demand for imports are really demand elasticities at all, but instead hodge-podges of demand and supply effects. Pins, though technically identical, are assumed to be treated by consumers as subjectively different according to their source of origin. Thus, it is as if the United Kingdom specialises in U.K. pins. The demand for French pins is characterised by a separate function. There are no supply effects involved, since the United Kingdom does not produce French pins by definition. Functions for imports and the demand for importables thus coincide. Secondly, this approach means that a country's imports and exports of the same commodity category are treated as being separate commodities.

However, there is a difficulty. While from a subjective point of view goods originating from different countries appear as different, from the technical, supply side they are identical. This is emphasised by the balance relation which indicates that the price of commodity i is determined when total world demand for that good equals world supply. This means that no substitution will be observed between the commodities of the same group but from different sources, not because consumers do not view them differently but because their prices are always identical. There is no mechanism to explain divergences in the price indices for a commodity or commodity grouping between countries. However, as we noted earlier, price indices for the same category do indeed differ between countries. We have noted that this may be due to different weighting schemes. It may also be because the commodities are genuinely different.

Personally, I doubt that consumers would view a commodity from one country as having 'snob' appeal yet an identical article from another as 'inferior'. A more reasonable explanation is that goods from different countries are indeed different. French, Italian or Californian wines all have different, identifiable properties. And the same is true of cars, computers or wheat. Thus it may be a reasonable approximation to assume that countries, in the above sense, completely specialise in production. It is true that we are not dealing with such widely diverse commodity categories as agricultural or manufactured products. But it is impossible to say that a Saab is identical to a Fiat.

Thus if there are basically m goods traded and n regions, each country will have demand schedules for nm 'products' where these items are now differentiated by region. For the entire model there are then n^2m demand functions, that is

$$D_{ij}^k = D_{ij}^k(Y_i, p_1, \ldots, p_m),$$

$$(i = 1, \ldots, n; j = 1, \ldots, m; k = 1, \ldots, n) \quad (6.14)$$

where D_{ij}^k represents country i's demand for commodity j produced in country k.

As in the previous approach we have n times m supply functions, that is

$$S_{ij} = S_{ij}(\text{basic immobile factors}, p_1, \ldots, p_m),$$

$$i = 1, \ldots, n; j = 1, \ldots, m, \quad (6.15)$$

where S_{ij} represents country i's supply of the jth commodity. Previously, however, we treated the summation $\sum S_{ij}$ as equal to the total world output of commodity j. Now every S_{ij} is treated as if it were a different good. Hence we have a set of balance relationships described by the equation,

$$\sum_i D_{ij}^k = S_{kj}, \quad i = 1, \ldots, n; j = 1, \ldots, m; k = 1, \ldots, n. \quad (6.16)$$

This system has two immediate advantages over the Armington approach. First, it offers a clearer economic rationale for distinguishing between commodities. Secondly, equilibrium prices for the nm separate price indices can now be calculated on the basis of the above balance relations. In the previous approach, we had difficulty in explaining the apparent divergent movement of price indices for the same commodity categories but for different countries. Now each index is interpreted as referring to a different commodity.

V CHOOSING A FUNCTIONAL FORM

Having now laid out some theoretical foundations for the study of international trade flows, let us now turn our attention to the choice of functional form. The theory of consumer behaviour for an individual imposes a number of constraints on the form that demand functions may take:

(1)   they must be additive in the sense that the sum of expenditure on each individual commodity must equal total expenditure;
(2)   they must be homogeneous of degree zero – a proportionate increase in prices and income does not affect the quantities demanded; and
(3)   they must also satisfy the so-called Slutsky equations – that is, they must be derivable from a preference system.

It is therefore of some interest to enquire whether the linear or logarithmic forms that have been used in the past satisfy some or all of these constraints. First, consider the linear form,

$$X_i = b_i \frac{Y}{p_i} + \sum_j a_{ij} \frac{p_j}{p_i}, \qquad i = 1, \ldots, n, \tag{6.17}$$

which can be expressed in the form of a linear expenditure system as

$$p_i X_i = b_i Y + \sum_j a_{ij} p_j, \qquad i = 1, \ldots, n. \tag{6.18}$$

First of all, we immediately see that equation (6.17) is homogeneous of degree zero. For additivity to occur, it appears that several restrictions must be imposed. First, $\sum_i b_i$ must equal one and the $\sum_i a_{ij}$ must equal zero for every j. This ensures that $\sum p_i X_i = Y$ for all possible levels of price and income. Secondly, the own price must always appear in the denominator of equation (6.17). Otherwise, it will not, in general, form an expenditure system such that the sum of spending on each commodity equals total spending.

Now let us turn to the additivity and homogeneity properties of the log-linear form. We have

$$\log X_i = b_i \log \frac{Y}{P_i} + \sum_j \gamma_{ij} \log \frac{P_j}{P_i}. \tag{6.19}$$

It is immediately obvious that this relationship is homogeneous of degree zero. However, it is not so clear what it takes to guarantee the additivity constraint. Let us rewrite equation (6.19) as

$$X_i = \left(\frac{Y}{P_i}\right)^{b_i} \prod_j \left(\frac{P_j}{P_i}\right)^{\gamma_{ij}}. \tag{6.20}$$

Thus each γ_{ij} must equal zero and all the b_i must equal one. This, of course, is highly restrictive. It means that forms such as (6.19) should not, in general, be estimated. Even if we do restrict the γ_{ij}, unitary b_i's imply that expenditure elasticities are everywhere one.

The third constraint is a bit more difficult to examine. Basically it's purpose is to generate a symmetric set of elasticities of substitution between various pairs of commodities. Klein and Rubin [12] were the first to discover the constraints on the linear expenditure system, but these have never been applied in an international-trade context. However, very early on, researchers in this field did attempt to directly estimate elasticities of substitution. One of the best examples of this work is a paper by Harberger [8]. Armington [1, 2] has recently set out a scheme making use of this approach and his work in turn has been extended within the *Link* project [5]. To appreciate what is involved consider Figure 6.2 where the indifference curve of Figure 6.1 has been redrawn. The elasticity of substitution in demand between the importable commodity wine and the exportable commodity cloth is defined as the percentage change in the ratio of consumptions X_w/X_c when there is a percentage change in relative prices, or, in algebraic terms,

$$\frac{d(X_w/X_c)/(X_w/X_c)}{d(P_c/P_w)/(P_c/P_w)}.$$ (6.21)

Now if we could describe consumer behaviour by the equation,

$$\log\left(\frac{X_w}{X_c}\right) = a + b \log\left(\frac{P_c}{P_w}\right),$$ (6.22)

it is easily determined that b is the elasticity of substitution. Although this form has been widely used in econometric work to estimate this parameter, it is none the less important to ask whether it is really a viable approach (Morrissett [16]).

Suppose that the underlying preference function of consumers is

$$U = a_1\left(\frac{Y}{p_1}\right)^{b_1} + a_2\left(\frac{Y}{p_2}\right)^{b_2}.$$ (6.23)

The a_i and b_i are parameters and the function itself is known as the indirect addilog [9]. If we maximise (6.23) subject to the budget constraint, $Y = p_1 X_1 + p_2 X_2$, we obtain

$$\log X_1 - \log X_2 = \log\left(\frac{a_1 b_1}{a_2 b_2}\right) + (1+b_1) \log\left(\frac{Y}{p_1}\right) - (1+b_2) \log\left(\frac{Y}{p_2}\right),$$

or $$\log\left(\frac{X_1}{X_2}\right) = A + (b_1 - b_2) \log Y - (1+b_1) \log p_2 + (1+b_2) \log p_1,$$

which in turn equals

$$\log\left(\frac{X_1}{X_2}\right) = A + (b_1 - b_2) \log Y + (1+b_1) \log\left(\frac{p_1}{p_2}\right) + (b_2 - b_1) \log p_1.$$ (6.24)

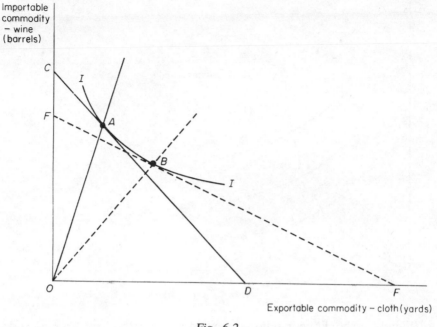

Fig. 6.2

The only way that this equation will collapse into the form which is estimated – (6.22) – is if $b_1 = b_2$. Then we obtain

$$\log \left(\frac{X_1}{X_2} \right) = A + (1 + b_1) \log \left(\frac{p_1}{p_2} \right). \tag{6.25}$$

For this form to be acceptable then, we must be willing to test the maintained hypothesis (that is that $b_1 = b_2$).

The implications of equation (6.24) can be seen from Figure 6.3. Suppose that b_1 is greater than b_2 and that prices are constant but that income changes so that we move from A to B. As a result the ratio of X_1 to X_2 increases. Thus the income expansion path curves upwards. If b_1 was equal to b_2, an increase in income would have no effect on the ratio of importables to exportables and the income expansion path would be a straight line through the origin.

Now suppose that income is constant but that prices of both commodities decrease in the same proportion so that we move from B to C. Thus if b_1 equals b_2, the ratio of the two commodities does not vary but if b_1 is less than b_2, the last term on the right-hand side will have a positive effect on the ratio as indicated. The problem is that, in general, the elasticity of substitution will not be a constant as in equation (6.25) but indeed a variable depending on the level of income as well as on the level of prices.

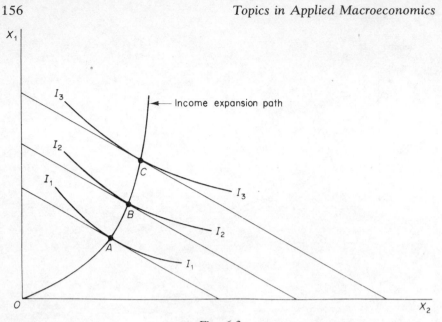

Fig. 6.3

Finally, it should be noted that while our discussion here has proceeded in terms of an elasticity of substitution between importables and exportables, actual empirical work involves data on imports. As a result the 'elasticities' will again be hodge-podges of demand and supply effects, and thus of little significance; an interesting but unfortunately useless approach which has received too much attention.

Dynamic Considerations

So far we have been concerned with describing situations which are in *full equilibrium*. However, in actual practice market demand and market supply will not always equal each other. And it may appear as if demand and supply respond to price and/or income variations only with a lag. Junz and Rhomberg [11] argue that such lags may be decomposed into five elements:

(1)   a *recognition lag* – the time it takes for buyers and sellers to become aware of changed competitive situations;
(2)   a *decision lag* – the time it takes for new business connections to be formed and new orders to be placed;
(3)   a *delivery lag* – published trade flows occur only when goods are delivered, months and perhaps years after the orders were placed;
(4)   a *replacement lag* – in certain circumstances, additional materials and equipment may not be purchased until existing stocks are used up or worn out; and
(5)   a *production lag* – producers must be convinced that current changes

in prices and/or sales are permanent and large enough before they will be willing to commit themselves to an expansion in productive capacity.

To determine the possible extent of such lags Junz and Rhomberg regressed percentage changes in market shares for thirteen exporting countries over the period 1958–69 against changes in relative prices. Their results, statistically significant, indicate that responses in trade flows to relative price changes stretch over four to five years.

An interesting procedure for studying the responsiveness of trade flows over time forms an important part of the Southampton econometric model of the United Kingdom (cf. Pearce [18]). Consider the following reasoning. Rather than immediately vary prices so as to clear a market, suppliers may decide to add to (or draw down) their inventories if supply is greater than market demand (and vice versa). Thus, in calculating the total demand for any product at any period of time, we must consider stock as well as market demand. Hence total excess demand for commodity i by country j, Z_{ij} equals

$$D_{ij} + \Sigma_{ij} - S_{ij}, \qquad (2.26)$$

where Σ_{ij} represents i's net inventory accumulation of commodity j.

If we explain each of the components of expression (2.26) there is no need to provide additional equations describing exports and imports. As was discussed in Section III, where we implicitly assumed that Σ_{ij} equalled zero, these variables are residuals determined by the rest of the model. However, it is also true that if we explain imports and exports as well as D_{ij} and S_{ij}, then inventory changes can be treated as residuals. To accomplish this, Pearce suggests estimating functions which describe the behaviour of foreign traders – a novel approach. For example, consider the following equation explaining imports:

$$M_{ij} = M_{ij}(V_{ij}, D_{ij} + \Sigma_{ij}^p - S_{ij}), \qquad (2.27)$$

where Σ_{ij}^p represents planned inventory change (cf. Chapter 5) and V_{ij} is the ratio of home to foreign prices for this particular commodity classification.

The interpretation of this relationship is as follows. First, when prices abroad are less than prices at home, there will be abnormal profits, and importers will tend to increase their purchases abroad. Secondly, even if there are no abnormal profits, imports will not necessarily equal actual excess demand if (a) planned and actual excess demand are not equal, and (b) if there is a non-zero inventory demand on the part of importers. In the above formulation, the latter consideration does not enter in, since it is assumed that only producers hold inventories.

VI ECONOMETRIC PROBLEMS

As noted in Chapter 1 applied econometric research faces a number of difficulties, and quantitative work in international trade is no exception.

Although the problems in this area are similar to those faced by others, some of the proposed solutions are specific to international-trade situations and thus they must be discussed in their own right. It is interesting to note that the problems raised by Orcutt in the 1950s still exist. Although considerable amount of estimation work has been undertaken, no concerted effort has been made to examine the importance of Orcutt's points. Let us now turn to these, singling out two arguments for specific attention: (1) simultaneous-equation bias; and (2) bias due to aggregation.

A.   *Simultaneous-Equation Bias*

In Section III above it was pointed out that an estimated import (or export) demand elasticity could very well represent a hodge-podge of the demand and supply elasticities for importable (or exportable) commodities. There is a separate, statistical problem, which arises irrespective of whether our *a priori* specification is based on the first approach mentioned (pp. 148–9) or the other two versions. When we estimate a demand function for a traded commodity we must also take into account the existence of a supply function. First, we must check to see whether the equation in which we are interested can be identified (see Chapter 1). Secondly, we must take into account the possibility of simultaneous-equation bias.

To see what is involved, consider Orcutt's diagram as depicted in Figure 6.4. Here we plot the variations in quantity demanded due to price variations, on the one hand, and the variations in quantity supplied, also

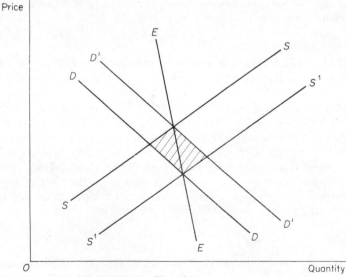

Fig. 6.4

due to price changes, on the other. Now our statistical specification for both demand and supply functions involves a random element which causes both relations to move about. In Figure 6.4 we assume that due to these random fluctuations the demand schedule shifts about between *DD* and *D'D'* and that the supply schedule varies between *SS* and S^1S^1. Let us also assume for the moment that the error terms for the demand and supply functions are distributed independently.

Now the points that are actually observed lie within the shaded parallelogram with the result that the fitted demand relationship between price and quantity will be *EE*. That is, it will appear as if the responsiveness of the quantity demanded to price changes is less than is actually the case. This point can be emphasised by considering a case where the random fluctuations in the supply relation are so small as to be negligible. In that case all the observed points would lie along S^1S^1, meaning that the price elasticity of demand for this traded commodity would be positive!

In more technical terms, what has happened is that one of the assumptions involved in the use of ordinary least-squares regression techniques has been violated. Every time there is a positive error term there is an upward shift in the *DD* schedule and this will generate a higher price. Similarly, a negative error term will yield a lower price. In other words, there will be a positive correlation between the error and one of the independent variables. But this violates one of the assumptions of the Gauss–Markov theorem. Hence the ordinary least-squares estimator is biased.

Several approaches to the solution of this problem of bias have been suggested. The most obvious is the use of simultaneous-equation procedures such as two-stage least squares or limited-information maximum likelihood. However, our criteria for evaluation are somewhat changed since these procedures can be considered to yield estimators which are unbiased asymptotically, that is only for large samples. In addition, if the entire model (of which the demand function of interest is but a part) involves more predetermined variables than there are observations on each variable, there are insufficient degrees of freedom to proceed.

It is perhaps for these reasons that there are relatively few simultaneous-equation studies involving traded commodities. In an oft-quoted work, Morgan and Corlett [15] estimated demand and supply relationships using both ordinary least squares and the limited-information maximum-likelihood procedure, and were unable to obtain satisfactory results in either case. That was in 1951, and very little has been done since to examine the importance of this problem.

In contrast, most economists have been concerned with looking for possible justifications for using the computationally simpler ordinary least squares. Rhomberg and Boisseneault [21] have taken the position that ordinary least squares may actually generate more accurate elasticities of demand than a simultaneous-equation procedure. They argue that ordinary least squares may yield results 'which, though biased, have a smaller variance around their (biased) expected value than some of the principal alternative estimation methods'. There are several difficulties with this reasoning. First, there is no particular *a priori* reasoning why the ordinary least-squares estimator should have a smaller variance; it could just as well be larger. Secondly, what exactly does a smaller variance mean if the estimator is highly inaccurate? If our concern is with forecasting, then biased estimates will also yield biased forecasts. Surely this is unsatisfactory.

There are, however, alternative arguments which might be used more successfully to justify the use of single-equation procedures. If the variations in the error term associated with the demand function are small compared to the variations in the supply schedule, then the slope of the estimated *EE* schedule in Figure 6.4 will be closer to the slope of the true relationship. In other words, the shifting supply schedule will trace out an 'almost unbiased' demand schedule.

Alternatively, if one could justify the assumption that the country under study were a price-taker in some sense then ordinary least squares would not yield biased results. In other words, if the price level could be considered a predetermined, rather than an endogenous variable, the simultaneous-equation problem could be assumed away. Two justifications are often suggested. First, if the country being studied is relatively small, then it may be thought of as a price-taker unable to influence events abroad. Unfortunately, this assumption has been applied to large and small countries alike, usually with no attempt to justify this maintained hypothesis. However, Houthakker and Magee [10] note that estimated supply functions appeared to be reasonably elastic for a number of countries. Unfortunately, they do not present their results nor do they indicate the differences in estimated demand parameters when estimated by ordinary least squares and a simultaneous-equation procedure.

Another approach, which enables prices to be treated as predetermined, is to assume that the entire model under consideration is recursive. There are very few activities in the real world where cause and effect occur simultaneously. As noted earlier, a change in a price does not usually lead consumers to adjust their buying patterns immediately. An alteration may not occur until at least the next period; and so forth for all economic units. The implication is that we can treat today's price as being inherited from economic activity in the past. Thus consumers act as price-takers for the current period and the price level can be treated as a predetermined variable. There are two important caveats to this argument, however. If the error term belonging to the demand function exhibits the property of auto-correlation then the estimated parameters will still be biased. Auto-correlation means that an endogenous variable – in this case the demand for a traded commodity – is affected not only by a contemporaneous error term, but also the error(s) for the previous period(s). Thus consider the impact of a positive error term in period $t-1$. This will increase the quantity demanded. The market price has been inherited from the previous period so this variable will have no direct impact. However, the interrelation of demand and supply during period $t-1$ will determine the market price for the subsequent period, t. Thus demand at period t will be related to an unexplained term which consists in part of the error associated with period $t-1$ and an increase in price also associated with that error. A predetermined variable and the unexplained term are thus correlated and the estimated parameters will be biased. Secondly, although economic activity itself may be recursive, most data are collected at discrete intervals; yearly, quarterly, sometimes monthly, and only rarely at weekly intervals. The implication is that the period of observation may be too long to pick up the recursive behaviour. It will indeed appear as if everyone is acting simultaneously and hence the appropriate statistical procedures must be used. For an extensive discussion of the estimation problems posed by systems of equations, see Fisher [7].

Finally, brief mention should be made of what happens when the error terms associated with the supply and demand schedules *are* correlated. Both Orcutt [17] and Liu [14] thought that this possibility was strong, though for different reasons. In such cases two-stage least squares and limited-information maximum liklihood are no longer asymptotically the best estimators and instead three-stage least squares or full-information maximum likelihood techniques are warranted. However, the loss of degrees of freedom is quite severe, particularly when the model being considered is bound to be quite large. To my knowledge, no attempts have been made to estimate systems of demand equations for traded goods using such a procedure.

B. *Bias Due to Aggregation*

At several points above, we have alluded to difficulties involved in the use of index numbers. With regard to the price elasticities being estimated, they may also cause difficulties. Consider the following example: a price index involving two commodities is constructed. One has a very low price elasticity of demand but not much of it is consumed, that is its weight is relatively low. The other commodity has a high price elasticity and its weight is relatively high. However, the variation of prices of goods with low elasticities is usually very great, and hence such movements will tend to dominate the index, even though the weight given to such prices is relatively low. At the same time, the variations in the quantities of the two commodities demanded will not be very great. In the one case because its elasticity of demand is low; in the other case because the price variation involved is relatively small. As a result, the estimated demand elasticity will also be small.

Whether such bias due to aggregation is common is still a matter for conjecture. In one study [19], Prais disaggregated U.S. imports into five major commodity groups and estimated the appropriate parameters. Finished manufacturers exhibited the highest elasticity, whereas crude materials possessed the lowest. The weighted average of the separately

estimated elasticities was −1·6 and this was exactly the value obtained
using aggregate price and quantity data. Ball and Marwah [4] also
concluded that little is lost by working with an aggregate relationship for
imports. In contrast, however, a more recent study by Barker [5] has
shown that 'relative price effects measured in an aggregate function are
both much smaller and less significant than those measured in disaggregated ones'. Obviously, the size of the bias will differ according to
circumstances. The answer then must be that if data are available and
there is sufficient time to process them, then estimate the appropriate
parameters on a disaggregated basis.

VII CONCLUSIONS

In their recent survey volume, *Quantitative International Economics*,
Leamer and Stern concluded that 'Orcutt's reservations about least
squares procedure are not quite as devastating as they may appear' ([13]
p. 34). First, lagged variables can be incorporated into any function
relating to a traded good, thereby enabling short-run and long-run
elasticities to be distinguished. Secondly, work has shown that, often,
over-all aggregate price elasticities may be the same as an average of
elasticities obtained from disaggregated data. Thirdly, there are a number
of *a priori* arguments that one can use to justify ordinary least-squares as
opposed to simultaneous-equation methods.

As far as results are concerned, future research would seem to hold the
key. It is indeed the case that recent work is not capable of generating the
'elasticity pessimism' that earlier work produced. However, current research is far from convincing. Houthakker and Magee [10] show many
price coefficients to be small or insignificant. However, ordinary least
squares procedures are used, and the basic methodology is open to
question on the grounds raised in this chapter. More research is certainly
warranted into the reasons for incorporating lags, and into the nature of
the particular adjustment process involved. As noted earlier, the work of
Junz and Rhomberg [11] suggests lags of considerable length. The importance of the aggregation problem may vary from case to case. We shall
never know just *how important* unless disaggregated data are used in every
instance. And the same argument could be applied to the estimation
procedures chosen. It is necessary to test whether a particular *a priori*
belief is indeed consistent with the data and this inevitably involves using
simultaneous-equation procedures.

BIBLIOGRAPHY

[1] P. S. Armington, 'A Theory of Demand for Products Distinguished
     by Place of Production', *International Monetary Fund Staff Papers*
     (Mar 1969) pp. 159–76.
[2] —, 'The Geographic Pattern of Trade and the Effects of Price
     Changes', *International Monetary Fund Staff Papers* (July 1969) pp.
     179–201.

[3] R. J. Ball (ed.), *The International Linkage of National Economic Models* (Amsterdam: North-Holland, 1973).

[4] — and K. Marwah, 'The U.S. Demand for Imports, 1948–1958', *Review of Economics and Statistics* (Nov 1962) pp. 395–401.

[5] T. S. Barker, 'Aggregation Error and Estimates of the U.K. Import Demand Function', in *The Econometric Study of the United Kingdom*, ed. K. Hilton and D. Heathfield (London: MacMillan, 1970).

[6] H. S. Cheng, 'Statistical Estimates of Elasticities and Propensities in International Trade: A Survey of Published Studies', *International Monetary Fund Staff Papers* (Aug 1959) pp. 107–58.

[7] F. M. Fisher, 'Dynamic Structure and Estimation in Economy-Wide Econometric Models', in the *Brookings Quarterly Econometric Model of the United States*, ed. J. Duesenberry *et al.* (Chicago: Rand McNally, 1965).

[8] A. C. Harberger, 'Some Evidence on the International Price Mechanism', *Journal of Political Economy* (Dec 1957) pp. 506–21.

[9] H. S. Houthakker, 'Additive Preferences', *Econometrica* (Apr 1960) pp. 244–57.

[10] — and S. P. Magee, 'Income and Price Elasticities in World Trade', *Review of Economics and Statistics* (May 1969) pp. 111–25.

[11] H. Junz and R. Rhomberg, 'Price Competitiveness in Export Trade Among Industrial Countries', *American Economic Review* (May 1973) pp. 63, 412–18.

[12] L. R. Klein and H. Rubin, 'A Constant Utility Index of the Cost of Living', *Review of Economic Studies*, no. 2 (1948) pp. 84–7.

[13] E. E. Leamer and R. M. Stern, *Quantitative International Economics* (Boston: Allyn & Bacon, 1970).

[14] T. C. Liu, 'The Elasticity of United States Import Demand: A Theoretical and Empirical Reappraisal', *International Monetary Fund Staff Papers* (1954).

[15] D. J. Morgan and W. J. Corlett, 'The Influence of Price in International Trade: A Study in Method', *Journal of the Royal Statistical Society*, Series A, Part III (1951) pp. 307–58.

[16] L. Morissett, 'Some Recent Uses of Elasticity of Substitution – A Survey', *Econometrica* (Jan 1953) pp. 41–62.

[17] G. H. Orcutt, 'Measurement of Price Elasticities in International Trade', *Review of Economics and Statistics* (May 1950) pp. 117–32.

[18] I. F. Pearce, *International Trade* (London: Macmillan, 1970) vol. II, ch. 19.

[19] S. J. Prais, 'Econometric Research in International Trade: A Review', *Kyklos*, fasc. 3 (1962) pp. 560–79.

[20] R. R. Rhomberg, 'Toward a General Trade Model' in [3] pp. 9–20.

[21] — and L. Boisseneault, 'Effects of Income and Price Changes on the U.S. Balance of Payments', *International Monetary Fund Staff Papers* (Mar 1964) pp. 59–124.

7

Consumption Functions

M. C. Timbrell
University of Southampton

I INTRODUCTION

We start our analysis of consumption by separating the problem into two distinct parts, distinguishing between the purchase of consumer durables and that of other, non-durable, goods and services. In purchasing a consumer durable a decision has been taken, not about present consumption, but about a flow of consumption services which that good will provide in the future. Similarly, the consumption of a durable good, that is the actual use of the service which the good provides, does not entail any contemporaneous expenditure. It is this divorce of the expenditure decisions from consumption decisions which sets the consumer-durable good apart from other goods and services.

In practice, this distinction is not as clear cut as it sounds. The accounting definitions used to separate these categories must be rather arbitrary. For example, certain types of footwear and household textiles clearly have elements of a durable nature yet are usually classified as non-durables. We shall follow the standard procedure and assume that the effect of these 'border-line' items upon the empirical results is insignificant. A more difficult problem is provided by the flow of consumption services from the existing stock of durable goods since this flow is unobservable. Were we able to estimate this flow we could add it to the total current consumption. One possibility is to assume that this current flow is a constant proportion of existing durable-good stocks. But the problem does not end there. Consider an individual with £100 to spend. We offer him the choice of buying a television set with a guaranteed life of five years or of investing his £100 at a fixed rate of interest such that over the next five years he could consume it at the rate of £26 per year. This sum just enables him to rent a television set. Whichever decision he makes, his consumption is the same, and so we would like the consumption function to reflect that fact. In the case of renting the set he has increased both consumption and income by £26 per year, and hence to deal properly with consumer durables in an aggregate consumption function we would have to allow for, not only the depreciation of the good, but also the implicit rate of interest payments. Furthermore, we should need to modify his measured income to allow for the implicit returns to ownership of the good just as in the case of buying bonds.

This is an oversimplification of the problem but it highlights the problems associated with constructing a true aggregate consumption function. A simpler approach, and that which is adopted here, is to separate out durable goods and estimate two distinct types of consumption function – one for non-durables and services, the other for durables. Most applied work has, explicitly or implicitly, concentrated on the former and the balance of this chapter will reflect this emphasis. We shall, however, return to the discussion of durable goods in the final section.

II NON-DURABLE GOODS AND SERVICES

The consumption function originates from Keynes's treatise of the 1930s, and in its simplest form may be represented as

$$C = f(Y). \tag{7.1}$$

Keynes then went on to argue that the marginal propensity to consume lies between zero and unity and that it will be less in the short run than in the long run, that is

$$0 < \frac{dC}{dY} < 1. \tag{7.2}$$

It is further postulated that the income elasticity of consumption is similarly bounded, that is

$$0 < \frac{d \log C}{d \log Y} = \frac{Y}{C} \frac{dC}{dY} < 1. \tag{7.3}$$

This specification leaves unanswered many problems of definition, aside from that outlined in the introduction. Closer inspection of Keynes's writing reveals that the correct income variable is personal disposable income and that we are concerned with real rather than monetary (nominal) magnitudes. In principle we could use nominal values and test for money illusion rather than assuming its absence, but multi-collinearity problems tend to obscure any conclusions. In contrast to most authors, Branson and Klevorick [6] conclude that consumers do suffer from a degree of money illusion in the short run. They argue that, since using either constant or current prices engenders mis-specification, the appropriate form is that which causes the lesser bias – which depends upon the extent of money illusion. A theoretically different reason for using current prices is provided by Duesenberry [11]. His justification is that price changes reflect quality changes. Inasmuch as this is the case, then an increase in nominal consumption expenditure is a change in real consumption. A more satisfactory approach to this problem would be to use a quality adjusted price deflator, and the retail price indices in the United Kingdom and the United States do try to allow for quality changes. There is also the question as to the actual deflator(s) that is (are) appropriate. This is discussed at length by Evans [12].

Keynes's justification of his theory is explicitly in terms of individuals' behaviour patterns and we require some further assumptions before we can interpret equations (7.1)–(7.3) as a theory of aggregate consumption. Theil [30] provides a systematic treatment of the effects of aggregation but the problems are considerable and rarely faced up to. The usual procedure is to specify the function in its simplest (linear) form and sum over all individuals giving

$$\sum_i^{N_t} C_{it} = \sum_i^{N_t} \alpha_i + \sum_i^{N_t} \beta_i Y_{it} + \sum_i^{N_t} U_{it}, \tag{7.4}$$

where N_t is population in time t, and U_{it} is the usual disturbance term. To turn this into a readily estimable form we require to assume either that the parameter β_i is the same for all individuals, or that each individual's income is a constant linear function of total income, that is

$$Y_{it} = \gamma_i + \delta \sum_{i=1}^{N_t} Y_{it}.$$

In addition we either require the population, N_t, to be fixed over time, or we can follow the more usual practice of dividing through by the population to arrive at a function specified in *per capita* terms, that is

$$\frac{C_t}{N_t} = \alpha + \beta \frac{Y_t}{N_t} + \frac{\sum_i^{N_t} U_{it}}{N_t}. \tag{7.5}$$

The assumptions that are made about the individual disturbance terms plus the assumption about the aggregation procedure will determine the nature of the aggregate disturbance term. In our simple case, if we make the usual assumptions about the original disturbances (i.e. zero mean, constant variance and no serial dependence), then the properties survive the aggregation. In more general circumstances this is not necessarily the case. Allowing the population to vary requires that we impose the further assumption that the variance be constant across individuals as well as over time.

All the problems considered so far are common to all the empirical work on the consumption function. We shall assume that it is possible to derive a meaningful aggregate consumption function of the form,

$$C_t = \alpha + \beta Y_t + U_t, \tag{7.6}$$

where the variables are in real terms and Y_t refers to personal disposable income. This hypothesis is known as the absolute-income hypothesis (A.I.H.).

A. The Case Against

Standard Keynesian doctrine was first challenged shortly after the Second World War. A number of variants of the simple absolute-income hypothesis were estimated using various sources of data and the results were far from encouraging and the forecasts very poor. Davis [10] analysed the predictive ability of a number of these consumption functions fitted to U.S. data (1929–40). R^2 were found to be high but so too were prediction errors. Specifically, the models under-predicted the level of consumption that pertained in the post-war period, suggesting strongly that either the models were mis-specified or that the underlying relationship had changed.

Earlier work by Brady and Friedman [5] on household-budget data demonstrated that, although the consumption function had a positive intercept, and hence the marginal propensity to consume (m.p.c.) was less than the average propensity (a.p.c.), the intercept shifted upwards over time. In one respect at least, this result is a red herring. The consumption-function theory as developed by Keynes is a theory about *changes* in consumption consequent upon *changes* in the level of income, whereas budget studies show the way in which consumption *differs* as income *differs* at a point in time. While it is aesthetically appealing to have one theory to explain both sets of data it is not prerequisite. In this respect Johnson's [19] defence of Keynes is misplaced. For Keynes the relevant consumption function is the short-run function estimated from *time-series* data. Previously Smithies [28] had used a time trend to capture a ratchet-like effect in his analysis of annual time-series data but the most important results were produced by Kuznets [22] a subset of which are reproduced in Table 7.1. Kuznets demonstrates that over fairly long periods the a.p.c. was high and stable, while the m.p.c. was lower than the average, lower in the short than the long run and tended to fluctuate in value, particularly during the war years. Clearly the absolute-income hypothesis, as it stood, was incapable of explaining the apparent contradictions.

One possible source of explanation was the estimation technique. Keynes's system had a second equation, or rather identify, of the form

$$Y_t \equiv C_t + A_t, \tag{7.7}$$

and it is easy to show that using ordinary least squares (O.L.S.) on the

TABLE 7.1
Estimates of average and marginal propensities

Period	C/Y	$\Delta C/\Delta Y$
1897–1906	0·89	0·72
1907–16	0·89	0·65
1919–29	0·88	0·60
1929–41	0·94	0·45
1897–1949 excluding war years	0·90	0·82
1897–1949 including war years	0·88	0·70

Source: U.S. National Income data in Kuznets [22].

structural equation will give rise to simultaneous-equation bias. Furthermore, if the underlying m.p.c. is stable, the O.L.S. estimate of β in equation (7.6) may nevertheless fluctuate. Important though this is, it does not rescue the A.I.H. Haavelmo [16] calculated the O.L.S. estimate, $\hat{\beta} = 0·732$, whereas, using an appropriate technique which provides a biased but consistent estimator (indirect least squares), $b = 0·672$. The problem however was that post-war predictions had been too low rather than too high and we must look elsewhere for a solution.

On a theoretical level the objection to the 'Keynesian' function is that it does not accord with what orthodox microeconomics would have you believe. We shall return to this point shortly.

B.   *Relative-Income Hypothesis*

The first attempt at modifying the theory has its roots in the work of Brady and Friedman [5] but the fullest exposition was provided by Duesenberry [11]. In this, and all subsequent work, we start from a consumption decision derived from a utility-maximisation procedure. Duesenberry argues that an individual's utility function cannot be taken as fixed. Specifically he argues that, at any moment in time, it will be determined by social conditions. (In other words, an individual's utility is not independent of the consumption of other individuals and hence of their utility functions. Under these circumstances the utility functions are said to be interdependent.) Also the utility function will change over time as the individual 'learns' new patterns of consumption. The result of the maximisation process is to produce a consumption function involving current income, current assets, expected future income and current consumption by other people. A comparative-static analysis shows that a change in aggregate income, *ceteris paribus*, leaves the aggregate savings (consumption) ratio unchanged, and so we have a proportional long-run consumption function. From the discussion of interdependent utility functions comes the conclusion that an individual with a high income relative to the norm will have a higher savings ratio than those towards the lower end of the income scale – this accounts for the 'flat' consumption functions estimated from cross-sectional data. Suppose that each individual function may be expressed as

$$\frac{C_{it}}{Y_{it}} = \alpha_0 + \alpha_1 \frac{\bar{Y}_t}{Y_{it}},$$

where $\bar{Y}_t$ denotes mean income level. Then we may write $C_{it} = \alpha_0 Y_{it} + \alpha_1 \bar{Y}_t$ and at any point in time there is a postive intercept, $\alpha_1 \bar{Y}_t$. This implies that high-income individuals will have higher saving ratios. Aggregating we have $C_t = (\alpha_0 + \alpha_1) Y_t$. The m.p.c. is $(\alpha_0 + \alpha_1)$ which is greater than that found in cross-section analysis and the lack of an intercept term gives consumption a constant share of income as income rises.

In order to explain the behaviour of the 'short-run' consumption function Duesenberry appeals to dynamic behaviour, utilising his concept of 'learning'. Under the A.I.H. the fall in income faced by an individual at a time of recession would lead him to reduce consumption. Duesenberry suggests that the influence of habit and the desire to maintain living standards will lead consumers to offset this *temporary* loss of income by consuming out of accumulated savings. He concludes that the past level of income (consumption) is an important determinant of current consumption. In particular he stresses the value of income at the previous cyclical peak. Duesenberry's estimating equation is

$$\frac{S_t}{Y_t} = \alpha_0 + \alpha_1 \frac{Y_t}{Y_0} + u_t, \tag{7.8}$$

where Y_0 is previous peak income.

Using U.S. annual data (we shall assume it is *per capita* and deflated unless otherwise stated) from 1929 to 1940 he estimates $\hat{\alpha}_0 = -0.196$ and $\hat{\alpha}_1 = 0.25$ with $R^2 = 0.81$. Assuming a growth rate of 3 per cent this generates a savings ratio of approximately 6 per cent which is quite consistent with Kuznets's data. With income falling the short-run m.p.c. is shown to be approximately 0.69 which is once again consistent with Kuznets's data. The short-run implications are more easily seen by reference to the model that Modigliani [24] used. His estimated form is

$$\frac{S_t}{Y_t} = \alpha_0 + \alpha_1 \frac{(Y_t - Y_0)}{Y_t}. \tag{7.9}$$

Rearranging this to the more standard form,

$$C_t = (1 - \alpha_0 - \alpha_1) Y_t + \alpha_1 Y_0, \tag{7.9a}$$

gives a positive intercept and, on Modigliani's estimates, a m.p.c. of 0.777. Rearrange as

$$C_t = (1 - \alpha_0) Y_t - \alpha_1 (Y_t - Y_0), \tag{7.9b}$$

and we have a long-run m.p.c. of 0.902 (Modigliani's estimates). Diagrammatically the path of consumption is given in Figure 7.1. As income

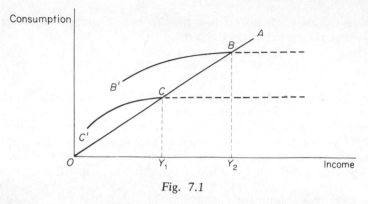

Fig. 7.1

increases consumption expands along *OA*. At some point, *C*, the income level begins to fall but consumption patterns are determined in part by the previous peak income, Y_1, and contraction of consumption is along the path of the short-run function *CC'*. When income rises again consumption will expand back along *C'C* until it reaches the previous peak at *C* and then resumes its path along *OA*. (A similar process could occur at Y_2.) The result is a ratchet-like progress.

Appealing as the theories are, problems do remain. The most important relates to the microeconomic foundation. If we accept the interdependence assumptions then we have a completely different model of consumer behaviour than that which underlies standard Hicksian demand analysis. The theory also predicts an asymmetry in behaviour that worried some authors. Brown [8] argues that the effects of past habits are continuous in both directions and substituted previous period consumption for previous peak income. The addition of the lagged dependent variable gives a consumption function of the form

$$C_t = \alpha + \beta_1 Y_t + \beta_2 C_{t-1}, \qquad 0 < \beta_1, \qquad \beta_2 < 1. \qquad (7.10)$$

This gives a short-run m.p.c. of β_1 which is less than the long-run value of $\beta_1/(1 - \beta_2)$. Brown allowed for the possibility of simultaneous-equation bias due to the existence of a second relationship between income and consumption by using an instrumental variable estimator. He found for Canadian data in the period 1926–49 excluding the war years, a short-run m.p.c. of 0·40 and a long-run one of 0·59. We shall reserve further comment upon what is really the addition of dynamic behaviour to the Keynesian theory until we have considered the other two major theories of the consumption function.

C.   *Permanent-Income Hypothesis*

The permanent-income hypothesis (P.I.H.) was developed by Friedman [15]. Unlike Duesenberry he started from standard consumer-choice theory and demonstrated that the simple Keynesian function is not readily derivable from orthodox microeconomics. Consider a typical consumer, who must decide between consumption today, C_t, and consumption tomorrow, C_{t+1}. We assume that he wishes to maximise utility, which is itself an increasing function of consumption, subject to an income constraint. This constraint on today's consumption therefore consists of today's income, Y_t plus what can be borrowed against tomorrow's income, Y_{t+1}, at the going interest rate, r. Assuming perfect capital markets and perfect certainty we have

$$C_t \leqslant Y_t + \frac{1}{(1+r)} Y_{t+1} = Y_t^*. \qquad (7.11)$$

Similarly, we can show that

$$C_{t+1} \leqslant Y_{t+1} + (1+r)Y_t = Y_{t+1}^*, \qquad (7.11a)$$

and we can represent the choice problem diagrammatically as in Figure 7.2. Current income and consumption are plotted on the horizontal axis and future quantities on the vertical axis. The line joining Y_t^* and Y_{t+1}^* is the budget line for it denotes all possible combinations of expenditure in the two periods, given the interest rate. The slope of the budget constraint is $-(1+r)$ and the utility function is assumed convex to the origin. The optimal solution is then given by the point of tangency between the indifference curve and the constraint. This says that current consumption is a function of this period's income, next period's income and the interest rate.

Now if the rate of interest between periods is constant we can generalise to n periods and in place of period $t+1$ we can substitute all future periods. The constraint is defined by the present discounted value of all

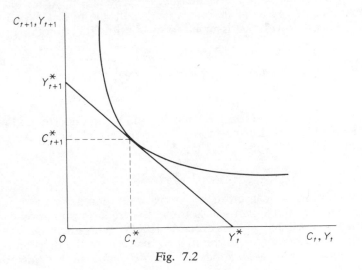

Fig. 7.2

current and future income streams, Y_t^*, and the slope, given by the interest rate. Friedman's conclusion is that the traditional 'Keynesian' consumption function was mis-specified, and hence its poor performance was not to be wondered at. His next step is to annuitise the constraint. This annuity which he calls permanent income, Y^p, is that which could be bought now, given the interest rate and the present value of the future income stream. Formally, if present discounted value is given by

$$\text{P.D.V.} = Y_1 + \frac{Y_2}{(1+r)} + \cdots + \frac{Y_t}{(1+r)^{t-1}} + \cdots = \sum_{t=1}^{\infty} \frac{Y_t}{(1+r)^{t-1}}, \quad (7.12)$$

then define Y^p such that

$$\text{P.D.V.} = Y^p + \frac{Y^p}{1+r} + \cdots = Y^p \sum_{t=1}^{\infty} \frac{1}{(1+r)^{t-1}}. \quad (7.12a)$$

Friedman now states that the utility function is such that consumption out of permanent income is strictly proportional. It follows that, unlike the two-period theoretical case we have just considered, where all income is exhausted by consumption, we now have a situation in which wealth will be perpetually increasing. As with all previous theories Friedman cannot claim for his an unimpeachable micro theoretic foundation.

Friedman's econometric work is worth considering in some detail for it is an excellent example of the way in which economic theory and econometric theory may be combined to explain a variety of apparent contradictions in the data. In terms of econometrics the analysis is one of errors in variables.

Following from Friedman's definition of permanent income we may divide measured income, Y, into two parts, permanent, Y^p, and transitory Y^T. By analogy we conceive of measured consumption, C, as the sum of two components, permanent (or planned) consumption, C^p, and transitory, C^T. Together with the assumed form of utility function this gives us

$$C = C^p + C^T; \qquad E(C^T) = \text{cov}(C^T, C^p) = 0, \qquad (7.13)$$

$$Y = Y^p + Y^T; \qquad E(Y^T) = \text{cov}(Y^T, Y^p) = 0, \quad \text{and} \qquad (7.14)$$

$$C^p = KY^p, \qquad (7.15)$$

the transitory elements having zero mean and being uncorrelated with the permanent elements. Furthermore, the transitory elements are assumed independent of each other, that is

$$\text{cov}(C_T Y_T) = 0. \qquad (7.16)$$

This assumption has caused more controversy than any of the others. It implies that a windfall gain will not affect current consumption except in as much as it may change the perceived level of permanent income. Note, however, that Friedman was the first to insist upon the division between durable and non-durable goods which we made in the introduction.

Hence we may allow windfall gains to be spent on durable goods which do not, by definition, form part of current consumption.

Under O.L.S. the estimate of the m.p.c. in function (7.6) is given by

$$\hat{\beta} = \frac{\text{cov}(C, Y)}{\text{var}(Y)}. \tag{7.17}$$

Using equations (7.13)–(7.15) we have $C - KY = C^T - KY^T$. Hence

(i) $\text{var}(C - KY) = \text{var}(C) - 2K\,\text{cov}(C, Y) + K^2\,\text{var}(Y)$
$= \text{var}(C^T) - 2K\,\text{cov}(C^T, Y^T) + K^2\,\text{var}(Y^T),$

(ii) $\text{var}(Y) = \text{var}(Y^p) + 2\,\text{cov}(Y^p Y^T) + \text{var}(Y^T)$, and

(iii) $\text{var}(C) = \text{var}(C^p) + 2\,\text{cov}(C^p C^T) + \text{var}(C^T)$.

Rearranging (i), substituting (ii) and (iii), and noting the conditions given by equations (7.13) and (7.14), we have $\text{cov}(C, Y) = \{\text{var}(C^p) + K^2\,\text{var}(Y^p)\}/2K$. Then using the relation, $C^p = KY^p$, gives us $\text{cov}(C, Y) = K\,\text{var}(Y^p)$. Hence under Friedman's assumptions,

$$\hat{\beta} = K\frac{\text{var}(Y^p)}{\text{var}(Y^p + Y^T)} = K\frac{\text{var}(Y^p)}{\text{var}(Y^p) + \text{var}(Y^T)} = K\left\{\frac{1}{1 + \dfrac{\text{var}(Y^T)}{\text{var}(Y^p)}}\right\}. \tag{7.18}$$

As long as there is a non-zero variance to transitory income the traditional estimate of the m.p.c. will be biased downwards, the degree of the bias depending upon the ratio of the variance of permanent to transitory income. In cross-section studies there are components of transitory income specific to individuals which result in a low estimated $\hat{\beta}$. Aggregating across individuals tends to cancel these out but there still remain transitory components caused by short-run cyclical fluctuations and random shocks. The variance of these is high relative to the variance of permanent income in the short run. As we extend the data period these transitory components decline in importance relative to the changes in permanent income, and consequently the estimated marginal propensity to consume rises as the time span increases.

D. *Life-Cycle Hypothesis*

Another approach which was developed simultaneously with, but independently from, the P.I.H. was the life-cycle hypothesis (L.C.H.). It is primarily the work of Modigliani and Brumberg [26] and Ando and Modigliani [1]. The intellectual basis for the work is the same as that of Friedman. The typical consumer has to choose a consumption stream to maximise a utility function, defined on present and future consumption, which is subject to a lifetime resource constraint, and which is itself stable over time. The major distinction lies in the choice of time horizon as the human lifetime. While this may be appropriate it is not *necessarily* correct. The typical consumer unit is a household and it is not clear that the household's planning horizon may be identified with that of an individual, nor that an individual within a household will use a planning horizon identical to his life span. Thus we cannot say *a priori* whether this hypothesis is more or less appropriate than the P.I.H. One of its advantages is that it generates an endogenous explanation of why saving is positive.

Like the permanent-income hypothesis we introduce a concept of 'normal income' and a proportionality assumption which implies that any increase in total resources will be allocated between consumption at different times in the same proportions as are existing resources. Formally, the individual chooses C_i, $i = t, t+1, \ldots, L$ subject to

$$\sum_{i=t}^{L} C_i = W_{t-1} + Y_t + \sum_{i=t+1}^{N} Y_i^e/(1+r)^{i-t}, \qquad (7.19)$$

where C_i is consumption in each period of lifespan, L, W_{t-1} is existing stock of wealth, Y_t is current income, and Y_i^e is expected income in each of the periods to retirement age N.

The proportionality assumption imposes the condition that the optimal consumption pattern shall be such that $C_t = K_1 C_{t-1} = K_2 C_{t-2}$, and so on. For simplicity of exposition it is commonly assumed that $K_1 = K_2 = K_3, \ldots, = 1$, that is the optimal consumption stream is constant. This results in a consumption function for an individual of age T of the form

$$C_t = \frac{1}{L-T} W_{t-1} + \frac{1}{L-T} Y_t + \frac{N-T}{L-T} Y_t^e, \qquad (7.20)$$

where $Y_t^e(N-T)$ is the present discounted value of expected future income stream (that is Y_t^e is 'normal income'). This predicts an m.p.c. out of current income which is low when the individual is relatively young, which increases with age and is very small relative to the m.p.c. out of 'normal' income. The similarity with the permanent-income hypothesis is obvious, and reconciliation of the apparent contradictions proceed along very similar lines. We shall not repeat them here, but it is useful to consider the extra element that this hypothesis introduces.

If the economy is static (that is assuming no changes in population, age distribution and technology) then aggregate saving will be zero. The cross section of the economy at a point in time will look like the behaviour of any individual throughout his lifetime, and the individual, by assumption, consumes all his resources. If we introduce an element of technical change, however, then those currently employed will have a greater set of resources and will therefore consume at a higher level in each period than those currently retired. In order to set aside sufficient for this increased level of consumption in their own retirement it follows that they must also be saving more than those currently retired are dissaving. Similarly, a growing income level or, analogously, a growing population will imply a positive level of saving for the economy. Furthermore, the faster the rate of growth, by whatever the cause, the higher will be the aggregate savings ratio – this, in principle, is a testable hypothesis.

E. *Making the Hypothesis Operational*

We have already discussed some of the problems of doing empirical work on the consumption function, problems of definition, measurement, and so on, but these apply equally to all the various hypotheses. By contrast the P.I.H. and the L.C.H. introduce a new problem in that one or more of the explanatory variables is unobservable. In the case of permanent consumption Friedman uses the simple expedient of substituting measured consumption. He argues that, with durable-goods expenditure already excluded, the differences are of a sufficiently small order of magnitude. In terms of econometrics the matter is irrelevant since we cannot distinguish between measurement error on the dependent variable and the disturbance term. For permanent income Friedman suggests a weighted average of past and present measured income, and in performing his empirical tests he used a geometrically declining weighting pattern on yearly income, such that

$$Y_t^p = (1 - \lambda) \sum_{i=0}^{\infty} \lambda^i Y_{t-i}, \qquad 0 \leq \lambda \leq 1. \tag{7.21}$$

Justification for this approach comes from Cagan [9]. Cagan's error-learning hypothesis states that to arrive at his expectation of future income an individual will adapt his last period's expectation, Y_{t-1}^e, by some proportion of the error he made in forecasting current income, Y_t. Formally

$$Y_t^e - Y_{t-1}^e = b(Y_t - Y_{t-1}^e), \qquad 0 \leq b \leq 1 \tag{7.22}$$

or equivalently

$$Y_t^e = bY_t + (1 - b)Y_{t-1}^e, \qquad 0 \leq b \leq 1. \tag{7.22a}$$

This is usually called the adaptive-expectations hypothesis. If we set $b = 1 - \lambda$ then by repeated back substitution we arrive at equation (7.21). Friedman in fact truncated the lag series after seventeen terms but, even so, the implementation of this definition is extremely time-consuming, for it necessitates constructing one Y_t^p series for each value of λ, running each regression and selecting that which gives the highest R^2. A simpler procedure is to perform a Koyck transformation on the consumption function as follows:

$$C_t = KY_t^p = K(1 - \lambda) \sum_{i=0}^{\infty} \lambda^i Y_{t-i}$$

$$\lambda C_{t-1} = K(1 - \lambda) \sum_{i=0}^{\infty} \lambda^{i+1} Y_{t-i+1}$$

$$C_t - \lambda C_{t-1} = K(1 - \lambda)Y_t$$

$$C_t = K(1 - \lambda)Y_t - \lambda(C_{t-1}). \tag{7.23}$$

This resolution provides us with an empirically testable version of the permanent-income hypothesis. In doing so it presents us with a different problem for it bears more than a passing resemblance to equation (7.10) as estimated by Brown [8]. There is, in fact, an important difference between the two, for Friedman's formulation implies a zero intercept. Consider, however, the following hypothesis. In the long run consumption is proportional to income, but for the reasons that Brown gives the individual is slow to adjust his consumption plans. Specifically

$$C_t^* = KY_t \tag{7.24}$$

and
$$C_t - C_{t-1} = (1 - \lambda)(C_t^* - C_{t-1}), \qquad 0 < \lambda < 1. \tag{7.25}$$

Equation (7.25) is known as a partial-adjustment process and if we combine it with (7.24) we arrive at a consumption function which is indistinguishable from (7.23). Yet another approach is provided by Spiro [29] and Ball and Drake [2] in which consumption is assumed to be a function of wealth only. But notice that savings is, by definition, both the change in wealth and also the difference between income and consumption. We have

$$C_t = Y_t - S_t = Y_t - (W_t - W_{t-1}), \tag{7.26}$$

where W_t is total wealth at time t. Combining this with the Spiro consumption function,

$$C_t = a + bW_t, \tag{7.27}$$

gives an estimating form

$$C_t = \frac{b}{b+1} Y_t + \frac{1}{b+1} C_{t-1}, \tag{7.27a}$$

which is also empirically indistinguishable from equation (7.23).

F.   *Some Empirical Evidence*

Friedman presents some time-series evidence in support of his theory, his estimate of $\hat{K} = 0.88$ is indeed very close to the observed a.p.c. over the period of 0.877. But then that is not very surprising. A regression line passes through the mean of the variables, and hence

$$\sum_{t=1}^{n} C_t = \hat{K}(1 - \hat{\lambda}) \sum_{t=1}^{n} Y_t + \hat{\lambda} \sum_{t=1}^{n} C_{t-1}.$$

Now $\sum_{t=1}^{n} C_t$ is approximately equal to $\sum_{t=1}^{n} C_{t-1}$, the closeness of the approximation depending on the number of observations, and hence

$$\hat{K}(1 - \hat{\lambda}) \sum_{t=1}^{n} Y_t \doteq (1 - \hat{\lambda}) \sum_{t=1}^{n} C_t,$$

$$\hat{K} \doteq \frac{\sum_{t=1}^{n} C_t}{\sum_{t=1}^{n} Y_t},$$

which is the aggregate average propensity to consume.

M.p.c. in this model is given by $k(1-\lambda)$ which Friedman estimates at 0·33 (which implies a consumer horizon of approximately three years). Modigliani and Ando present estimates for the regression coefficients on income in the range 0·52–0·60. Since then there have been a large number of studies of aggregate time-series data which have attempted to test variants of P.I.H. and L.C.H. on the same data. One such extensive survey is given in Evans [12]. He infers from the results that wealth has no place in the consumption function but his conclusions are open to debate. We shall not consider this evidence in any more detail since it is very difficult to come to any definite conclusions. Not least of the reasons for this is the similarity of estimation forms, which we have discussed above. Such small differences as do exist appear even less significant in view of the econometric problems involved. We shall return to these in the next section.

Faced with the inability of time-series data to provide any discriminatory power, Friedman, Ando and Modigliani and many researchers since, have turned to cross-section data for help. Under Friedman's hypothesis the C^p/Y^p ratio is independent of the value of Y^p. It need not, however, be the same for all individuals, which suggests that we might use data on different communities with widely differing incomes. The proposition is that, over a whole community, the transitory incomes will average out at zero. By careful choice of samples, the other factors such as age and composition of the population may be kept very similar for the different communities. Friedman presents results for white and non-white groups based on the U.S. 1935–6 cross-section survey. Neither he nor Ando and Modigliani (in a similar inter-city study using 1950 U.S. data) find any correlation between C/Y and Y and therefore conclude that the P.I.H. and the L.C.H. are consistent with the data while the A.I.H. is not.

One of the major problems in testing these models is the difficulty of obtaining independent estimates of permanent or normal income. Modigliani and Ando argue that housing expenditure provides a good proxy. If we accept that proposition then their results represent substantial evidence in favour of the P.I.H. A summary of these results is given by Evans [12] and is reproduced in Table 7.2. For comparison the results obtained when the same individuals are classified by income are also presented.

Unfortunately no one has yet produced evidence to distinguish between the P.I.H. and L.C.H. or between the many variants of either, despite the ever increasing number of studies since the mid-1960s. Indeed one of the most recent, Mayer [23], suggests that a compromise is the most likely explanation and produces evidence in support of a 'standard' theory. If all this work has not produced the answer there is little value in presenting it here. Rather we shall briefly consider one particular line of research.

In an attempt to provide an independent source of evidence on the P.I.H., Bodkin [4] analysed the behaviour of certain war veterans who received an unanticipated National Service Life Insurance Dividend. He

TABLE 7.2
C/Y ratios for groups classified by housing expenditure and by income

Value of house ($)	Ave. Y	C/Y	Income class	C/Y
<5,000	3,606	0·98	<1,000	4·79
5,000–7,500	4,274	0·98	1,000–2,000	1·19
7,500–10,000	4,649	0·99	2,000–3,000	1·03
10,000–12,500	5,191	0·99	3,000–4,000	0·98
12,500–15,000	5,729	0·98	4,000–5,000	0·96
15,000–17,500	5,948	1·00	5,000–6,000	0·96
17,500–20,000	7,547	0·95	6,000–7,500	0·95
20,000–25,000	9,607	0·99	7,500–10,000	0·87
>25,000	11,267	0·99	>10,000	0·82

Source: Evans [12].

estimates that

$$C = \$959{\cdot}30 + 0{\cdot}5597Y + 0{\cdot}722d, \qquad R^2 = 0{\cdot}60,$$

where d is the windfall gain. Friedman has argued that such windfall gains would only affect consumption in as much as they changed permanent income. With an horizon of three years and a proportionality constant of about 0·9 this implied that the coefficient on d should be of the order of 0·3. Since Bodkin's estimate was significantly different this implies a refutation of the P.I.H. Since then, work by Kreinin [21] on restitution payments by Germany to Israeli families, and Reid [27] on the National Service data have estimated a very low m.p.c. out of windfalls. Finally Bird and Bodkin [3] have reworked their data. Following the lead of Reid they add extra explanatory variables to allow for the ownership and purchase of housing, the age and educational level of the head of the household and geographical location. As each explanatory variable is added the coefficient on windfall income falls until Bird and Bodkin concede that the tests are inconclusive.

This controversy provided a good example of yet another problem we face when doing empirical work. Our theories are always developed on *ceteris paribus* assumptions. Bird and Bodkin demonstrate that a failure to take account of variations in extraneous factors can greatly influence our conclusions. While their work is on cross-section data the same general comment may be made of time-series analysis, and much of the recent work on the consumption function has been the refinement of theory by the addition of explanatory variables.

G.   Some Econometric Problems

We have considered two ways in which econometrics has been used to explain the early results (Haavelmo's simultaneity-bias and Friedman's errors-in-variables approaches) but otherwise we have ignored the problems of the actual estimation process. This has simplified the exposition but we must now set about rectifying the omission if we are to justify the conclusion of the previous section that the small differences produced by the evidence are insignificant in the light of the estimation problems.

In particular we shall consider two sources of error, namely misspecification of the disturbance term and multi-collinearity. For example, if we assume that the correct specification of the P.I.H. is given by

$$C_t = K(1-\lambda) \sum_{i=0}^{\infty} \lambda^i Y_{t-i} + U_t, \qquad (7.28)$$

where U_t is a serially uncorrelated disturbance term with zero mean and constant variance, then performing a Koyck transformation on the estimating equation gives us a new estimating equation of the form,

$$C_t = K(1-\lambda)Y_t - \lambda C_{t-1} + (U_t - \lambda U_{t-1}), \qquad (7.29)$$

and we have introduced a first-order moving-average process into the disturbance term. This invalidates the assumptions necessary for ordinary least-squares estimates, and such estimates of the parameters will be biased, as will be the standard statistical tests. Various techniques have been suggested to cope with this problem but the only correct procedure is to use a more sophisticated estimation procedure which allows the moving-average disturbance term to be taken into account.

In an attempt to estimate the importance of such mis-specifications Zellner and Geisel [32] consider a general form of the consumption function (7.29), utilising four different assumptions about the disturbance term, and calculating the maximum-likelihood estimates. The four assumptions are

(i) $U_t - \lambda U_{t-1} = \varepsilon_t$;

(ii) $U_t = \varepsilon_t$;

(iii) $U_t = \rho U_{t-1} + \varepsilon_t$; and

(iv) $U_t - \lambda U_{t-1} = \gamma(U_{t-1} - \lambda U_{t-2}) + \varepsilon_t$,

where ε_t is normally distributed, with zero mean, variance σ^2, and is serially uncorrelated. These four assumptions may be interpreted as: (i) ignore the problem and use O.L.S. on the estimating equation – if this assumption is valid the estimates of K and λ are consistent; (ii) the disturbance term is indeed a moving-average process; (iii) that the original disturbance in equation (7.28) exhibited first-order auto-correlation; and (iv) approximate the true disturbance term by a first-order auto-regressive process. The results are listed in Table 7.3.

Notice that the estimate of K, the long-run propensity, is relatively insensitive to changes in specification, but the estimates of b, the short-run propensity, range from 0·22 to 0·52. Their results suggest that assumption (i) is the most acceptable though the stability of these results is in doubt. The problem is that the sophisticated estimation techniques

TABLE 7.3
Estimated coefficients under alternative assumptions

	λ	K	b	ρ		$\lambda + b$
(i)	0·66	0·89	0·31			0·97
(ii)	0·45	0·94	0·52			0·97
(iii)	0·66	0·94	0·32	0·69		0·98
(iv)	0·77	0·96	0·22		−0·13	0·99

where $b = K(1 - \lambda)$

Source: U.S. quarterly data 1947–60 [32].

used require far longer runs of data than are usually available to the researchers. Be that as it may, the important lesson to be learnt from the Zellner and Geisel study is that the specification of the error term is an integral part of the model and may considerably affect the estimated parameters. Another problem given little attention is that of multi-collinearity, the trend factors in income and lagged consumption giving the two variables a high cross correlation. Klein [20] presents some evidence on this point. The result of this is that the sum of the two coefficients will remain roughly constant under different estimators but the values attached to each may vary considerably. Thus it is difficult to determine the short-run m.p.c. In general, multi-collinearity is more likely to distort the estimates the more complex is the estimation technique. This provides us with an alternative point of view on the estimates presented by Zellner and Geisel for if we look at Table 7.3 we see that the sum of the estimated coefficients $\lambda + b$ is exceedingly stable, while the collinearity between income and lagged consumption is high.

H.   *Other Models, Other Influences*

We have presented the basic theories of the consumption function and a few variations. We have also presented some of the evidence and some of the problems which most commonly arise. The body of literature which now exists on the consumption function is considerable, and the number of empirical studies is increasing all the time. Some of these will be referred to in the final section on consumer durables but we cannot attempt to summarise them all here. The interested reader is recommended to a survey of consumer behaviour by Ferber [14]. This lists not only most of the recent work on consumption functions but also developments in other areas of economics and other social sciences which impinge upon consumer behaviour (for example the allocation of time, human capital, decision-making in the household, advertising, and so on).

III CONSUMER DURABLES

In the introduction we gave several reasons for excluding the purchase of durable goods from the consumption function *per se*, and during the course of the preceding section this distinction was emphasised, particularly with respect to the P.I.H. Nevertheless, simply to exclude consumer durables is not a sufficient answer, even if we were able to define our variables exactly in the way that theory would suggest.

Let us suppose that, although we cannot clearly distinguish *the* 'correct' theory of the consumption function, we can come to a consensus view as to the estimated parameters. If we accept Evans's estimates [13] as being representative we have a quarterly m.p.c. of 0·30–0·35, a yearly m.p.c. of 0·35–0·45 and an a.p.c. of 0·80. This suggests that changes in income will have an effect on consumption patterns which will vary with the time interval since the changes occurred. This result is of fundamental importance to the operation of government stabilisation policies. It tells us, for example, that a tax cut or an increase in government expenditure will have a multiplier effect upon income that will continue over time in a much more complicated way than simple Keynesian multiplier analysis would have one believe. It is only when we look at the purpose to which the information will be put that we see just how important it is to have good estimates of the propensities to consume, long- and short-run, marginal and average, and from different sources of income, of consumers' time horizons, and so on. Considering the problem faced by the government also tells us why our consumption function is inadequate, since the government is interested in a theory of consumption *expenditure*. The purchase of consumer durables creates a multiplier expansion in just the same way as does the purchase of non-durables. As a result of this it is often suggested that we should estimate consumption functions both including and excluding durable-goods' purchase, and hence derive two estimates of the various propensities. Since these will bracket the 'true' propensities this would enable us to set limits upon the likely effect of government policies. The argument is ill-conceived. Stabilisation policy requires that one knows the long-run effects of past policies which have still to work themselves out as well as the short-run impact of the current policies. Hence the time path of adjustment of consumption to income changes, and the *timing* of the purchase of durables in particular, is essential to the successful operation of stabilisation policy.

Let us first make some general observations about the purchase of durables. Unlike non-durable goods, they are made sporadically, and past purchases tend to reduce current purchases. Unlike most capital goods they can be purchased almost immediately. The only qualification to the last of these statements would be that it depends upon the degree to which available credit has already been used. We have already indicated that the purchase of a consumer durable is a purchase of a flow of future services. If we assume that this flow of services is proportional to the stock of durables owned, then it would seem a reasonable hypothesis that the stock of durables will be made proportional to the level of permanent income, such that

$$D_t = \alpha Y_t^p = \alpha \sum_{i=0}^{\infty} \lambda^i Y_{t-i}, \qquad (7.30)$$

where D_t is stock of durables at time t.

Now the consumer's expenditure on durables is the difference between the stock now and what it was in the previous time period. If we also assume that the stock of durables depreciates at a rate δ then we have

$$C_t^D = D_t - (1 - \delta)D_{t-1}, \qquad (7.31)$$

where C_t^D is the purchase of consumer durables in time t.

If we perform a Koyck transformation on equation (7.30) and then substitute in equation (7.31) we have

$$C_t^D = \alpha Y_t - (1 - \lambda - \delta)D_{t-1}, \qquad (7.32)$$

which has the *negative* response to previous stocks (that is past purchases) that we suggested above. This process is known as a stock-adjustment process and has been very successfully used to study a wide variety of goods by, among others, Harberger [17] and Wu [31]. In practice it is common to add some other terms to the estimating equation. We shall not present a formal derivation of these here but we can illustrate their intuitive plausibility.

We know from standard consumer theory that the demand for any good is a function of its price, the prices of other goods, income and attitudes or tastes. Applying this to the demand for durable goods in general we would expect income and attitudes to be important as will the relative price between durable and non-durable goods. A rise in the price of durables, relative to non-durables, will cause a substitution away from durables. Perhaps less obvious is the influence of credit availability. In general, consumer durables require the outlay of a greater percentage of current income than is the case for other goods. This suggests that either saving must have occurred in the past to accumulate the necessary purchasing power or, alternatively, that the payment need not all be made at the time of purchase. The higher is the outlay required the more likely is the availability of credit to be important. For example, more than 50 per cent of new cars sold require credit finance. The addition of these factors suggest that the consumer-durables function will be of the form,

$$C_t^D = a Y_t - b D_{t-1} - c\left(\frac{P^D}{P^{ND}}\right)_t + d A_t + e R_t, \qquad (7.33)$$

where $(P^D/P^{ND})_t$ is relative prices of durables to non-durables, A_t is an attitudes variable, and R_t is the credit variable.

Evans [13] presents a discussion of some of the work done on this form of equation in addition to his own empirical results. Of particular interest are the discussion of car purchases and the relationship of consumer durables and liquid assets. Houthakker and Taylor [18] provide the best-known attempt to incorporate the work on durables and non-durables. They start by assuming expenditure to be of the form,

$$q_t = \alpha + \beta S_t + \gamma x_t,$$

where q_t is expenditure on a good at time t, S_t is existing stocks at time t, and x_t is income at time t. They argue that if $\beta < 0$ then we have a durable good and if $\beta > 0$ we have a non-durable good. (In the latter case the influence of past purchases or habit outweighs the stock-adjustment element.) A brief exposition of this work is given by Bridge [7] and we shall not devote any more space to it here. Note, however, that this provides us with a rather different definition of durable goods which need not necessarily correspond to the accounting definitions.

The more closely one looks at consumption behaviour the more difficult such definitions become. If we allow the existence of second-hand markets for goods then many commodities previously deemed as durables may be incorrectly defined, since the decision to consume can be retaken each year. For this and other reasons we must expect our consumption functions to become increasingly specialised to goods with particular characteristics.

IV FINAL COMMENTS

If there is one conclusion that is clear from the theoretical and empirical work of the last fifteen years it is that consumers' expenditure, on all categories of commodities, is best explained with reference to a dynamic view of income and consumption patterns. Whether they derive from permanent-income, stock-adjustment, habit-persistence of some other hypothesis, the final testable forms of the hypotheses bear a very close resemblance to each other, and in particular they often include a term in lagged consumption. A great deal more work is needed to explore the true role of this variable, and if progress is to be made, we need both a more general theory which can incorporate the various features of the different hypotheses and an expanded data base with which to test it. For example, data relating to the same consumer units over time is essential to the study of the changing consumption over the life cycle.

The second point is that experience has shown that as we include more and more of the *ceteris paribus* variables, that is those hitherto assumed not to change, the majority of our evidence becomes inconclusive. Future research will have to pay careful attention to the role of these other variables and, indeed, much work has already begun (for example on the effect of advertising, changes in interest rates, interregional differences, and so on). An adequate treatment however of all these factors requires that we can establish their role in consumption behaviour on a theoretical level. Only by doing so can we produce hypotheses which can be tested against the empirical evidence, and thus determine the importance of the various factors.

BIBLIOGRAPHY

[1] A. Ando and F. Modigliani, 'The Life-cycle Hypothesis of Saving: Aggregate Implications and Tests, *American Economic Review*, vol. 53, no. 1 (1963).

[2] R. J. Ball and B. S. Drake, 'The Importance of Credit Control on Consumer Durable Spending in the U.K., 1957–61', *Review of Economic Studies*, vol. 30 (1964).

[3] R. C. Bird and R. G. Bodkin, 'The National Service Life Insurance Dividends of 1950 and Consumption: A further test of the strict 'Permanent Income' Hypothesis', *Journal of Political Economy*, vol. 73 (1965).

[4] R. G. Bodkin, 'Windfall Income and Consumption', in *Consumption and Savings*, ed. I. Friend and R. Jones, vol. 2 (University of Pennsylvania Press, 1960).

[5] D. S. Brady and R. D. Friedman, 'Savings and the Income Distribution', in *Studies in Income and Wealth*, vol. 15 (New York: National Bureau of Economic Research, 1947).

[6] W. H. Branson and A. K. Klevorick, 'Money Illusion and the Aggregate Consumption Function', *American Economic Review*, vol. 59 (1969).

[7] J. Bridge, *Applied Econometrics* (Amsterdam: North-Holland, 1971).

[8] T. M. Brown, 'Habit Persistence and Lags in Consumer Behaviour', *Econometrica*, vol. 20 (1952).

[9] P. Cagan, 'The Monetary Dynamics of Hyperinflations', in *Studies in the Quantity Theory of Money*, ed. M. Friedman (University of Chicago Press, 1958).

[10] T. E. Davis, 'The Consumption Function as a Tool for Prediction', *Review of Economics and Statistics*, vol. 34 (1952).

[11] J. Duesenberry, *Income, Saving and Theory of Consumer Behaviour* (Harvard University Press, 1949).

[12] M. K. Evans, 'The Importance of Wealth in the Consumption Function', *Journal of Political Economy*, vol. 75 (1967).

[13] —, *Macroeconomic Activity* (New York: Harper & Row, 1969).

[14] R. Ferber, 'Consumer Economics, A Survey', *Journal of Economic Literature* (1973).

[15] M. Friedman, *A Theory of the Consumption Function* (Princeton: National Bureau of Economic Research, 1957).

[16] T. Haavelmo, 'Methods of Measuring the Marginal Propensity to Consume', *Journal of the American Statistical Association*, vol. 42 (1947).

[17] A. C. Harberger, *The Demand for Durable Goods* (Chicago University Press, 1960).

[18] H. S. Houthakker and L. D. Taylor, *Consumer Demand in the U.S. 1929–70* (Harvard University Press, 1966).

[19] M. B. Johnson, *Household Behaviour* (Harmondsworth: Penguin, 1971).

[20] L. E. Klein, 'Problems in the Estimation of Interdependent Systems', in *Model Building in the Human Sciences*, ed. H. Wold (Monaco: Union Europeanne d'Editions, 1967).

[21] M. E. Kreinin, 'Windfall Income and Consumption – Additional Evidence', *American Economic Review*, vol. 51 (1961).

[22] S. Kuznets, *Uses of National Income in Peace and War*, Occasional Paper, no. 6 (New York: National Bureau of Economic Research, 1942).

[23] T. Mayer, 'The Propensity to Consume Permanent Income', *American Economic Review*, vol. 56 (1972).

[24] F. Modigliani, 'Fluctuations in the Saving–Income Ratio', *Studies in Income and Wealth*, vol. 2 (New York: National Bureau of Economic Research, 1949).

[25] — and A. Ando, 'Tests of the Life-Cycle Hypothesis of Savings', *Bulletin of the Oxford Institute of Statistics*, vol. 19 (1960).

[26] — and R. Brumberg, 'Utility Analysis and the Consumption Function; an Interpretation of Cross-section Data', in *Post-Keynesian Economics*, ed. K. K. Kurihara (Rutgers University Press, 1954).

[27] M. G. Reid, 'Consumption, Savings and Windfall Gains', *American Economic Review*, vol. 52 (1962).

[28] A. Smithies, 'Forecasting Post-War Demand', *Econometrica*, vol. 13 (1945).

[29] A. Spiro, 'Wealth and the Consumption Function', *Journal of Political Economy*, vol. 70 (1962).

[30] H. Theil, *Linear Aggregation of Economic Relations* (Amsterdam: North-Holland, 1954).

[31] De Min Wu, 'An Empirical Analysis of Household Durable Good Expenditure', *Econometrica*, vol. 33 (1965).

[32] A. Zellner and M. S. Geisel, 'Analysis of Distributed Lag Model with Application to Consumption Function Estimation', *Econometrica*, vol. 38 (1970).

8

The Demand for Money

P. G. Saunders and D. J. Taylor*
University of Stirling

I INTRODUCTION

The purpose of this chapter is to discuss some of the problems associated with the empirical investigation of the demand for money. We shall also consider some aspects of the supply of money but the emphasis will be on the complications which these introduce into the analysis of the demand for money. In order to clarify the relevance to policy of the issues dealt with below, we consider first the importance of the demand for money function to the general problem of the relationship between money-stock changes and changes in the level of economic activity.

Consider the following simple closed economy macroeconomic framework in which the symbols have their usual meaning:

$$Y = E(Y, r) + G \tag{8.1}$$

and
$$M = L(Y, r). \tag{8.2}$$

This is the familiar *ISLM* model which can be solved for the equilibrium level of income, Y, and the equilibrium interest rate, r, on the assumption that the authorities control the money stock, M, and government expenditure, G. The authorities can attempt to manipulate the level of income in order to attain their policy objectives by changing G and M. The impact of fiscal and monetary policy can be seen most clearly by taking total differentials of (8.1) and (8.2) and solving for the change in equilibrium

* We wish to acknowledge the helpful comments of Maurice Townsend on an earlier draft of this chapter.

income, that is

$$dY = \frac{L_r}{L_r(1-E_y)+E_rL_y}\left(\frac{E_r}{L_r}dM + dG\right),$$ (8.3)

where subscripts refer to partial differentiation, for example $L_r \equiv \frac{\partial L}{\partial r}$. This reduced-form equation relates changes in G and M to changes in income through constant multipliers. The fiscal multiplier (F.M.) is given by

$$\text{F.M.} = \frac{dY}{dG} = \frac{L_r}{L_r(1-E_y)+E_rL_y},$$ (8.4)

and the monetary multiplier (M.M.) by

$$\text{M.M.} = \frac{dY}{dM} = \frac{E_r}{L_r(1-E_y)+E_rL_y}.$$ (8.5)

Note that the numerical values of both these multipliers are crucial to the effective operation of stabilisation policy and depend on all the parameters of the system.

The question of the effectiveness of monetary policy can be framed in two ways. We can ask what the quantitative impact of a given change in the money stock will be, that is calculate the value of M.M., which depends on, among other things, the value of the interest sensitivity of the demand for money function, L_r. Alternatively, we could compare the relative effectiveness of monetary and fiscal policy, that is calculate the difference between M.M. and F.M. It follows directly from equations (8.4) and (8.5) that M.M. $= (E_r/L_r)$F.M. The higher the interest elasticity of expenditure and the lower the interest elasticity of the demand for money, the more effective is monetary policy relative to fiscal policy. The smaller is L_r the larger will be the change in the rate of interest for a given change in the money stock, whilst the more sensitive expenditure is to interest-rate changes the larger will be the impact on income of any given change in the money stock, while the more sensitive is expenditure to interest-rate changes the greater will be the impact on income of any impact on income. The smaller is L_r the greater will be the increase in r for a given money stock, while the larger is E_r the greater will be the dampening effect of a given interest-rate change. Thus the larger is E_r/L_r the less effective will fiscal policy be, relative to monetary policy. The extreme case of the demand for money being completely insensitive to interest-rate changes, $L_r = 0$, gives the simple Quantity Theory result in which monetary policy is all-powerful and fiscal policy ineffective. To see this, substitute $L_r = 0$ in equation (8.5), which gives

$$dY = \frac{1}{L_y}dM.$$ (8.6)

Clearly the numerical value of L_r is an important element in determining the effectiveness of monetary policy, regardless of the interpretation

188   *Topics in Applied Macroeconomics*

of the term 'effectiveness'. However, it is only one of a number of important elements. In addition, it is not necessarily the case that each element of M.M. and F.M. needs to be calculated independently. Empirical work in this area has taken two different methodological approaches. The first, initiated by Friedman and Meiselman [14], attempts to calculate the value of monetary and fiscal multipliers directly from reduced-form equations like (8.3). The essence of this approach is that it does not require any specific view of the transmission mechanism between money-stock and income changes. The alternative approach is represented by the estimation of separate structural equations for different sectors. These might be single-equation studies or part of a full-scale, economy-wide, econometric model. The objective in both cases is to test underlying theory as well as to derive estimates of the structural parameters. In this approach equation (8.3) becomes a particular transformation of the model, rather than an estimating equation, and the monetary and fiscal multipliers are calculated from structural estimates. (For a fuller discussion of this distinction and some empirical results for the United States, see Fisher and Sheppard [10].) The investigation of the demand for money function represents part of this latter methodology.

The *ISLM* model outlined above is highly simplified – in particular it assumes a rather simple transmission mechanism for the effect of a change in money stock on income. However, it does demonstrate that the interest elasticity of the demand for money is potentially an important link in the chain of causation even though it is only one of the many possible routes through which a change in the money supply could influence income. In addition the numerical value of L_r is only one aspect of this link that is relevant to the effectiveness of monetary policy. The other major factor is the stability of the link. If the money-demand function is a stable function of a few variables then, to the extent that at least one of these variables (for example the interest rate) must adjust to maintain equilibrium in the money market when the money stock changes, the effects of monetary policy will be stable and predictable. We shall discuss the meaning of stability more fully later. At this stage it is only necessary to understand that the stability of the demand for money function and the role of interest rates are crucial issues for monetary policy. The empirical investigation of these issues requires that a correctly specified theoretical model be used as the basis for estimation. Consequently we now turn to a discussion of alternative theories of the demand for money.

II THEORY

We shall consider two approaches to the theory of the demand for money, the modern quantity theory as expounded by Friedman [11] in his restatement of the Quantity Theory of Money, and the Keynesian approach based on the original formulation by Keynes [23]. Both approaches consider the demand for money as part of the general problem of wealth allocation but place emphasis on different aspects of the problem. Keynes identified four motives for demanding money: 'income', 'business', 'precautionary' and 'speculative' motives. The 'transactions' motive includes both the income and business motives and arises from the lack of synchronisation between receipts and payments. It depends primarily on the level of income, as does the precautionary motive, although this motive arises from uncertainty about the pattern and size of future receipts and payments. The speculative motive depends on the relationship between the current rate of interest and expectations of future interest rates. Assuming a given expected rate of interest we obtain the familiar Keynesian liquidity-preference schedule,

$$m^d = m_1 + m_2 = L_1(Y) + L_2(r), \tag{8.7}$$

where m^d represents the total demand for money, m_1 is transactions plus precautionary demand, and m_2 is speculative demand.

The Keynesian approach based on schedule (8.7) has been refined and developed by Baumol [2] and Tobin [35]. Baumol showed that the transactions demand for money would itself be responsive to the rate of interest. This arises because individuals can increase their incomes by holding bonds rather than cash between transactions. However, they do not hold all of their transactions balances in the form of bonds because there is a positive cost, a brokerage fee, associated with any switch from cash to bonds or from bonds to cash. If there were no brokerage fee, then the transactions demand for cash would be zero. Baumol's analysis suggests that the transactions demand for money is related directly to the square root of the volume of transactions and inversely to the square root of the rate of interest. This suggests an interest elasticity of -0.5 and an income elasticity of 0.5, implying that there are economies of scale in money holding (see p. 124).

Tobin's work concentrated on the speculative demand for money, and provided an alternative rationale for Keynes's original idea that individual choice concerning the holding of cash or bonds was based on the relationship between the current and expected rate of interest. In Keynes's view, expectations of rising interest rates would imply expected capital losses from the holding of bonds. If this capital loss outweighs the interest earned from the bond, the expected holding-period yield of the bond is negative (unless held to maturity), so that an individual would wish to hold his wealth entirely in the form of money. If, in addition, individual interest-rate expectations are diverse then, at any given interest rate, some individuals will hold money while others will hold bonds. The inverse relationship between speculative demand and the rate of interest arises from the concept of a 'normal' expected rate of interest around which individual expectations cluster. Thus the higher is the actual rate of interest, the more likely is it to exceed the normal rate, so that the market will, on average, expect a capital gain from holding bonds, and the speculative demand for money will be lower. At lower interest rates the reverse argument applies, although there may be some low rate of interest which lies below all individual expected rates so that all individuals prefer to hold money rather than bonds. This tendency for the speculative demand to become perfectly elastic at some low interest rate has been called the 'liquidity trap'. The main problem with Keynes's formulation in terms of the diversity of expectations is that it implies that any given individual will at any moment in time hold either all money or all bonds but not both.

In contrast, Tobin's approach emphasises uncertainty rather than expectations as the prime determinant of the speculative demand, and he is able, within this framework, to show why individuals may hold a mixed portfolio of both money and bonds. Individual asset choice is made on the basis of the return and the risk associated with different assets. Uncertainty concerning future interest rates means that bonds, although earning a return in the form of interest payments, also involve a risk in the form of a possible capital loss. Even if the expected capital gain is zero, Tobin shows that individuals will, in most cases, prefer a mixed portfolio, assuming that they do not obtain positive pleasure from taking risks, that is individuals are assumed to be risk-averters. A rise in the rate of interest induces a substitution effect leading to increased bond holdings and an income effect acting in the opposite direction. The rise in the interest rate also lowers the value of the wealth held by bond holders who will thus reduce their demand for money if the wealth elasticity of the demand for money is positive. The over-all effect of an increase in the rate of interest on the demand for money is theoretically uncertain and can only be ascertained by empirical investigation.

Whilst Tobin's analysis regards money and bonds as alternative assets within individual portfolios, Friedman's restatement of the Quantity Theory emphasises the flow of services which money bestows on its owner. The demand for money is thus analysed within a standard choice theory model. Individuals hold money until the marginal convenience from so doing equals the marginal cost in terms of forgone interest payments on alternative assets. The demand for money thus depends upon the 'prices', that is the expected holding-period yields of all other assets, and total wealth, which constrains the over-all value of the portfolio. The wealth variable in Friedman's model incorporates human and non-human wealth since, in his wider view of portfolio choice, individuals are free to hold their wealth in a human form, by being educated for example, as well as in non-human forms such as cash, bonds and equities. To allow for the non-marketability of human wealth Friedman argues that the greater is the ratio of non-human to human wealth (ω), the lower will be the demand for money. Friedman's equilibrium demand for money function then becomes

$$m^d = f\left(P, r_b, r_e, \frac{1}{p}\frac{dp}{dt}, \omega, W, u\right), \tag{8.8}$$

where P is the price level, r_b and r_e are the bond and equity rates respectively, $(1/p)(dp/dt)$ is the expected rate of inflation, ω is the ratio of non-human to human wealth, W is human plus non-human wealth and u is a taste variable. The wealth variable in function (8.8) may be replaced by its income counterpart since wealth is equal by definition to the capitalised value of an income stream. Thus $W = y/r$, where r is a weighted average of individual interest rates, so that function (8.8) becomes

$$m^d = f\left(P, r_b, r_e, \frac{1}{p}\frac{dp}{dt}, \omega, y, u\right). \qquad (8.9)$$

The income term in equation (8.9) is a wider concept than the usual accounting concept of income since it includes the income flow from all forms of wealth holding. Following Friedman we shall refer to this income term as 'permanent income' (see pp. 170–3). If we further assume that interest rates move together and that expectations of inflation are fully incorporated into nominal interest rates, we can consider a single representative interest rate in our empirical work. If we further assume that the ratio of non-human to human wealth is constant, as are tastes, equation (8.9) becomes

$$m^d = f(P, r, y^p), \qquad (8.10)$$

where r is the representative rate of interest and y^p is permanent income. Finally, we note that Friedman argued that the permanent-income elasticity of the demand for money exceeds unity so that money is a luxury good. This, however, is an empirical rather than a theoretical proposition, and evidence either way cannot be taken as providing any information on the theoretical propositions of the Friedman approach.

The two approaches to the demand for money produce quite similar structural relationships although there are a number of important differences. Friedman emphasises the importance of a rather broad concept of wealth whereas the Tobin analysis is restricted essentially to non-human wealth. The Keynesian analysis also considers separately the role of current income in determining transactions demand. The two theories also have different implications for the definition of money. By concentrating on the utility yield of money, Friedman views money as a 'temporary abode of purchasing power' which suggests a rather broad definition of money, perhaps inclusive of some capital-certain, interest-bearing assets as well as currency and demand deposits. Although the Keynesian theory of the transactions demand suggests a narrow definition of money with short-term interest rates and current income as the main explanatory variables, the total Keynesian demand function incorporates Tobin's analysis which is concerned primarily with the demand for capital certainty. Thus the total demand function suggests a very broad definition of money, inclusive of all capital-certain assets, upon which wealth, longer-term interest rates and expectations of future interest rates would all be expected to have significant impacts. Since the definition of money in the Friedman model is not very clear theoretically, the appropriate definition of money is probably not a good basis on which to distinguish empirically between the two theories. The Keynesian analysis stresses the substitution between financial assets, and one might expect to find a high interest elasticity, while the Quantity Theory approach, in which money is seen as the most liquid of a complete asset spectrum, does not suggest that the demand for money is highly elastic with respect to any particular asset yield.

In both theories the expected holding-period yields represent the relevant opportunity costs of holding money, although the Keynesian analysis is more explicit in its handling of expectations. Since expected capital gains and the expected rate of inflation are not directly observable, and as neither approach provides a theory of the determination of these expectations, empirical formulations of the demand for money function often omit any consideration of expectations. If expectations are an important determinant of the demand for money, and fluctuate substantially, then an estimated demand function which omits them will tend to be unstable, and hence estimated coefficients may be biased. If the estimated relationships explain most of the variation in the demand for money, and display stable coefficients over time, we may conclude that expectations are either stable or unimportant so that observed rates of return are good proxies for expected holding-period yields. The same kind of results will hold if other important variables have been omitted (e.g. risk). Stability in this sense has been an important point of contention between the advocates of the two theories. Friedman's argument that the demand for money is a stable function of a few variables lies at the core of the monetarist position. Keynesians, however, have traditionally argued that the demand for money is unstable, particularly in the short run (see, for example the *Radcliffe Report* [5]). It is with the theoretical distinctions between the two approaches in mind, and in particular the resulting policy implications, that we now turn to the empirical evidence on the demand for money.

III EMPIRICAL MODELS

In order that we can use the empirical results to test individual theories and distinguish between them, we must first formulate the theories so that their predictions are explicit. The predictions of economic theory generally take the form of restrictions on the sign and size of the parameters of the estimated model, or restrictions on the relationships between individual parameters.

The more restrictions that the theory imposes on the parameters of the model the better, since we can have more confidence in the theory if the evidence fails to reject the implied restrictions. Acceptance or rejection of the models is decided by the application of standard techniques of statistical hypothesis testing, as outlined in Chapter 1. The answers we require of these tests relate to the choice of the most suitable theoretical approach to the demand for money, as well as to the question of the over-all stability of the demand for money function.

We have concentrated in the theoretical section entirely on the determination of the equilibrium demand for money, m^*. Most empirical work on the demand for money explicitly recognises the problem that the adjustment towards this equilibrium position may not be complete within the time period between observations. Thus the models in general consist of two separate components:

(*a*) the determination of the optimal (equilibrium) demand for money; and
(*b*) the disequilibrium behaviour of individuals and the adjustment process undergone in attaining equilibrium.

Although in the long run all individuals will hold their equilibrium money stocks this is not necessarily true in the short run, where, for example, adjustment costs may make it optimal not to adjust immediately to equilibrium. We turn first to the determination of the equilibrium demand for money.

The first model is the simplified Keynesian theory which we can write as

$$m_t^* = \alpha_0 + \alpha_1 r_t + \alpha_2 y_t + Z_t. \qquad (8.11)$$

Several points of a general nature can be made at this stage. First we shall interpret all of the models as being linear in the logarithms of the variables, which means that we are considering a multiplicative demand function. The advantage of this approach is that the estimated parameters are equivalent to the elasticities. Z_t represents the stochastic error term in the structural equation which is assumed to possess the usual properties such that the application of ordinary least squares yields unbiased estimates and enables the standard statistical tests to be applied. The interest rate (a short-term rate on the Keynesian active demand interpretation) is given by r_t, whilst y_t represents current measured income. The Keynesian total demand for money function replaces current income with a wealth variable, W_t, this being the appropriate constraint in the portfolio-choice model. In this case we replace model (8.11) by

$$m_t^* = \alpha_0 + \alpha_1 r_t + \alpha_2 W_t + Z_t. \qquad (8.12)$$

The Keynesian emphasis on the money–bonds choice suggests that the appropriate interest-rate variable is a long-term rate. This model is very similar to a simplified version of the Quantity Theory in which we replace the spectrum of interest rates which enter the function in theory (equation (8.8)) with a single representative interest rate. This procedure is normally adopted in empirical work because of the serious multi-collinearity problems which arise once a number of interest rates are included in the function.

As we have seen in the preceding section on theory, Friedman preferred to introduce the inclusive wealth concept as the constraint variable, which incorporates both non-human and human wealth. This variable in turn can be replaced by the permanent income variable, y^p, which represents the flow of services from this inclusive wealth concept. In this case we have

$$m_t^* = \alpha_0 + \alpha_1 r_t + \alpha_2 y_t^p + Z_t. \qquad (8.13)$$

This does not of course solve the empirical problems associated with the measurement of the inclusive wealth concept unless permanent income can be measured. Friedman suggests that one can obtain an estimate of permanent income by calculating expected future income, which he in turn specifies as being related to current and past levels of actual income. Permanent income is calculated as a weighted average of all past income levels, the weights declining geometrically so that in the formation of expectations more weight is placed on recent income than on income in the distant past. Following Friedman,

$$y_t^p = \lambda \sum_{i=0}^{i=\infty} (1-\lambda)^i y_{t-i} \qquad (0 \leqslant \lambda \leqslant 1) \qquad (8.14)$$

Subtracting $(1-\lambda)y_{t-1}^p$ from both sides of equation (8.14) and rearranging the right-hand side gives

$$y_t^p - y_{t-1}^p = \lambda(y_t - y_{t-1}^p). \qquad (8.15)$$

We can interpret λ as the elasticity of permanent income (or expected income) so that equation (8.15) states that permanent income is adjusted by some fraction of the discrepancy between actual and previous permanent income. Combining the two structural equations (8.13) and (8.15) gives the model,

$$m_t^* = \alpha_0\lambda + \alpha_1 r_t - \alpha_1(1-\lambda)r_{t-1}$$
$$+ \alpha_2\lambda y_t + (1-\lambda)m_{t-1}^* + Z_t - (1-\lambda)Z_{t-1}. \qquad (8.16)$$

Estimation of the model in this form produces estimates of the elasticities of the money-demand function as well as of the elasticity of permanent income, λ. Empirically we have three alternative models of the equilibrium money-demand function, equations (8.11), (8.12) and (8.16), although we would not expect the interest rate to be necessarily the same in each case. We turn now to the problem of the adjustment of actual money holdings to the desired position.

The standard adjustment model used in empirical work is the partial-adjustment model which assumes that individuals adjust their money holdings by some fraction, θ, of the difference between the actual and desired levels, such that

$$m_t - m_{t-1} = \theta(m_t^* - m_{t-1}), \qquad 0 \leqslant \theta \leqslant 1. \tag{8.17}$$

This can be shown to be optimal behaviour, in the sense that costs are minimised, if total costs consist of a disequilibrium cost and an adjustment cost. Assuming costs are proportional to the square of the extent of the disequilibrium and the square of the adjustment, we have the cost function,

$$C_t = \alpha(m_t^* - m_t)^2 + \beta(m_t - m_{t-1})^2. \tag{8.18}$$

Minimising costs we arrive at the partial-adjustment model in which $\theta = \alpha/(\alpha + \beta)$. If the disequilibrium cost is much greater than the adjustment cost, then α dominates β, and θ tends to one. When $\theta = 1$, equation (8.17) becomes $m_t = m_t^*$ and adjustment is instantaneous. Alternatively, if the adjustment cost dominates, then θ tends to zero and in the limit when $\theta = 0$ equation (8.17) becomes $m_t = m_{t-1}$ and no adjustment occurs.

Many writers have implicitly assumed that adjustment is instantaneous, and hence do not distinguish between actual and desired money demand. In this case the optimal money-demand equations derived above can be estimated directly since $m_t^* = m_t$. However, the partial-adjustment model represents a more general formulation and is thus more desirable; if adjustment is actually instantaneous, then the estimate of θ should be unity. To impose a value of unity in a situation in which adjustment is only partial, will result in the estimation of a mis-specified model and could produce biased parameter estimates. If we combine the partial-adjustment model (8.17) with (8.11), (8.12) and (8.15) respectively, we obtain the following reduced forms:

$$m_t = \theta\alpha_0 + \theta\alpha_1 r_t + \theta\alpha_2 y_t + (1-\theta)m_{t-1} + \theta Z_t; \tag{8.11a}$$

$$m_t = \theta\alpha_0 + \theta\alpha_1 r_t + \theta\alpha_2 W_t + (1-\theta)m_{t-1} + \theta Z_t, \text{ and} \tag{8.12a}$$

$$m_t = \theta\alpha_0\lambda + \theta\alpha_1 r_t - \theta\alpha_1(1-\lambda)r_{t-1} + \theta\alpha_2\lambda y_t + (2-\theta-\lambda)m_{t-1}$$
$$- (1-\lambda)(1-\theta)m_{t-2} + \theta Z_t - \theta(1-\lambda)Z_{t-1}. \tag{8.16a}$$

If the elasticity of permanent income, λ, is unity then the forms (8.16a) and (8.11a) are identical, although one might expect a different interest rate to be appropriate in each case. This follows from (8.15) since if $\lambda = 1$ then $y_t^p = y_t$, that is permanent and current incomes are equivalent. This is, of course, only an empirical equivalence and should not be confused with the real theoretical differences which remain, although it becomes more difficult to compare the theories empirically. In a recent paper Feige [8] has estimated a model equivalent to (8.16a), although he interprets it in a different way to Friedman's permanent-income approach. Feige prefers to regard money as being demanded for transactions purposes following Keynes, but argues that expected rather than actual income is the appropriate determinant of transactions balances. He defines expected future income, y_t^e, in an identical way to Friedman's permanent income, so that

$$y_t^e - y_{t-1}^e = \lambda^*(y_t - y_{t-1}^e),\qquad(8.19)$$

where λ^* is the elasticity of income expectations. Combining the model of (8.17) with (8.19) and an amended version of (8.11), in which y_t^e replaces y_t, produces equation (8.16a) with λ^* replacing λ. Again we find that different theoretical approaches to the demand for money (Feige's approach is strictly Keynesian) produce models which are empirically identical.

Yet another model was proposed by Chow [4], and is a slightly amended version of the partial-adjustment model in which we have

$$m_t - m_{t-1} = \theta(m_t^* - m_{t-1}) + \Phi(A_t - A_{t-1}).\qquad(8.20)$$

Here $A_t - A_{t-1}$ represents the change in total assets and Φ measures the proportion of this change which takes the form of increased money holdings. By definition, the change in assets is equal to savings whilst savings equals income minus consumption. Following Friedman's work on consumption theory [12], consumption is proportionally related to permanent income, that is $C_t = ky_t^p$. In this case model (8.20) becomes

$$m_t - m_{t-1} = \theta(m_t^* - m_{t-1}) + \Phi(y_t - ky_t^p).\qquad(8.21)$$

Chow combines this with a short-run (equilibrium) money-demand function equivalent to that in (8.13) so that the constraint variable is wealth proxied by permanent income. Combining (8.13) and (8.21) gives the model,

$$m_t = \theta\alpha_0 + \theta\alpha_1 r_t + \Phi y_t + (\theta\alpha_2 - \Phi k)y_t^p + (1-\theta)m_{t-1} + \theta Z_t.\qquad(8.22)$$

If $\theta\alpha_2 - \Phi k \approx 0$ model (8.22) becomes very similar to (8.11a), although once again the structural models are quite distinct.

This brief review of the conventional empirical models of the demand for money highlights the difficulties confronted, in practice, of distinguishing between alternative theoretical approaches. These difficulties arise largely from the problem of implementing different constraint variables. It could then be argued that since the theories differ mainly in their predictions for the role of the interest rate, in particular the size of the interest elasticity, we should not worry unduly about the constraint variable but concentrate our attention on the interest elasticity. This, however, ignores the fact that the interest elasticity will be correctly estimated only if the full model is properly specified, so that the choice of the constraint variable will affect the estimated interest elasticity. It follows that the full model must be correctly specified and it is therefore important to distinguish carefully between different theoretical specifications, and in particular the role of adjustment and/or expectations lags.

IV ESTIMATION PROBLEMS

Several initial problems need to be considered before we can discuss the empirical results. The first of these is the possible endogeneity of the money supply.

The models developed in the previous section are concerned with the specification of desired money holdings. Even the partial-adjustment mechanism represents desired or planned adjustment to a target level of demand. However, what we actually observe is the value of the money stock. The supply of money only equals the demand for money if the money market is in equilibrium. Thus, any empirical investigation of the demand for money requires a model with at least three relationships, a demand function, a supply function and an equilibrium condition. However, most studies of the demand for money function have only specified a demand function which has been estimated using single-equation estimation techniques with the money stock as the dependent variable. Even if we assume that the money market is continually in equilibrium, it does not necessarily follow that the estimated relationship is in fact the demand function. It may be the supply function, or a combination of the demand and supply functions. In either case biased estimates of the demand function will be obtained. To see this problem more clearly consider initially the case where the money supply varies positively with the rate of interest while the demand for money depends only on the interest rate. If the money-supply function shifts due, for example, to the authorities manipulating the reserve base whilst the money-demand function remains fixed, then we can be sure that single-equation estimation methods applied to the observed levels of M and r will yield unbiased estimates of the interest elasticity of the demand for money (see Figure 8.1(a)).

However, because the demand for money depends on variables other than the rate of interest, the demand curve itself may shift. In this case the observed values of r and M will represent a combination of the demand and supply functions. Single-equation methods applied to these observations will yield biased estimates of the interest elasticity. The line EE in Figure 8.1(b) represents the estimated regression line which clearly does not estimate either a demand or supply function. Thus, if the money supply is itself endogenous, we must use simultaneous estimation techniques in order to be able to separate the demand and supply functions and provide unbiased estimates of the parameters of both functions (see pp. 26–31). These methods have been employed by some investigators and their results are discussed later.

In order that the use of single-equation estimating techniques will produce unbiased estimates of the demand function we require the explanatory variables appearing in the function to be truly exogenous.

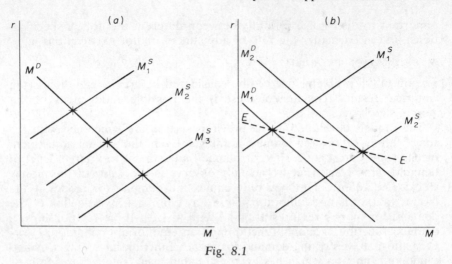

Fig. 8.1

Given a negative relationship between the demand for money and the interest rate, it follows immediately that the authorities can control the money stock or the interest rate, but not both. In other words either the money stock or the interest rate is truly exogenous, whilst the other is endogenously determined. The problem reduces to specifying the demand function so that the exogenous variable appears on the right-hand side of the equation. Thus, if the authorities control the level of interest rates then the money stock is demand-determined and a conventional money-demand function, $m^d = f(r, y)$ will produce unbiased estimates, whilst if the authorities seek to control the money stock then this becomes the exogenous variable and the demand for money determines the interest rate. In this case the money-demand function should be estimated in the form $r = f(m, y)$ in order to obtain unbiased parameter estimates.

In general it is true to say that during most of the post-war period the authorities in both the United States and the United Kingdom have operated their monetary policies with the objective of influencing interest rates rather than controlling the money stock (although recently the emphasis of monetary policy has been changing). To this extent the use of the money stock as a dependent variable is acceptable. However, the ability of the authorities to control the money stock independently of the behaviour of the public and banking system is less clear. The important issue from the point of view of estimating the money-demand function is whether the variables which determine money demand also enter a money-supply function. The simple credit-multiplier theory of money supply postulates that changes in the reserves of the banking system generate multiple changes in the money stock via the attempts of the public and banks to maintain their fixed, desired ratios of cash to deposits and reserves to deposits respectively. The model is

$$M \equiv C + D, \tag{8.23}$$

$$H \equiv R + C, \tag{8.24}$$

$$C \equiv cD, \tag{8.25}$$

and

$$R \equiv lD. \tag{8.26}$$

where M = money stock, C = cash with the non-bank public, D = deposits of commercial banks, R = reserves of commercial banks, and H = high-powered money. Equations (8.25) and (8.26) specify respectively the public's demand for currency and the banks' demand for reserves.

These relationships can be combined to give

$$M = \left(\frac{1+c}{c+l}\right)H. \tag{8.27}$$

This can be interpreted as generating either the change in money stock for a given change in the quantity of high-powered money, or as generating the required change in H for the authorities to meet a given change in the demand for money, as in the case of interest-rate stabilisation. Regardless of the assumed objectives of the authorities, as long as they can control H, and c and l are constants, the money stock is determined independently of the variables that enter the money-demand function. However, the constancy of c and l is not supported by the evidence. The public's desired cash ratio fluctuates seasonally and from year to year (see Newlyn [31]). It does not appear to depend on the rate of interest although the level of income does seem to be a significant determinant (Gibson [15]). Tobin [36] has argued that we would expect the banks' desired asset ratio to depend inversely on the rate of interest. The reserve assets of the banking system represent part of the portfolio of assets held by the banks. Typically, they represent the capital-certain part of the banks' portfolios, and as such play a role analogous to an individual's money holdings in portfolio theory. The opportunity cost of holding reserve assets is the rate of interest, so that the higher is the interest rate the lower will be the proportion of total bank assets held as reserve assets. If the rate of interest is such that the banks' desired ratio is above the legal minimum, then changes in the interest rate will change the money supply by altering the credit multiplier. Thus the possibility exists that the money stock increases as the rate of interest increases. Evidence on the observed reserve ratios of banks suggests that this effect may be significant, especially in the United States where banks are observed to hold reserves substantially in excess of the legal minimum. In the United Kingdom the banks tend to hold reserves close to the minimum, irrespective of the interest rate, largely because of the existence of a well-developed market in riskless reserve assets in which transactions costs are low. However Newlyn [31] has calculated that, for the U.K. banking system as a whole, the cash ratio varied between 0·094 and 0·105 over the period 1959–69 in the presence of an 8 per cent legal minimum. Thus the possibility exists that, over a certain range of interest rates, endogeneity of the money stock may be important and require the use of simultaneous estimation techniques when analysing the demand for money.

We turn now to the problem of the appropriate definition of money. Although there is broad agreement that notes and coins in circulation and demand deposits should be defined as money, there is less agreement about the inclusion of time deposits. As far as individual behaviour is concerned, money is a subjective concept; the definition of money will be chosen such that the individual has a much greater degree of substitutability amongst those assets he defines as money, than between money and other financial assets. It follows that, since money and other assets are distinguished behaviourally, one can only decide on the appropriate definition of money by studying individual behaviour. The definition of money is best regarded as an empirical question. The two most common definitions used are (1) a narrow definition which includes notes and coins plus demand deposits and (2) a broader definition which also incorporates time deposits. In fact, as Johnson has recently noted, 'different definitions of money give consistent results so that the definitional problem is not an obstacle to discovering regularities in monetary phenomena' ([21] p. 123).

Theoretically, we expect individuals to be interested in the real rather than the nominal value of their cash balances. This suggests that, in an aggregate money-demand function, the dependent variable should be specified in real *per capita* terms, as should the appropriate constraint variable. The assumption that the money-demand function is homogenous of degree one in prices is one of the basic propositions of monetary theory, whilst homogeneity of degree one in population is intuitively correct. These propositions can be tested by including both the price level and the population as separate independent variables in a nominal money-demand function and testing whether or not their elasticities are unity. Thus if p is the price level and n is the population we could estimate the model,

$$m_t = A r_t^{\alpha_1} y_t^{\alpha_2} p_t^{\alpha_3} n_t^{\alpha_4}, \tag{8.28}$$

where y_t represents the constraint variable in real *per capita* terms. Estimates of model (8.28) for both the United States and the United Kingdom suggest that $\alpha_3 = 1$ although there is no such agreement on the size of α_4. Meltzer [30] finds that for the United States $\alpha_4 \neq 1$ and argues that this may be due to the increased urbanisation which has accompanied population growth, making savings banks more readily available. The U.K. evidence is severely restricted by the lack of accurate regular data on population size, a factor which Goodhart and Crockett [17] argue accounts for their finding that $\alpha_4 \neq 1$.

If $\alpha_3 = \alpha_4 = 1$ the dependent variable in model (8.28) can be expressed in real *per capita* terms, and this is the procedure most commonly adopted. Biased estimates of model (8.28) are obtained if the constraint variable is itself expressed in nominal terms, since then the model becomes

$$m_t = Ar_t^{\alpha_1}(y_tp_tn_t)^{\alpha_2}. \qquad (8.29)$$

In this case the income elasticity is biased towards unity because it represents an amalgam of the true income elasticity and the price and population elasticities, both of which are equal to unity.

V RESULTS

Turning to the evidence in some detail, we shall consider first the problem of interest elasticity. The size of the elasticity will depend upon the precise definitions employed for both the interest rate and the money stock. The interest elasticity should be greater for a narrow definition of money than for a broad definition, since in the latter case substitutions towards interest-bearing money (time deposits) will not be picked up by the data whereas they will if narrow money is the dependent variable. Also, one should expect the interest elasticity to be greater for a long-term interest rate than for a short rate, since the former is much less variable than the latter. Since the size of the interest elasticity is crucial in distinguishing the alternative theories of the demand for money, the evidence must be viewed with these *a priori* predictions in mind.

As Laidler has commented, 'there is an overwhelming body of evidence in favour of the proposition that the demand for money is stably and negatively related to the rate of interest' ([27] p. 97). One famous early study by Friedman [13], in which the author could find no role for the rate of interest, has been shown by Laidler [26] to have been incorrectly estimated, and that a significant relationship emerges once the correct estimation procedure is employed. (Friedman's method involved correlating the residuals, from an equation in which the interest rate was omitted, with the interest rate itself. He found no evidence of association, but by omitting the interest rate from the model he obtained biased estimates, and thus his residuals were themselves biased. If the interest rate is included as an explanatory variable in the model, Laidler shows that it appears with a significant negative elasticity.)

Estimates of the interest elasticity for the United States and the United Kingdom indicate a long-term interest-rate elasticity of about -0.8 and a short-term interest-rate elasticity of about -0.3 when a narrow definition of money is used, these elasticities falling to about -0.7 and -0.2 respectively for a broad definition of money. There does not seem, to date, to be strong evidence in favour of either the long rate or the short rate being the most suitable to include, evidence for both the United States and the United Kingdom supporting both views. We are not able to decide with any confidence which of the two theories is the more appropriate on the basis of the size of the interest elasticity, although the evidence does suggest strongly that the extreme monetarist position in which the interest elasticity is zero, and the extreme Keynesian position in which the interest elasticity is infinite, are both inconsistent with all the available evidence. Tests of the liquidity-trap hypothesis, in which the interest elasticity rises as the rate of interest falls, have produced no evidence in its favour. The test can, however, be criticised since the theory suggests that the interest elasticity rises when the rate of interest falls relative to the expected rate of interest, which does not necessarily coincide with a low level of the actual interest rate.

Turning to the appropriate constraint variable, there is strong evidence in this case favouring the use of wealth rather than income. Meltzer [30], for example, finds that if both current income and non-human wealth are included together, the income term is completely insignificant whilst the wealth term is highly significant. His results indicated that the non-human wealth variable performed better than the inclusive wealth variable measured by permanent income, a result which was contradicted by Laidler's results [25] where he found that the permanent-income model was preferable for both narrow and broad definitions of money. Meltzer found the non-human wealth elasticity to be roughly equal to the permanent-income elasticity, both declining from about $1 \cdot 5$ for the period 1900–29 to about $1 \cdot 3$ for the period 1930–58 using a broad definition of money. Evidence for the United Kingdom, using a non-human wealth variable, is hampered by the lack of an adequate series for non-human wealth, although we consider below some recent estimates of the permanent-income model.

Evidence for both the United States and the United Kingdom confirms the importance of lags in the money-demand function. The lagged dependent variable is always highly significant, although we emphasised earlier the problems involved in distinguishing empirically between adjustment lags and expectations (permanent-income) lags. In the lagged-adjustment model (8.11a) we must distinguish between short-run and long-run elasticities. The long-run interest rate and income (wealth) elasticities are given by α_1 and α_2 respectively, whilst the short-run elasticities are $\theta\alpha_1$ and $\theta\alpha_2$. In general, the short-run elasticities will be smaller since $\theta < 1$, whilst if $\theta = 1$ the distinction between the long-run and short-run elasticities is redundant. Rather than discuss estimates of the simple adjustment model (8.11a) we consider the full dynamic model (8.16a) in which both adjustment lags and expectations lags are incorporated. The full dynamic specification presents quite formidable estimation problems because of the moving-average error process and the fact that the model is over-identified. Six coefficients are estimated whilst there are only five structural parameters, so that there exist some direct relationships between individual parameters of the estimated model. These relationships take the form of non-linear constraints on the estimated parameters. In estimating model (8.16a) Feige [8], for the United States, and Laidler and

TABLE 8.1

| | United States | United Kingdom | |
		(i)	(ii)
income elasticity	1·07	0·54	0·54
interest elasticity	−0·14	−0·02	−0·01
adjustment coefficient	1·09	0·20	0·80
income expectations elasticity	0·30	0·80	0·20

Source: Feige [8], Laidler and Parkin [29].

Parkin [29], for the United Kingdom, approximate the moving-average error process by a first-order serial-correlation process which they allow for in estimation. In a recent simulation study of this problem Hendry and Trivedi [19] conclude that 'taking some account of autocorrelation, even if the form is mis-specified, is a superior policy to ignoring it altogether' ([19] p. 127). However, the model really requires to be estimated taking explicit account of the moving-average error process. In both studies, the restrictions are imposed in estimation and an iterative procedure produces the best estimates. The restrictions themselves are, however, not tested independently (by the use, for example, of a likelihood ratio test; see Silvey [33]), and until such tests are performed we cannot conclude that the underlying theories have been rigorously tested. The structural parameter estimates are shown in Table 8.1 for the United States and the United Kingdom assuming a broad definition of money. The U.S. results indicate an income elasticity insignificantly different from unity whilst the adjustment coefficient suggests instantaneous adjustment.

Lags result from the formation of expectations of future income, which Feige argues is the correct determinant of the transactions demand for money. The U.K. results by Laidler and Parkin are presented in two forms since two local optima were obtained. The authors were unable to distinguish adjustment lags from expectations lags. The relevant parameters, θ and λ, enter the model symmetrically, except in the lagged interest-rate coefficient. In the Laidler and Parkin study this coefficient was insignificantly different from zero and herein lies the explanation of their inability to separate θ and λ. The income elasticities in both cases reject Friedman's hypothesis that money is a luxury good, although Laidler and Parkin's results are consistent with Baumol's view that there exist economies of scale in money holdings. While the dynamic specification of the demand for money has much to recommend it, further work needs to be done, particularly for the United Kingdom, before we can choose with any confidence between alternative theories of the demand for money and between alternative justifications for the presence of lags in the function.

The results presented so far have all been obtained using single-equation estimation techniques. We indicated in the last section that there is a strong possibility that the money supply is endogenous, in the sense that variables which determine the demand for money may enter the money-supply function. If this is the case then simultaneous estimation techniques are required and the results reported in single-equation studies are suspect. Brunner and Meltzer [3] and Teigen [34] have estimated both demand and supply functions for the United States using simultaneous techniques. While the interest rate appears to enter significantly in the supply function, the results for the demand function do not differ substantially from single-equation studies. This is encouraging, but to the extent that the specification of the money-demand function does not correspond with the full dynamic model, that is (8.16a), these conclusions are tentative. In addition, the correct specification of the money-supply function is still in dispute, especially in the United Kingdom (see, for example, Goodhart [16]).

An aspect of the demand for money function which has, to date, been possibly neglected in the empirical work is the role of the expected rate of inflation. Friedman's theory explicitly introduces the expected inflation rate as the expected return to holding physical goods, whilst it may also have an effect if nominal interest rates do not fully reflect changes in the expected rate of inflation, since in this case the nominal interest rate does not measure the true opportunity cost of holding money. (This latter reason was suggested by Laidler and Parkin as being the cause of the insignificant role which the rate of interest played in their model; the interest rate will not reflect the true opportunity cost if the monetary authorities adopt a policy of controlling nominal interest rates.) A recent empirical study for the United States by Shapiro [32] found a significant role for the expected rate of inflation proxied by a distributed lag of past actual inflation rates. An associated problem is concerned with the possibility of flexible adjustment coefficients. Goodhart and Crockett [17] have argued that the adjustment coefficient may depend upon the size of the initial disequilibrium, and possibly its source as well. Indeed, the adjustment coefficient may well be a function of the expected rate of inflation. As in many other areas of empirical economics, the demand for money function has entered the arena of distributed-lag models. Great care is required, particularly in estimation, before we can distinguish alternative dynamic specifications.

We conclude with a discussion of the implications of these results for the policy issues of the size and stability of interest-rate elasticity. The evidence is generally in support of the presence of a significant interest-rate effect on the demand for money, but the precise numerical value and the most relevant interest rate are still open to question. This arises largely because of the difficulties, already discussed, in implementing the theoretical models. Evidence on stability takes the form of the explanatory power of functions which include only an interest rate and constraint variable, and the values of the interest elasticity estimated over different time periods. Since most estimated functions incorporate a lagged dependent variable the explanatory power as measured by R^2 tends to be high, so that this is not a particularly stringent test of stability. The values of interest-rate elasticities appear to be relatively stable over long periods. In the United States, for example, the value of the short-rate elasticity appears to vary between -0.15 and -0.20 over a period of approximately one hundred years (Laidler [28]). If the parameters of the model are stable and if no important variables are omitted then one would expect the model to predict future changes in the demand for money. Recent prediction tests along these lines presented by Hacche [18] suggest that since 1971 the simple form of the demand for money function in the United Kingdom has become somewhat less stable. Hacche uses a demand function estimated from quarterly data over the period 1963–71 to predict money demand after 1971, and these predictions are then compared with actual behaviour. This new instability may be the result of the new banking regulations introduced in 1971 which redefined reserve assets in such a way as to leave the banks with a reserve ratio above the legal minimum. The adjustment of the banks over the period since December 1971 to the new minimum reserve ratio and the more competitive role envisaged for banks in the new regulations (see [6]) may have introduced some important aspects of simultaneity. Alternatively, it may be that the greatly accelerated rate of inflation over this period has introduced significant uncertainty and variability into the expected rate of inflation, making its omission an important source of instability. These recent developments clearly illustrate that the precise form of the demand for money function, and the associated policy issues of stability and interest elasticity, remain open to further investigation.

BIBLIOGRAPHY

[1] A. D. Bain, *The Control of the Money Supply* (Harmondsworth: Penguin, 1970).

[2] W. J. Baumol, 'The Transactions Demand for Cash: An Inventory Theoretic Approach', *Quarterly Journal of Economics*, vol. 66 (Nov 1952) pp. 545–56.

[3] K. Brunner and A. H. Meltzer, 'Predicting velocity: implications for Theory and Policy', *Journal of Finance*, vol. 19 (May 1964) pp. 240–83.

[4] G. C. Chow, 'On the Long Run and Short Run Demand for Money', *Journal of Political Economy*, vol. 74 (Apr 1966) pp. 111–31.

[5] Committee on the Working of the Monetary System, *Radcliffe Report*, Cmnd. 827 (1959).

[6] 'Competition and Credit Control', *Bank of England Quarterly Bulletin* (June 1971).

[7] F. de Leeuw, 'The Demand for Money: Speed of Adjustment, Interest Rates and Wealth' in *Monetary Process and Policy: A Symposium*, ed. G. Horwich (New York: Irwin, 1967).

[8] F. L. Feige, 'Expectations and Adjustments in the Monetary Sector', *American Economic Review*, papers and proceedings, vol. 57, no. 2 (May 1967) pp. 462–73.

[9] D. Fisher, 'The Demand for Money in Britain: Quarterly Results 1951 to 1967', *Manchester School*, vol. 36, no. 4 (Dec 1968) pp. 329–44.

[10] G. R. Fisher and D. K. Sheppard, 'Interrelationships between real and monetary variables: some evidence from recent U.S. empirical studies', in *Issues in Monetary Economics*, ed. H. G. Johnson and A. R. Nobay (Oxford University Press, 1974).

[11] M. Friedman, 'The Quantity Theory of Money: A Restatement', in *Studies in the Quantity Theory of Money*, ed. M. Friedman (University of Chicago Press, 1956).

[12] —, *A Theory of the Consumption Function*, National Bureau of Economic Research (Princeton University Press, 1957).

[13] —, 'The Demand for Money: Some Theoretical and Empirical Results', *Journal of Political Economy*, vol. 67, no. 4 (Aug 1959) pp. 327–51.

[14] — and D. Meiselman, 'The relative stability of monetary velocity and the investment multiplier in the United States, 1897–1958', in *Stabilisation Policies*, Research Study Two, one of a series prepared for the Commission on Money and Credit (Englewood Cliffs, N.J.: Prentice-Hall 1963).

[15] N. J. Gibson, *Financial Intermediaries and Monetary Policy*, Hobart Paper, no. 39 (London: Institute of Economic Affairs, 1970).

[16] C. A. E. Goodhart, 'Analysis of the determination of the stock of money', in *Essays in Modern Economics*, ed. M. Parkin (London: Longmans, 1973).

[17] — and A. D. Crockett, 'The Importance of Money', *Bank of England Quarterly Bulletin*, vol. 10, no. 2, pp. 159–78 and vol. 10, no. 3 (1970) pp. 181–97.

[18] G. Hacche, 'The demand for money in the United Kingdom: experience since 1971', *Bank of England Quarterly Bulletin* (Sep 1974) pp. 284–305.

[19] D. F. Hendry and P. K. Trivedi, 'Maximum Likelihood Estimation of Difference Equations with Moving Average Errors: A Simulation Study', *Review of Economic Studies*, vol. 39 (Apr 1972) pp. 117–46.

[20] H. G. Johnson, 'Monetary Theory and Policy', *American Economic Review*, vol. 52 (June 1962) pp. 335–84.

[21] —, *Macroeconomics and Monetary Theory* (London: Gray-Mills, 1971).

[22] N. J. Kavanagh and A. A. Walters, 'The Demand for Money in the

United Kingdom, 1877–1961: Preliminary Findings', *Bulletin of the Oxford University Institute of Economics and Statistics*, vol. 28, no. 2 (May 1966) pp. 93–116.

[23] J. M. Keynes, *The General Theory of Employment, Interest and Money* (London: Macmillan, 1936).

[24] A. M. Khusro, 'An Investigation of Liquidity Preference', *Yorkshire Bulletin of Economic and Social Research*, vol. 4, no. 1 (Jan 1952) pp. 1–20.

[25] D. Laidler, 'Some Evidence on the Demand for Money', *Journal of Political Economy*, vol. 74, no. 1 (Feb 1966) pp. 55–68.

[26] —, 'The Rate of Interest and the Demand for Money – Some Empirical Evidence', *Journal of Political Economy*, vol. 74, no. 6 (Dec 1966) pp. 543–55.

[27] —, *The Demand for Money – Theories and Evidence* (Scranton: International Textbook Co., 1969).

[28] —, 'The Influence of money on economic activity – a survey of some current problems', in *Monetary Theory and Monetary Policy in the 1970s*, ed. G. Clayton, J. C. Gilbert and R. Sedgwick (Oxford University Press, 1971).

[29] — and M. Parkin, 'The Demand for Money in the United Kingdom, 1955–1967: Preliminary Estimates', in *Readings in British Monetary Economics*, ed. H. G. Johnson (Oxford University Press, 1972).

[30] A. H. Meltzer, 'The Demand for Money: The Evidence from the Time Series', *Journal of Political Economy*, vol. 71 (June 1973) pp. 219–46.

[31] W. T. Newlyn, *Theory of Money* (Oxford University Press, 1971).

[32] A. A. Shapiro, 'Inflation, Lags, and the Demand for Money', *International Economic Review*, vol. 14, no. 1 (Feb 1973) pp. 81–95.

[33] S. D. Silvey, *Statistical Inference* (Harmondsworth: Penguin, 1970).

[34] R. Teigen, 'Demand and Supply Functions for Money in the United States', *Econometrica*, vol. 32, no. 4 (Oct 1964) pp. 477–509.

[35] J. Tobin, 'Liquidity Preference as Behaviour Towards Risk', *Review of Economic Studies*, vol. 25 (Feb 1958) pp. 65–86.

[36] —, 'Commercial Banks as Creators of Money', in *Banking and Monetary Studies*, ed. D. Carson (New York: Irwin, 1963).

9

Models and Forecasting

George McKenzie
University of Southampton

I INTRODUCTION

Most households and firms, no matter how small or humble, engage in some form of forecasting analysis. For example, a small firm or shop will usually base its decisions on recent events. If times have been good, it will continue to re-order goods in anticipation that they will be readily sold. Similarly, a household whose breadwinner is employed in a cyclical industry may attempt to build up a buffer stock of savings in anticipation of periodic lay-offs. However, if times are good then there is less likely to be any great urgency in adding to such liquid assets.

Forecasting macroeconomic activity involves many of the same elements contained in the above decision processes – a careful assessment of the current situation and some form of extrapolation based on history. However, unlike small firms and households, the authorities are likely to have the necessary expertise and financial resources to utilise fairly sophisticated and complex statistical techniques. The purpose of this chapter is to examine some of these procedures for organising available economic data so as to obtain meaningful forecasts. As we shall see, it is not easy to say that any one form of analysis is superior to all others.

II SOME ALTERNATIVES

A. *The Intuitive Approach*

This is what we might call an 'educated guess'. No formal statistical analysis of the data is undertaken. Rather, the policy-maker simply assesses the situation (perhaps with the visual examination of relevant data) and its relationship to previous events, and makes a decision. The problem with this approach is that it is very difficult to check its validity, since the various elements that enter into a subjective, intuitive evaluation are usually never made explicit. Thus even when such 'educated guesses' are wildly incorrect, it is difficult to suggest improvements.

B. *The National Bureau Approach*

The National Bureau for Economic Research is a private, non-profit organisation in the United States funded by government and private-foundation grants. The aim of its procedure is to forecast turning points in economic activity by identifying variables which may signal possible changes *in advance*. In the past the National Bureau has classified seventy-three individual data series, currently collected by the U.S. Department of Commerce, into three categories:

(*a*) thirty-seven *leading indicators*, changes in which precede any general change in economic activity;

(*b*) twenty-five *coincident indicators*, which vary concurrently in the same direction as general business activity; and

(*c*) eleven *lagging indicators*, which change direction only after a change in economic activity has occurred.

Since we are concerned with forecasting in this chapter, I shall only discuss the leading indicators. To simplify things, the National Bureau specifies a short list of only twelve leading indicators. This eliminates any duplication of similar series. In addition, a single composite index is constructed from these twelve. The names of the various components of this short list are given in Table 9.1, together with an analysis of their past performance. Although the indicators have turned in a reasonably good record of forecasting directional changes in economic activity, there have been errors in the past. As a result a new set of leading indicators has been proposed, particularly with a view to eliminating the distorting effects of inflation. Four of the original series are to be included in the new composite: average workweek, net business formation, stock prices, and new housing starts. Important additions include real money balances and the percentage change in total liquid assets as well as the percentage change in sensitive prices (for example the wholesale price index of crude materials excluding food and feeds).

The two approaches so far discussed are capable of generating qualitative forecasts, that is predictions as to the *sign* of change in a particular variable. However, in very many cases, we shall also be interested in forecasting the actual *magnitude* of change. We might want to forecast population increases, or changes in sales, or the seasonal variation in employment. For the authorities, interested in the effect of changes in official spending, taxation or monetary variables on real economic activity, quantitative information is indispensible. Several procedures are available.

TABLE 9.1

Performance record of twelve leading indicators, 1945–71

Series Name	Mean lead time* Peaks (mos)	Mean lead time* Troughs (mos)	False signals (no.)	Failure to signal (no.)	Average† score (percentage)
Average workweek, production workers, manufacturing	11	2	3	0	66
Average weekly initial claims, State unemployment insurance	15	1	2	0	73
New building permits, private housing units	16	7	2	0	67
Net business formation	15‡	2	2	0	68
New orders, durable-goods industries	7	3	2	0	78
Contracts and orders, plant and equipment	6	2	2	1	64
Change in book value, manufacturing and trade inventories	6	1	4	0	65
Industrial materials' prices	12	4	2	0	67
Stock prices, 500 common stocks	9	5	2	0	81
Corporate profits after taxes	9	2	2	0	68
Ratio, price to unit labour cost, manufacturing	14	0	1	0	69
Change in consumer installment debt	13	3	3	0	63
Composite index, reverse trend adjusted	5	4	2	0	

* The 1948–9, 1953–4, 1957–8, 1960–1, 1969–70 recessions were used to determine lead times.
† Based on a range of 0 to 100 per cent. See Geoffrey H. Moore and Julius Shiskin, *Indicators of Business Expansions and Contractions* (New York: National Bureau of Economic Research, 1967).
‡ Index of net business formations was not available in determining lead time prior to the 1948 peak.
Source: U.S. Department of Commerce, *Business Conditions Digest* (June 1971).

C. Straight Extrapolation

This approach assumes that the value of a particular variable, Y_t, is generated by a model of the form,

$$Y_t = \alpha + \beta t + u_t, \tag{9.1}$$

where t represents the time period, from one to n, where n is the total number of observations. The variable u_t is the random or unexplained component of changes in Y.

Once least-squares estimates, a and b (of α and β) have been obtained, these can then be used to obtain forecasts of Y for period $n+1$, $n+2$, and so on. Consider Figure 9.1. Given the slope and intercept of the regression line, it is then a straightforward matter to extend or *extrapolate* it beyond the period of observation. Simply insert the value of $n+1$ into the linear equation to obtain a forecast for Y in that period, $\hat{Y}_{n+1}$, and so on for each subsequent period.

There are a number of variations on the above theme. For example, equation (9.1) could be modified to describe a polynomial relationship in time, that is

$$Y_t = \alpha + \beta_1 t + \beta_2 t^2 + \cdots + \beta_k t^k + u_t, \tag{9.2}$$

where k is the order of the polynomial. Or equation (9.1) might be estimated in logarithmic form such that

$$\log Y_t = \alpha + \beta \log t + u_t, \tag{9.3}$$

where β is interpreted as the elasticity of Y with respect to time.

However, all these procedures suffer a very strong defect. They assume a much stronger degree of regularity in Y than is likely to exist in practice. For example, suppose that we are interested in forecasting income. Past experience indicates that there are observable cycles in this variable between recession and boom. Thus a straight line may not even offer a good explanation of past behaviour let alone the future.

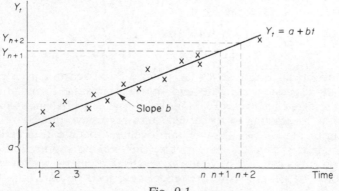

Fig. 9.1

D. *Auto-regressive Forecasting*

This approach assumes that a particular variable, Y_t, is generated on the basis of its own past history. A fairly broad class of models having this property may be described by the equation,

$$(1 - \phi_1 L - \cdots - \phi_p L^p)(1 - L)^d (Y_t - u) = (1 - \theta_1 L - \cdots - \theta_q L^q) u_t, \quad (9.4)$$

where p, d and q are non-negative integers and are assumed parameters of the model; L is the lag operator – for example $LY_t = Y_{t-1}$ and $L^p Y_t = Y_{t-p}$; ϕ_i, θ_j are parameters of the model which are to be estimated; u is a constant disturbance term; and u_t is a random disturbance independently distributed as $N(0, \sigma^2)$.

Thus, if $p = 1$, $d = 0$ and $q = 0$, we obtain $(1 - \phi_1 L)(Y_t - u) = u_t$, or

$$Y_t = u(1 - \phi_1) + \phi_1 Y_{t-1} + u_t. \quad (9.5)$$

Ordinary least squares can be used to estimate ϕ and the intercept $u(1 - \phi)$. Then to obtain a forecast for period $n + 1$, the value of Y_n would be substituted into equation (9.5) to obtain

$$\hat{Y}_{n+1} = u(1 - \phi_1) + \phi_1 Y_n.$$

The forecast for period $n + 2$ would be calculated using $\hat{Y}_{n+1}$. Thus

$$\hat{Y}_{n+2} = u(1 - \phi_1) + \phi_1 \hat{Y}_{n+1},$$

and so forth. It should be noted that if $|\phi_1| > 1$, the forecast values will tend to plus or minus infinity over time. If, however, $|\phi_1| < 1$, this will not occur. If, instead, we had a situation where $p = 0$, $d = 1$ and $q = 0$, the forecast model would be written as

$$(1 - L)Y_t = u_t$$

or
$$Y_t - Y_{t-1} = u_t,$$

that is, changes in Y are generated by a random walk process, determined solely by the disturbance term.

Another model of some interest is the one where $p = 1$, $d = 0$, $q = 1$ and $\phi_1 = \theta_1 = \lambda$. It is of the form

$$(1 - \phi_1 L)(Y_t - u) = (1 - \theta_1 L)u_t$$

or
$$Y_t = (1 - \lambda)u + \lambda Y_{t-1} + u_t - \lambda u_{t-1},$$

which is identical to the Koyck lag process discussed in earlier chapters. For a full discussion of these and other interesting formulations, the reader is referred to Box and Jenkins [6], Jorgenson [14] and Almon [2].

As far as forecasting is concerned, auto-regressive procedures represent, in principle, a considerable improvement over extrapolation. If a trend dominates a particular variable, this will be captured. But these models are also capable of capturing cyclical regularities. For example, cycles could be generated in the model described by equation (9.5) if u was of the same order of magnitude as Y, and $-1 < \phi_1 < 0$. However, like the extrapolative procedure, auto-regression is really a 'black-box' technique in that there are no other predetermined variables influencing Y. Hence the validity of this approach rests on the assumption that the underlying economic environment remains relatively unchanged.

E. *Forecasting with Econometric Models*

In Chapter 1, procedures were discussed for estimating systems of structural equations designed to describe the behaviour of an economy during the period of estimation. In a very real sense, econometrics is one of the major tools for the study of economic history for it enables us to ascertain whether there have been any significant regularities in human behaviour during that *past* period. Then, if we are willing to believe that these regularities will continue into the future (that is that history, in this sense, can repeat itself), it is but a simple step to use the estimated system of equations for forecasting purposes.

Suppose that the model which has been estimated is a simple one consisting of but two equations which are

$$Y_1(t) = a_{12}Y_2(t) + b_{11}Y_1(t-1) + b_{12}Y_2(t-1) + c_1Z(t) + u_1(t) \quad (9.6a)$$

and $$Y_2(t) = a_{21}Y_1(t) + b_{21}Y_1(t-1) + b_{22}Y_2(t-1) + c_2Z(t) + u_2(t), \quad (9.6b)$$

where $Y_1(t)$ and $Y_2(t)$ are the values of the dependent variables during period t, Z is an *exogenous*, predetermined variable, $Y_1(t-1)$ and $Y_2(t-1)$ being also classified as predetermined but not exogenous, since their values were determined by the past behaviour of the economy as described by the model, and the residuals associated with the two equations are denoted by $u_1(t)$ and $u_2(t)$. The results of this section can be generalised for larger, more complex models through the use of matrix algebra (see Fisher [7]).

Now it is possible to rewrite the model described by (9.6a) and (9.6b) in a number of ways which are useful for forecasting purposes. First let us solve for the two dependent variables in terms of the predetermined variables, such that

$$Y_1(t) = g_{11}Y_1(t-1) + g_{12}Y_2(t-1) + h_1Z_1(t) + du_1(t) \quad (9.7a)$$

and $$Y_2(t) = g_{21}Y_1(t-1) + g_{22}Y_2(t-1) + h_2Z_1(t) + du_2(t), \quad (9.7b)$$

where $$d = \frac{1}{1 - a_{12}a_{21}}$$

and
$$g_{11} = d(b_{11} + a_{12}b_{21}) \qquad g_{12} = d(b_{12} + a_{12}b_{22})$$
$$g_{21} = d(b_{21} + a_{21}b_{11}) \qquad g_{22} = d(b_{22} + a_{21}b_{12})$$
$$h_1 = d(c_1 + a_{12}c_2) \qquad h_2 = d(a_{21}c_1 + c_2).$$

The parameters h_1 and h_2 represent the *impact* or first-period *multipliers* associated with any change in the exogenous variable Z. They indicate the initial response of these endogenous variables to any change in Z.

Subsequent changes in Y_1 and Y_2 can then be determined by iteration, that is the values for $Y_1(1)$ and $Y_2(1)$ can be substituted back into equations (9.7a) and (9.7b) to obtain values for $Y_1(2)$ and $Y_2(2)$. This process can then be repeated *ad infinitum*. This, however, raises the interesting question: under what conditions will the system converge to new *equilibrium* values for Y_1 and Y_2. Unfortunately, space limitations do not permit us to answer this question fully. The necessary and sufficient mathematical conditions for such a model to be stable in the above sense do not have a straightforward economic interpretation. Often, however, meaningful sufficient conditions can be obtained. For example, in the case of a multi-country multiplier analysis, a sufficient condition for stability is that the sum of the propensities to consume in each country should be less than one. An excellent discussion of this example, and of the more general mathematical conditions, is given in Goldberg [9].

However, assuming that these requirements are met, we can calculate the final equilibrium multipliers as follows. Rewrite equations (9.6a) and (9.6b) by substituting in the equilibrium values for Y_1 and Y_2; hence we obtain

$$(1-b_{11})Y_1-(a_{12}+b_{12})Y_2 = c_1Z_1 \qquad (9.8a)$$

and
$$-(a_{21}+b_{21})Y_1+(1-b_{22})Y_2 = c_2Z. \qquad (9.8b)$$

This can then be solved for Y_1 and Y_2 such that

$$Y_1 = 1/r[(1-b_{22})c_1+(a_{12}+b_{12})c_2]Z_1 \qquad (9.9a)$$

and
$$Y_2 = 1/r[(a_{21}+b_{21})c_1+(1-b_{11})c_2]Z_1, \qquad (9.9b)$$

where $r = (1-b_{22})(1-b_{11})-(a_{12}+b_{12})(a_{21}+b_{21})$. The above coefficients are called the final *equilibrium multipliers*.

It should be noted that the ultimate forecasting equations can be obtained in two ways. Either of the reduced-form equations, (9.7a) and (9.7b), can be estimated directly and subsequently used for forecasting. Or the structural equations, (9.6a) and (9.6b) can be estimated and used to construct the required reduced form. The latter is often referred to as the *constrained* reduced form whereas the former is said to be *unconstrained*, that is the assumptions implicit in the structural equations have not been formally taken into account.

Another type of reduced-form estimation is also of interest. Reconsider equations (9.6a) and (9.6b) but assume, for the purpose of simplicity, that both a_{12} and a_{21} equal zero. In other words, the dependent variables are related only to the exogenous variable, the error term and the *lagged* dependent variables. Thus for period one we have

$$Y_1(1) = b_{11}Y_1(0) + b_{12}Y_2(0) + c_1Z_1(1) + u_1(1) \tag{9.10a}$$

and
$$Y_2(1) = b_{21}Y_1(0) + b_{22}Y_2(0) + c_2Z_1(1) + u_2(1). \tag{9.10b}$$

Now let us concentrate solely upon constructing an equation describing the behaviour of Y_1 in terms of the exogenous variable and error terms. In period two,

$$Y_1(2) = b_{11}Y_1(1) + b_{12}Y_2(1) + c_1Z_1(2) + u_2(2), \tag{9.11}$$

which, upon substitution of (9.10a) and (9.10b), becomes

$$Y_1(2) = b_{11}[b_{11}Y_1(0) + b_{12}Y_2(0) + c_1Z_1(1) + u_1(1)]$$
$$+ b_{12}[b_{21}Y_1(0) + b_{22}Y_2(0) + c_2Z_1(1) + u_2(1)] + c_1Z_1(2) + u_2(2). \tag{9.12}$$

The value of $Y_1(2)$ has been written as a function of the initial values, $Y_1(0)$ and $Y_2(0)$, of the dependent variables, the current and lagged value of the exogenous variable and the error terms. This same procedure can then be undertaken for Y_2. Next, equations can be constructed for the variable values in periods 3, 4 and so on such that only the *initial* values of the dependent variables appear. Further, provided that the necessary stability conditions hold, these terms will be negligible with the result that an approximate final form can be created, containing only the current and lagged values of the exogenous variables. Thus

$$Y_1(t) = \sum K_i Z(t-i). \tag{9.13}$$

As Smith [22] has argued, this analysis provides a rationale for the construction of a single-equation forecasting model such as was undertaken by Anderson and Jordan [3]. Their approach attempts to explain changes in U.S. gross national product in terms of government expenditure, tax variables and the money supply.

III PROPERTIES OF LINEAR PREDICTORS

In Chapter 1 it was argued that the least-squares estimators a and b of α and β from the model,

$$C_t = \alpha + \beta Y_t + u_t \tag{9.14}$$

were best (because they minimised the variance of a and b) in the class of linear, unbiased estimators, under certain assumptions (see p. 7). These assumptions are (with slightly differing notation)

(A.1) Y_t is a fixed non-stochastic, known number for all t;
(A.2) $E(u_t) = 0$ for all t;
(A.3) $V(u_t) = \sigma^2$ for all t; and
(A.4) $\text{Cov}(u_t, u_s) = 0$ for all $t \neq s$.

If these assumptions are extended to cover the period of forecast, as well as the period of observation, then it is possible to show that the linear predictor, $\hat{C}_0$ of C_0,

$$\hat{C}_0 = a + bY_0, \qquad (9.15)$$

is unbiased and that the variance of the forecast error, $e_0 = \hat{C}_0 - C_0$, is at a minimum (cf. Johnston [13] or Goldberger [11]).

It is easy to establish that the expectation of e_0 is zero, that is $E(\hat{C}_0) = C_0$. We have

$$E(\hat{C}_0) = E(a + bY_0) = E(a) + E(b)Y_0. \qquad (9.16)$$

If a and b are unbiased, then $E(a) = \alpha$ and $E(b) = \beta$. Hence

$$E(\hat{C}_0) = \alpha + \beta Y_0 = C_0, \qquad (9.17)$$

and $E(e_0)$ equals zero. Thus the predictor described by equation (9.16) is unbiased.

It is more difficult to establish that this predictor has minimum variance in the class of linear, unbiased predictors. However, we need to establish an expression for the variance of e_0 for statistical inference, that is

$$
\begin{aligned}
V(e_0) &= V(\hat{C}_0 - C_0) \\
&= V(a + bY_0) + V(\alpha + \beta Y_0 + u_0) \\
&= V(a) + Y_0^2 V(b) + 2Y_0 \operatorname{Cov}(a, b) + V(tu_0).
\end{aligned}
$$

By assumption, in the least-squares formulation, $V(u_0) = \sigma^2$. The first three terms represent the variance of the forecast and can be calculated from the variances of a and b and their covariance.

As noted in Chapter 1, there are many circumstances when ordinary least-squares procedures are statistically not the most satisfactory. The most relevant example for our discussion is the estimation of a set of simultaneous equations such as described by the matrix formulation in (9.6). In these circumstances, two-stage or three-stage least squares or maximum-likelihood procedures are more desirable. Unfortunately, it is not in general possible to establish small-sample properties for such estimators. Rather resort must be made to asymptotic sampling theory. The same must also be the case in trying to describe the statistical properties of predictors based on these more complex procedures. In general, however, if the errors in the observation and forecast periods are distributed independently, then the characteristics of the estimators will carry over to the predictor. Thus two-stage least-squares estimators are asymptotically unbiased but are not of asymptotically minimum variance. In this case, the associated predictor will be asymptotically unbiased but will not be of asymptotically minimum variance.

An econometric model represents the formal organisation of a given body of data in such a way that economic hypotheses can be subjected to vigorous statistical tests. However, although the procedures are in some sense 'scientific' this does not mean that they are perfect or foolproof.

This must be explicitly recognised when such models are used for fore-casting purposes. Specifically, there are four potential sources of error.

First, as was pointed out in Chapter 1, the best that we can do is to say that a particular model is *consistent* with the data. But we do not know whether or not that model is the *true* one. It may always be possible to construct, at a subsequent date, a model which more closely fits that data, according to standard statistical criteria. But at the time that a model is to be used for forecasting purposes, we will, of course, not know whether improvements are feasible. Hence we must reconcile ourselves to the possibility that our forecasting model is *mis-specified* over its period of estimation.

Secondly, *even if* the model is a good representation of reality, some structural change may have occurred during the period of estimation such that it is not relevant for the forecast period. People's taste or behaviour patterns may change, or a variable which had no impact during the estimation period may now become quite significant. In either case, however, such changes will not become apparent until *after* the forecast has actually been undertaken.

Thirdly, the specified model includes the random disturbance, u. If its deviations from zero are quite large this can have a significant impact on prepared forecasts, an impact which cannot be assessed *a priori*.

Finally, the values of many if not all of the predetermined variables may not be accurately known for the duration of the forecast period. This may even be true of policy instruments which may subsequently be changed in response to unforeseen circumstances. Thus, even if the model being used is a valid representation of the world, it may still yield poor forecasts if the values of the predetermined variables are incorrect.

Despite the above shortcomings, econometric forecasting procedures are the best available. To reject this approach means the adoption of 'off the cuff' *ad hoc* forecasts which involve implicit or vague assumptions, and which possess no formal structure. As a result, it is difficult if not impossible to discern the causes of any errors. Of course, an econometric model is not the only information which should be used in preparing forecasts. Qualitative as opposed to purely quantitative information may also be important. For example, information that most businessmen are highly pessimistic about future sales could represent an important reason for doubting econometric forecasts of higher levels of business activity. All bits of data must be brought together and cross-checked one against the other.

A particularly important use to which forecasting models can be put is to enable government decision-makers to check to see whether their diverse plans are mutually consistent. The various policy proposals can be assembled and the model used to simulate the behaviour of national product, prices and other key variables. If the results are not consistent with over-all economic objectives then further study along two lines is called for.

(1) One possibility is that the various policy proposals themselves are inconsistent. In this case greater co-operation among government departments is required to formulate a set of actions which do produce the desired results.
(2) However, for the reasons noted above, the model itself may be at fault. Thus continuing efforts must be made to check alternative hypotheses in an attempt to reformulate the model.

The implications of this last point need to be emphasised. Forecasting is not a static, mechanical exercise. Even a simple model may take several years to perfect to the point where it yields reliable results. Much trial and error will be involved: forecasting with a model, determining *ex post* the extent of the errors, and then trying to reformulate the model in such a way that future results are more accurate. This highlights the fact that econometrics is really an art (one where the artist's tools are statistical techniques).

IV AN EXAMPLE

Once forecasts have been made, it is important that these can be subjected to *ex post* tests to assess the extent and reasons for any errors. First, it is necessary to check whether the actual and assumed values for predetermined variables are close and whether any differences have an important impact on the forecast. Then it is necessary to check the model itself. Correct values of the exogenous variables are used to generate *ex post* forecasts. These can then be checked against some *a priori* criteria or compared with alternative, *naive* models. If a model incorporating hypotheses derived from economic theory does not perform as well as one which embodies no economics, then obviously modifications are necessary.

To see what is involved let us evaluate forecasts generated from a rather simple Hicksian *ISLM* model. The basic approach is similar to one used by Scott [21] and involved the estimation of two functions:

(1) an *IS* schedule describing real-sector behaviour and relating gross national product, Y, to government spending, G, taxes, T, and an interest rate, R; and
(2) an *LM* schedule describing financial-sector behaviour and relating an interest rate to gross national product and the money supply, M.

The main differences between Scott's work and the results below are that I have (a) used seasonally unadjusted data, and (b) incorporated lagged endogenous and exogenous variables to reflect the fact that adjustments take place over time. All variables are in real terms, that is they have been divided by the gross domestic product deflator.

The two equations, estimated by two-stage least squares for the period 1964(3) to 1972(2), are used to create the unconstrained reduced form. This, in turn, is used to forecast U.K. gross national product for the four quarters 1972(3) to 1973(2). Actual values of the exogenous variables are used. However, in the case of lagged endogenous variables values generated by the model are used. These forecasts are then compared with the changes as they actually occurred and forecasts obtained from (*a*) the unconstrained reduced form associated with the above model (that is the first stage of the two-stage least-squares procedure, (*b*) a final form model, (*c*) straight extrapolation, and (*d*) an auto-regressive scheme.

The estimated equations, together with standard errors, are as follows:

(*a*)   straight extrapolation: — *seasonal dummies.*

$$Y_t = 9371 + 55T - 388S_1 - 3S_2 + 34S_3$$
$$\quad (43) \quad (2) \quad (36) \quad (36) \quad (36)$$

$R^2 = 0.96$; Durbin–Watson statistic $= 2.25$.

(*b*)   auto-regressive scheme:

$$\Delta Y_t = 190.16 - 0.88\Delta Y_{t-1} - 0.75\Delta Y_{t-2} - 0.67\Delta Y_{t-3}$$
$$\quad (27.88) \quad (0.13) \quad\quad (0.15) \quad\quad (0.14)$$
$$\quad - 208.87S_1 - 19.60S_2 + 64.13S_3$$
$$\quad (80.15) \quad (87.24) \quad (85.83)$$

$R^2 = 0.95$; Durbin–Watson statistic $= 1.78$.

(*c*)   a simple structural model estimated by two-stage least squares:

$$\Delta Y_t = 54.42 + 0.60\Delta G_t + 0.35\Delta G_{t-1} + 0.38\Delta T_t$$
$$\quad (22.31) \quad (0.20) \quad (0.26) \quad\quad (0.14)$$
$$\quad - 0.09\Delta T_{t-1} + 43.50\Delta R_t - 157.66\Delta R_{t-1} - 0.40\Delta Y_{t-1}$$
$$\quad (0.17) \quad\quad (80.34) \quad (107.61) \quad\quad (0.17)$$
$$\quad - 431.94S_1 - 197.92S_2 + 227.73S_3$$
$$\quad (96.84) \quad (126.62) \quad (48.35)$$

$R^2 = 0.96$; Durbin–Watson statistic $= 2.56$.

$$\Delta R_t = 0.06 + 0.0003\Delta M_t + 0.0003\Delta M_{t-1}$$
$$\quad (0.05) \quad (0.0002) \quad\quad (0.0002)$$
$$\quad + 0.0001\Delta Y_t - 0.0005\Delta Y_{t-1} + 0.5263\Delta R_{t-1}$$
$$\quad (0.0002) \quad\quad (0.0003) \quad\quad (0.1618)$$
$$\quad + 0.3259S_1 - 0.0802S_2 + 0.0546S_3$$
$$\quad (0.2219) \quad (0.2054) \quad (0.1357)$$

$R^2 = 0.56$; Durbin–Watson statistic $= 1.37$.

TABLE 9.2

Summary of forecasts 1972(3)–1973(2) (first differences)

Quarter	Actual	Extrapolaive scheme	Auto-regressive scheme	Final-form system	ISLM First stage of 2 S.L.S.	ISLM Second stage of 2 S.L.S.
1972(3)	−65	+84	+183	−38	−182	−175
1972(4)	+706	+378	+415	+722	+740	+711
1973(1)	−489	−690	−980	−333	−499	−474
1973(2)	+295	−439	+601	+168	+342	+254
Annual	+447	−211	+219	+519	+401	+316

(*d*) 'Final' reduced-form estimation:

$$\Delta Y_t = 21 \cdot 20 + 0 \cdot 67 \Delta G_t + 0 \cdot 11 \Delta G_{t-1} + 0 \cdot 20 \Delta G_{t-1}$$
$$(20 \cdot 84) \quad (0 \cdot 19) \quad (0 \cdot 24) \quad\quad (0 \cdot 25)$$

$$+ 0 \cdot 50 \Delta G_{t-2} + 0 \cdot 44 \Delta T_t - 0 \cdot 53 \Delta T_{t-1} - 0 \cdot 15 \Delta T_{t-2}$$
$$(0 \cdot 21) \quad\quad (0 \cdot 15) \quad (0 \cdot 17) \quad\quad (0 \cdot 17)$$

$$- 0 \cdot 40 \Delta T_{t-3} + 0 \cdot 07 \Delta M_t - 0 \cdot 16 \Delta M_{t-1} - 0 \cdot 19 \Delta M_{t-2}$$
$$(0 \cdot 16) \quad\quad (0 \cdot 10) \quad (0 \cdot 12) \quad\quad (0 \cdot 11)$$

$$+ 0 \cdot 06 \Delta M_{t-3} - 364 \cdot 37 S_1 - 6 \cdot 54 S_2 + 191 \cdot 18 S_3$$
$$(0 \cdot 10) \quad\quad (92 \cdot 55) \quad (89 \cdot 13) \quad (74 \cdot 40)$$

$$R^2 = 0 \cdot 97; \text{ Durbin–Watson statistic} = 2 \cdot 22.$$

The forecasted and actual changes are summarised in Table 9.2. The first comparison that we shall make concerns the sign of these changes – the extrapolative and auto-regressive schemes both fail to predict the correct direction of change in 1972(3). The other three models score 100 per cent. Quantitative comparisons can be made utilising a number of measures. Klein [15] prefers the mean absolute percentage on the grounds of 'simplicity and ease of understanding'. This measure is written as

$$\text{mean absolute percentage error} = \sum_{t=1}^{N} \frac{|Y_t^F - Y_t|}{Y_t} \times 100.$$

Results for this statistic using, both first differences and absolute levels are shown in Table 9.3. Again the extrapolative and auto-regressive schemes fare poorly. The final-form system scores highest marks for both first differences and levels, whereas the constrained reduced form comes second for first differences and a close third using absolute levels. The main reason for the different ranking is that, with levels, the forecast levels represent a cumulation of the forecast changes, and with first differences we are averaging actual and forecast changes for each quarter. A third possible comparison is to calculate the annual percentage error on an annual basis. Here the unconstrained reduced-form forecasts are the best. Three other statistics, however, indicate that the constrained reduced form produces the best results. Theil has suggested something called the *U*-statistic. It can be written in the form,

$$U = \sqrt{\frac{\sum (Y_t^F - Y_t)^2}{\sum Y_t^2}}.$$

With this the final form comes third. Another approach involves regressing forecasted against actual values. A perfect score would be achieved with a zero intercept and unitary slope. There is a bit of ambiguity here, however, since the slope coefficient associated with the constrained reduced form is the best, whereas the unconstrained reduced form yields the lowest intercept. A sixth statistic is the average absolute error – which

TABLE 9.3

Analysis of forecast errors (ranking in parentheses)

Statistic	Extrapolative scheme	Auto-regressive scheme	Final-form system	ISLM First stage of 2 S.L.S.	ISLM Second stage of 2 S.L.S.
Mean abs. percentage error (first differences)	108 (4)	157 (5)	34 (1)	51 (3)	47 (2)
Mean abs. percentage error (levels)	2·07 (4)	2·33 (5)	0·75 (2)	0·75 (1)	0·95 (3)
Annual percentage error (levels)	2·04 (5)	1·97 (4)	0·62 (2)	0·40 (1)	1·13 (3)
U-statistic (first differences)	0·59 (5)	0·76 (4)	0·23 (3)	0·14 (2)	0·13 (1)
Regression of forecast on actual values* (first differences)	$b = 0·90$ $a = -48·36$ (3)	$b = 1·17$ $a = -76·27$ (5)	$b = 0·86$ $a = 34·10$ (4)	$b = 1·07$ $a = -19·47$ (2)	$b = 1·01$ $a = -33·60$ (1)
Average absolute error (first differences)	256 (4)	334 (5)	84 (3)	52 (2)	43 (1)

* Ranking based on slope coefficient.

shows that the constrained reduced-form forecasts are almost twice as good as those obtained from the final-form model. Unfortunately, we have no *a priori* criteria by which to choose between these measures, as Klein [15] has pointed out. This is particularly embarrassing if we have a situation, such as shown in Table 9.3, where three of the procedures yield reasonably small forecast errors (on the basis of absolute levels).

Over the past twenty years several conscientious attempts have been made to construct useful forecasting models. With a few exceptions, these are quite large and complex, and thus it is impossible to discuss them in any detail. However, several works stand out as being worthy of further study. Certainly the pioneering research of Klein and Goldberger [16] and Goldberger [10] has had considerable influence on subsequent model formulation in the United States, the United Kingdom and elsewhere. Another important paper by the Adelmans [1] subjects the Klein–Goldberger model to random shocks. This results in cycles very close to those actually observed.

The Wharton School model [18] is a particularly important recent attempt at constructing a forecasting framework. Klein [15] discusses the actual procedures used to forecast with this model. A comparison of this with other U.S. models has recently been prepared by Fromm and Klein [8]. Their conclusions are that, with some exceptions, errors are within 'reasonable' bounds. Interestingly, the relatively simple model constructed by Anderson and Jordan [3] is one of the best performers.

BIBLIOGRAPHY

[1] F. and I. Adelman, 'The Dynamic Properties of the Klein–Goldberger Model', *Econometrica*, 29 (Oct 1959) pp. 596–625.

[2] S. Almon, 'The Distributed Lag Between Capital Appropriations and Expenditures', *Econometrica*, 33 (Jan 1965) pp. 178–96.

[3] L. Anderson and J. Jordan, 'Monetary and Fiscal Actions: A Test of Their Relative Importance in Economic Stabilization', *Review of the Federal Reserve Bank of St Louis* (Nov 1968) pp. 11–24.

[4] R. J. Ball *et al.*, *The International Linkage of National Economic Models* (Amsterdam: North-Holland, 1973).

[5] —, 'The London Business School Quarterly Econometrics Model of the U.K. Economy', in *Modelling the Economy*, ed. G. A. Renton (London: Heinemann, 1975).

[6] G. Box and G. Jenkins, *Time Series Models for Forecasting and Control* (San Francisco: Holden-Day, 1970).

[7] F. Fisher, 'Dynamic Structure and Estimation in Economy-wide Econometric Models', in *Brookings Quarterly Econometric Model of the United States*, ed. J. Duesenberry *et al.* (Amsterdam: North-Holland, 1965).

[8] G. Fromm and L. Klein, 'A Comparison of Eleven Econometric

Models of the United States', *American Economic Review*, 63 (May 1973) pp. 385–93.

[9]   S. Goldberg, *Introduction to Difference Equations* (New York: Wiley, 1961).

[10] A. S. Goldberger, *Impact Multipliers and Dynamic Properties of the Klein–Goldberger Model* (Amsterdam: North-Holland, 1959).

[11] —, *Econometric Theory* (New York: Wiley, 1964).

[12] D. F. Heathfield and I. F. Pearce, 'A View of the Southampton Econometric Model of the U.K. and its Trading Partners', in *Modelling the Economy*, ed. G. A. Renton (London: Heinemann, 1974).

[13] J. Johnston, *Econometric Models*, 2nd edn (New York: McGraw-Hill, 1972).

[14] D. Jorgenson, 'Rational Distributed Lag Functions', *Econometrica*, 34 (Jan 1966) pp. 135–49.

[15] L. Klein, *An Essay on the Theory of Economic Prediction* (Helsinki, 1968).

[16] — and A. S. Goldberger, *An Econometric Model of the United States, 1929–1952* (Amsterdam: North-Holland, 1955).

[17] L. M. Koyck, *Distributed Lags and Investment Analysis* (Amsterdam: North-Holland, 1954).

[18] M. D. McCarthy, *The Wharton Quarterly Econometric Forecasting Model Mark III* (Philadelphia, 1972).

[19] G. H. Moore and J. Shiskin, *Indicators of Business Expansions and Contractions* (New York: National Bureau of Economic Research, 1967).

[20] I. F. Pearce, *International Trade* (London: Macmillan, 1970) vol. II, ch. 19.

[21] R. H. Scott, 'Estimates of Hicksian *LS* and *LM* Curves for the United States', *Journal of Finance*, 21 (1966) pp. 479–87.

[22] W. L. Smith, 'On Some Current Issues in Monetary Economics', *Journal of Economic Literature* (Sep 1970) pp. 767–82.

Index